ESSAYS ON **HITLER'S EUROPE**

ISTVÁN DEÁK

ESSAYS ON **HITLER'S EUROPE**

UNIVERSITY OF NEBRASKA PRESS
Lincoln & London

© 2001 by the University of Nebraska Press
All rights reserved
Manufactured in the United States of America

⊗

Library of Congress Cataloging-in-Publication Data
Deák, István.
  Essays on Hitler's Europe / István Deák.
    p. cm.
  Includes bibliographical references and index.
  ISBN 0-8032-1716-1 (cl.: alk. paper)—ISBN 0-8032-6630-8 (pbk.: alk. paper)
  1. Jews—Persecutions—Europe. 2. Holocaust, Jewish (1939–1945)—Europe.
3. National socialism—Europe. 4. Fascism—Europe. I. Title.
DS135.E83 D43 2001
940.53'18—dc21   2001017103

*For Gloria, Kiséva,
Nagyéva, Fruzsa,
and Panka*

CONTENTS

Preliminary Notes IX   *Introduction* XI

1 GERMANS
Who Were the National Socialists? 3
Who Were the Fascists? 16
Perpetrators 23
The Nazi Past in the Two Germanys 35

2 JEWS AMONG "ARYANS"
In Disguise 47
Cold Brave Heart 51

3 VICTIMS
The Incomprehensible Holocaust 67
A Mosaic of Victims 89
Memories of Hell 94
The Goldhagen Controversy in Retrospect 100

4 THE HOLOCAUST IN OTHER LANDS
A Ghetto in Lithuania 113
Romania: Killing Fields and Refuge 129
The Europeans and the Holocaust 137
A Hungarian Admiral on Horseback 148
The Holocaust in Hungary 159
Poles and Jews 163

5 ONLOOKERS
The Pope, the Nazis, and the Jews 169
The British and the Americans 185

Notes 195   *Index* 207

PRELIMINARY NOTES

Writing reviews for the *New York Review of Books* and the *New Republic* means writing about books that the editors have assigned to you. Bunched together more or less to fit the reviewer's fields of interest, these works have some common themes; still, this is a rather haphazard process, dictated by what is new and what attracts the editor's attention in the mountains of books that rise in every nook and corner of his office. From time to time I was assigned only a single book to review; in the most demanding assignment, I had to review sixteen volumes within a single essay and in addition was asked to refer, either in the text or in the footnotes, to several other new works.

An unexpected offer recently came my way when the director of the University of Nebraska Press presented me with the opportunity of publishing a selection of my essays that had appeared up to then. Now, I was confronted with the dilemma of how to organize and to systematize a collection of work that, by its very nature, defies organization. A major rearrangement would have amounted to writing a new book; also, the original flavor of the essays would have been lost. I therefore compromised by shifting—but only in a few instances—segments of a review from one essay to another when it seemed absolutely necessary.

Because it is always the journal editor and not the author who decides on the title of an essay and because editors like to use splashy titles for very obvious reasons, I found it impossible to keep some of the original essay titles. Otherwise, several articles would have had nearly identical titles, generously spiced with such words as "Hell", "Hero," "Horror," and "Survivor." The beginning of each essay in the book indicates precisely when, where, and under what title the original essay was printed.

Needless to say, I was tempted to rewrite some of the articles, especially where historical hindsight has proven me wrong. I resisted the temptation and rewrote only a handful of sentences where omissions made this absolutely necessary. I also took the liberty of correcting a handful of small factual errors (I see no reason why errors should be perpetuated).

Journal essays, especially in the *New York Review of Books,* often lead to exchanges between the readers and the author. In one case, that of "The Incomprehensible Holocaust," the exchanges lasted for one and a half years. I wish I could have included at least some samples of these letters here but space did not allow it. At the beginning of some of the articles, I have indicated in a few sentences the nature of the controversies between reviewer and reader. Mostly these arose because readers found my judgment either too harsh or not harsh enough; others complained that I neglected to include yet another aspect of the subject under review. But responses to the reviews also elicited many, many fascinating letters from which I profited enormously.

It seems to be only right to express my thanks here to my friend and colleague, Robert Scott, and to my wife, Gloria Deák, both of whom read, corrected, and edited my essays. My wife, who is an art historian, was able to assist me while writing and publishing several books, the most recent being the lively *Picturing New York: The City from Its Beginnings to the Present* (New York: Columbia University Press, 2000). Finally, I can only think with gratitude and enthusiasm of Robert Silvers of the *New York Review of Books* and Leon Wieseltier of the *New Republic,* both of whom presented welcome challenges to me in my writing career.

INTRODUCTION

It was some twenty years ago that Robert Silvers, the editor of the *New York Review of Books,* first asked me to write a review critiquing a book about the 1848 revolutions in Central Europe—my specialty at that time. Many other essays have followed since then, although the subjects of the books I have reviewed have moved increasingly forward in time to World War II and particularly to coverage of the domestic fronts, the persecution of minorities, the policies of the German and other occupation forces, collaboration, resistance, war crimes, postwar retribution, and, mainly, the genocide of the European Jews. Throughout the process, Robert Silvers has continued to be a conscientious, erudite, brilliant, charming, witty, demanding, impatient, and exasperating collaborator. All the essays I conceived for the journal bear the marks of his editorial pen; all were born after titanic struggles, not only over content but often over a sentence, sometimes a single word. It is through association with him that I have retrained myself as a historian of the tragic and yet ultimately hopeful events of World War II. Hopeful because, even though World War II was the bloodiest conflict in human history as well as the cruelest and the most devastating, it was also a just war. Witness its entry into American popular consciousness as the conflict that had to be fought against a vile tyranny and that was indeed fought victoriously by a united citizenry and by millions of willing civilians in uniform.

In time, another brilliant editor entered on the scene: Leon Wieseltier, a celebrated writer who solicited reviews for the *New Republic,* often on similar World War II themes. Because both editors sent me many more works than I could possibly review for their journals and because some authors and publishers voluntarily mail me their publications, hundreds of new books on the war now line my shelves. They serve to remind me that my essays in the two journals discuss only a small section of the vast literature in English on Hitler's

Europe (and that the articles reprinted here are only some of those I had the pleasure of contributing to the *New York Review,* the *New Republic,* and other journals).

Recent works on the war range from memoirs of the "I Was Hitler's Moustache" variety, through discussions of the Waffen SS, German army and navy uniforms, and the British commandos, all the way to studies of secret warfare, life in Europe during the war, the horrors of the POW camps, the cruelties of the Gestapo, the problems of anti-Nazi resistance, and the crimes and suicidal behavior of the collaborators as well as the Nazi persecution of homosexuals, Gypsies, Communists, Socialists, and Jews. Recent Holocaust literature alone could fill libraries: it includes a few unforgettable novels, many valuable memoirs, and profound philosophical, psychological, and theological analyses but also, unfortunately a growing number of invented reminiscences, other forgeries, and Holocaust denials. I often wonder what harms the memory of the Holocaust more: pseudomemoirs by real or alleged survivors, or pseudoscientific allegations that no Jew was ever gassed? I am afraid it is the former, because the public tends to believe the false or partly falsified memoirs, whereas Holocaust denials are accepted only by extremists. One thing that has inspired my writings on the genocide of the Jews is the desire to combat the harmful and confusing legends, myths, and general misinformation.

How are we to explain the public's seemingly inexhaustible appetite for Nazism and World War II in Europe as historical and literary themes? This fascination is one of the many subjects I attempt to discuss in my essays.

From time immemorial, war, violence, brutality, and the exploits of war heroes have proved spellbinding. In the twentieth century, many Germans proved themselves such brutes and such super-soldiers, provoking bewilderment that the inhabitants of one of the world's most civilized nations were capable of committing such abominable crimes. Fear, too, swells the fascination: fear that the German-Nazi phenomenon could arise anew, in some other form, in some other place. How to prevent it? How to recognize it? How, and at what point, to stop it? During the first three or four decades after World War II, rejuvenated fascism was detected, depending on one's political persuasion, in most countries of the Third World as well as in the Soviet Union, West and East Germany, and the United States. Today, however, the danger is unmistakably less acute than at a time when dictatorial and ultranationalist regimes seemed to be the wave of the future.

There is yet one more major explanation for our fascination with Nazism and World War II, namely, that no other major state, probably, has ever been so utterly defeated, had more of its secrets seized by the victors, and ironically,

Introduction XIII

taken greater pains to document its own crimes. As a result, we know a great deal about the Nazi system, which does not, however, mean that we fully understand it. In fact, many insoluble dilemmas of the Third Reich and the Holocaust remain.

One of our main problems regarding Nazism—and indeed, fascism in general—is one of definition. What was fascism? Was National Socialism one of the many varieties of that elusive concept called fascism or was it a phenomenon *sui generis*? I will suggest in this book that even though there is no agreed-on definition of fascism, its followers can be fairly easily identified. One can at least draw up a sort of laundry list of the tenets and practices of fascism, including such particulars as a mania for marching, fascination with martial display, and a philosophical commitment to violence. The greater its conformity to this list, the more a movement approaches what one might call "ideal fascism." Of course, there has never been a perfect or pure fascist movement. What sets German National Socialism apart from other fascist movements is that it is unlikely to have survived without violence and war (at least this was Hitler's own view) and that the desire to exterminate Jewry was the alpha and omega of its creed. Franco's Spain has demonstrated that fascism can exist without war and all the Mediterranean fascist movements were almost entirely devoid of racism and radical anti-Semitism.

Virtually no Holocaust literature emerged in the period immediately following the war. There was not even a commonly used term to describe the event. It is frequently forgotten today that the postwar years in Europe actually witnessed a resurgence of anti-Semitism, even in places where the "Jewish question" had not been a major consideration. Fear of Jewish revenge and an unwillingness to return plundered booty played major roles in these events. The Jewish survivors themselves tended to keep silent about their experiences, both in order to be reaccepted into the society that had expelled them and to wash away the shame of "otherness." Postwar governments, invariably made of wartime resisters, had an interest in boosting the number of wartime antifascist fighters; Jewish survivors in concentration camps were often classed with political deportees. Jews gladly accepted such a categorization because it was better to be a homecoming hero than a returning expellee.

Only in the last thirty-odd years has the Holocaust become a major topic, if not the most important topic of World War II research and memory. This was inevitable, not only because of our recent preoccupation with history's victims and with victimization but also because of the ever growing documentation of the genocide of the Jews. We have come to understand that the annihilation of Jewry was Hitler's major goal, sometimes even more important for him than the pursuit of the war. At the same time, some interpretations born of popular fascination with the Holocaust arguably go too far; certainly it would be a mistake to view all politics and military events, from the movement of troops to aerial bombing, through the prism of the genocide of the Jews. The war had to be fought and won; some Allied moves that hastened victory over Nazism also cost thousands of Jewish lives.

The debates over the historic significance of the Holocaust, its place in World War II history, and the best scholarly approach to an event that remains fundamentally incomprehensible are opening new avenues of research. Some of the present-day targets of interest are the perpetrators, the collaborators, the bystanders, as well as the non-German assisters to the German Nazis in the so-called Final Solution. The latter relates to the controversial issue of Jewish "collaboration"—by members of Jewish Councils, ghetto policemen, and Jewish Gestapo agents. I hold that no Jew can be charged with collaboration because the very term indicates a choice. Non-Jews could choose to work or not to work with the Germans; Jews, who were under a collective death sentence, could at most try to save their lives. While so doing, some behaved in an undignified or even criminal manner. But many others would have done the same in the face of death.

Other favored and rewarding avenues of research include the study of non-Jewish victims of Nazism, especially the mentally or physically handicapped "Aryans" whose mass extermination prepared the way for the gassing of the Jews. Additionally many books have been written by and about Jews who were able to pass as Aryans. Their stories are often so adventurous as to raise the question of credibility, yet at least some are demonstrably true. Consider the case of Oswald Rufeisen, narrated in this volume, a young Polish Jew who became successively an armed German police auxiliary, a refugee in a convent wearing a nun's habit, a Soviet partisan, a Bolshevik commissar, a Catholic priest, and finally a Catholic monk in an Israeli monastery.

Recently, much has been written on the crucial difference between the Western and Eastern European situations regarding the Jews. One has only to consider that in occupied Poland one courted death by giving a cigarette to a Jew; in occupied Denmark and many other places, one incurred no danger even by hiding a Jew.

The conduct of the major European institutions, especially the Catholic Church, toward the Jewish victims of Nazism is another subject of protracted debate. To put it bluntly, no European government, trade union, church, political party, police force, resistance movement, and so forth was blameless. Many sinned by commission, many others by omission, but none, except the National Socialists and their dedicated European ideological sympathizers, was fully committed to the Nazi plan of total annihilation. In any case, the result was the death of millions whom the Nazis would have been unable to annihilate without non-German assistance. On the other hand, we have the survival of millions of Jews, often protected by the same criminally guilty politicians, governments, and organizations. This was mainly because national and individual interests had changed over time. However, one cannot deny the role of humanitarian feelings either.

For a number of decades, specialists have debated whether the Holocaust was the outcome of a blueprint drawn up well before the extermination of the Jews became practicable or whether it was the result of economic and other pragmatic considerations by persons in whose eyes the Jews—and often other non-Germans—were no better than worms. Today, however, these somewhat crude "intentionalist" and "functionalist" interpretations are no longer acceptable, though no compromise has arisen; Nazi motivations are too complex for any generalization.

During the first half of the twentieth century, Europe was pocked with concentration camps; recent research comparing the Soviet Gulag, the Nazi Konzentrationslager, and camps in Italy and elsewhere have yielded important insights, as has the study of the concentration camp hierarchies. The latter, research suggests, resembled in many ways the social, ethnic, and religious hierarchies of the outside world, only that in the camps there were fewer pretenses. In my view, the experience of the camps suggests that prewar adherence to liberal or illiberal views, left-wing or conservative persuasions, religious devotion or atheism, had little to do with the way a person behaved in such an extreme situation. It would appear that dignified behavior and charitable actions welled up instead from some unfathomable inner source. The only generalization I can allow myself is to suggest that the European aristocracy as a whole seems to have shown more decency in the camps than most other castes, classes, and groups.

If it is permissible to compare concentration camps that flourished under mutually hostile dictatorships, then one should not hesitate either to compare the despots who put millions of Europeans into those camps. Recent studies reveal great similarities between the personalities of Hitler and Stalin, whereas Mussolini, Franco, and other dictators seem to belong to a more familiar and less terrifying world. It is not too difficult, either, to draw parallels, despite significant differences, between Soviet Communism and German National Socialism. Such an approach can be a risky one, however; witness the recent, often ugly historical controversies in Germany between those who argue that

Hitler both took his inspiration from and reacted to Russian Bolshevism, and those who see such views as an attempt to lift the moral burden from German shoulders and make Russian Bolshevism the primary culprit in the horrors of the twentieth century.

The Soviet regime survived for seventy-two years, the Third Reich for only twelve. In the last four decades of its existence, Soviet Communism mellowed considerably; it was also gradually undermined by corruption, economic failure, and intellectual dissent. What would have happened to Hitler's system had it survived World War II? Would it have mellowed also? While there is no answer to this question, it should be food for thought.

A considerable part of this book deals with countries other than Germany—their governing systems and their wartime policies. One can postulate, as a general rule, that most countries in Hitler's Europe enjoyed some degree of autonomy under Nazi tutelage. In this respect there was less difference than it is usually assumed between the countries officially allied to Germany, such as Italy, Hungary, Romania, Slovakia, Croatia, Bulgaria, and Finland, and the countries occupied by the German army, such as Denmark, Norway, the Netherlands, Belgium, France, the Czech Protectorate, Serbia, and Greece. In both groups, local or national authorities were able to make important decisions on, for instance, the extent of economic cooperation with Germany or compliance with the German request for the "Final Solution of the Jewish Question." In fact, all the above-named states, except Denmark and Finland, assisted the Nazis in the Final Solution, though only to a certain extent, and often only so as to be able to use the remaining Jews as a bargaining tool. The Finns remained their own masters during the war; in occupied Denmark the national government took no measures against the Jews, but then the Danes were subjected to much less Nazi pressure in this respect than any other country. Also, Denmark earned this tolerant treatment on the part of Germany because of its full and highly valuable economic cooperation. This certainly prolonged the war and thus indirectly contributed to the killing of more Jews.

Some European governments, such as that in Romania, engaged in their own territorially restricted Holocaust project, but Romania never surrendered any of its Jews to the Germans. Hungary alternately protected its Jews and handed them over to Adolf Eichmann. With regard to the Holocaust, hardly a European government can be considered guiltless. Because the Germans did not create even a puppet government in Poland, the Baltic states, or the occupied parts of the Soviet Union the question of national responsibility does not arise in those areas. We must also remember, however, that these last named countries did, nonetheless, provide the Germans with plenty of willing helpers in their genocide program.

Note that, with time, nearly every German satellite turned against Nazi Germany and, accordingly, often had to face devastating consequences. Romania suffered very heavy losses fighting both for and against Germany. Bulgaria, a German ally from April 1941 to September 1944, lost very few soldiers during that period but suffered terrible losses in the final campaign against the Third Reich. Note also that in many countries, especially in eastern and southeastern Europe, World War II deteriorated into a civil war in which the exceptionally brutal occupation forces ultimately inflicted less suffering on a country's population than that country's citizens inflicted upon one another.

How much did the free world know about the German decision to annihilate the Jews and to enslave others? It has been demonstrated that the British and U.S. governments were well informed but hesitated to make their knowledge public, in part because of the anti-Semitism of some key British and American officials, in part because of popular anti-Semitism in the two countries, and in part so as not to betray the Allies' ability to decode secret German communications. Whether or not the Allies could have done more to save the Jews during the war remains a subject of heated debate. Suffice it to say here that when it was still clearly possible to do something—before the war—little or nothing was done; later, only minimal help could be extended to the Jews. The greatest help was a speedy defeat of the Third Reich.

There is, finally, the endlessly debated question of German guilt. In this collection of essays I hold that it is wrong to call all Germans "willing executioners," as Daniel Goldhagen does in his famous work of 1996. If nothing else, the German Jew Victor Klemperer's wartime diaries, also discussed in this book, contradict this wholesale indictment. On the other hand, it would be equally unacceptable to lay blame solely on the shoulders of the Nazi Party leadership and the SS; an enormous number of Wehrmacht officers, civil servants, businessmen, policemen, and other ordinary Germans were also guilty. And those who did nothing one way or another were not without responsibility either—whether we are speaking of Germany during the Nazi period, the United States under slavery, or anywhere else in the world where rank injustices are or were committed.

An absolutely unique feature of World War II is that, when the fighting was over, the leaders of defeated Germany were called to task in an international court constituted for that purpose. A few dozen Nazi leaders were actually executed, but most others, including thousands of mass murderers, were soon released or were never even charged. They were all allowed to continue and to thrive as if nothing had happened. Paradoxically, the countries that had been allied to Germany or had suffered German military occupation were far more thorough in their purges than the two halves of Allied-occupied Germany. In these countries, from Norway to Italy, from the Netherlands to Eastern Europe, thousands were executed for treason and war crimes—no doubt many innocent people among them. The outrageously lenient treatment of the Nazi criminals, especially in West Germany, was a consequence of the cold war and thus of a time frame that does not preoccupy us here.

I do not wish to pretend that all the problems mentioned in this introduction are discussed, even less that they are resolved, in this book. My purpose here has been to inform the reader of some of the preoccupations of historians regarding that terrible and yet often encouraging war. As for myself, I have lived with these thoughts and dilemmas for many, many years. Though only a teenager, I was there when these dramatic events took place. Even today, the memories are enough to spoil one's sleep.

1
GERMANS

WHO WERE THE NATIONAL SOCIALISTS?

We can organize the problem of National Socialism around some major questions. First, who in Weimar voted for Hitler, and who became a party member? What made the Nazis popular, and how did they come to power? How anti-Semitic were the Germans? Was anti-Semitism the main attraction of the Nazi movement? Did the Germans uphold the Nazi proposition that the Jews should be murdered, and how much did they know about the Final Solution? Related to this last theme is another: was the Third Reich totalitarian? Was Nazism merely a theory of mass murder, and if so, were all those who supported the Nazis accomplices in murder? The ultimate question, then, is the eternal one: were Hitler's German contemporaries guilty?

Who Were the Nazis?

The Nazis and their sympathizers are carefully identified by Thomas Childers in *The Nazi Voter: The Social Foundation of Fascism in Germany, 1918–1933* (Chapel Hill: University of North Carolina Press, 1983) and by Michael Kater in *The Nazi Party: A Social Profile of Members and Leaders, 1919–1945* (Cambridge MA: Harvard University Press, 1983). Both books are thorough social histories, enriched—some would say weighted down—by many charts and statistical tables. Kater in particular provides a large number of tables on such themes as the growth of Nazi party membership from 1919 to 1945; "Nazi newcomers" between 1930 and 1944, in big cities, small towns, and the country; Nazi newcomers in the professions; and even "female Nazi newcomers in relation to corresponding percentages for male Nazi newcomers."

This somewhat abbreviated version of an article entitled "How Guilty Were the Germans" originally appeared in the May 31, 1984, issue of the *New York Review of Books*.

Thomas Childers, a professor of history at the University of Pennsylvania, effectively demonstrates that in the Weimar Republic, people voted for the National Socialist Party (NSDAP), as the Nazi Party was formally known, for diverse reasons, of which anti-Semitism was but one. He undermines the engrained notion that the petty bourgeoisie were the Nazis' major support before 1933, showing that Hitler in fact was acclaimed by representatives of many different social groups. He admits, however, that the petty bourgeoisie was the group most susceptible to the cruder forms of anti-Semitism.

Childers reinforces Richard Hamilton's recent findings in *Who Voted for Hitler?* (Princeton NJ: Princeton University Press, 1982) that the NSDAP before 1933 won many followers among the higher circles of German society, especially among university students—then, unlike today, a highly privileged and exclusive group. The Nazis were popular among civil servants and in the well-to-do suburbs of Berlin, Hamburg, and other big cities. But Hitler also secured an ever-increasing number of supporters from among factory workers. Childers demonstrates that those who voted for Hitler, especially between 1930 and 1933, were not—as is commonly held—primarily young people and freshly enfranchised youngsters in particular. On the contrary, he suggests, the party "found its greatest electoral support among groups composed of older voters." Turning to the denominational composition of the Nazi vote, Childers corroborates Hamilton's conclusion that German Catholics were far more resistant to Nazi ambitions than were Protestants, even though German National Socialism had begun in Catholic Bavaria. Throughout the Weimar years, Catholic Germans showed their preference for the moderate Zentrum Party, which, like the NSDAP or the Marxist parties, provided its followers with a well-defined belief system.

According to Childers, Nazism signified "a fundamental rejection of the social and political implications of modernization." Those who saw modern industrial society as a threat—for example, farmers, artisans, domestic servants—were more likely to cast their vote for Hitler than those, like technicians or factory workers, who were themselves a part of the industrial process. Small wonder, then, that the NSDAP appealed to women, who generally still believed in the ideals of *Kinder, Küche und Kirche* (Children, Kitchen, and Church). By attacking both Marxist socialism and liberal capitalism, the NSDAP appealed to the conservative instincts of its mostly Protestant small-town or rural sympathizers. To this we might add, as one of the many ironies of the situation, that Hitlerism, once in power, reneged on its earlier promises to restore bucolic rural life and continued the process of industrialization and urbanization. Moreover, it ended up conscripting millions of women for factory labor.

At the same time, Childers points out, it must be kept in mind that the Nazi electorate was volatile and diverse. After its resounding success in the parliamentary elections of July 31, 1932, in which it received 37.3 percent of the vote, the NSDAP began to decline, faring less well on November 6, 1932 (33.1 percent). At this dramatic point a number of reactionary politicians and businessmen came to the rescue of Hitler, making him chancellor in January 1933. They were mistaken, however, in their belief that they could control and guide the Nazi momentum.

Kater, a professor of history at York University in Toronto, does not contradict Childers's or Hamilton's conclusions. He is, however, a bit more cautious and does not discuss "class support" for Hitler. Instead, he carefully constructs a German society made up of three complex social layers: at the bottom, the wage earners; in the middle, tradespeople, artisans, peasants, professionals, and lower civil servants; and at the top, an elite consisting of managers, higher civil servants, academically trained professionals, entrepreneurs, and students. Nazi party members came from all three layers, but there was a considerable social difference between Nazi leaders and their followers, the social elite being strongly overrepresented in the party leadership.

One of Kater's most interesting conclusions concerns age patterns within the Nazi leadership. To put it simply, the party leaders were becoming senescent by the 1940s, and this prompts Kater to speculate what would have happened to the NSDAP had it survived the war. He suggests that its bosses would most likely have come to resemble the superannuated former revolutionary leaders of the Soviet Union and China. Would age have mellowed the Nazi bosses? Perhaps not, Kater writes, but certainly they would have become more skeptical and conservative.

Kater sees the Nazis as revolutionary levelers; they wished to create a true *Volksgemeinschaft*, a society without class distinctions. They failed to achieve their goal. Kater also attributes the remarkable stability of West German society since 1945 to this failure. German class structure was basically not changed by the events of 1918, or by those of 1933, or, finally, even by those of 1945.

What all of this shows is that the National Socialist movement appealed to a highly diverse cross section of German society. It attracted support from among radicals and conservatives, the young and the old, the rich, the middle class, and the poor, the well-integrated and those on the fringes of society. Still, if we were to draw some kind of composite portrait of the Nazi voter or Nazi Party member, one exhibiting the most frequently occurring characteristics, we would find that he or she was a Protestant, north or central German, living in a small town, and engaged in a "traditional" profession. That there were millions of exceptions to this portrait only shows that although some groups were more likely to cast their votes for Hitler than others, no part of German society was immune to his appeal.

Why Did They Become Nazis?

Social historians have been able to explore in detail the Nazi Party membership and the National Socialist electorate. They have much greater difficulty explaining how and why the NSDAP gained so many followers. Gordon Craig, the "Dean of German History," presents a version of the classical explanation in his stimulating book *The Germans* (New York: Putnam's, New American Library, 1982). According to Craig, it all began with the German Romantics. At the risk of overstating and oversimplifying a complex and elegant argument, we can perhaps sum up Craig's views as implying that Nazism would not have arisen had nineteenth-century Germans succeeded in absorbing the Enlightenment. Instead of exercising their critical faculties, they chose escapism in, to cite two of many examples, the music of Wagner and the adventure stories of Karl May—both, incidentally, favorites of Hitler. Political romanticism characterized twentieth-century Germans as well: "It impressed the educated middle class, and especially academic youth, and helped both to weaken their confidence in the democratic system and to strengthen their latent tendency to escapism. The beneficiary of [the political romantics'] work was Adolf Hitler." Despite his bitter indictment of the German intellectual tradition, Craig is very optimistic about today's Germans. He sees a sharp break after 1945, when most Germans finally awakened to reality and chose the path of rationalism. It is true, he writes, that irrationality lingers, as typified by the activities of the Baader-Meinhof gang and the Red Army faction, but in general, the age of political romanticism in Germany is over. (His book was published before the rise of the Greens.)

The left-wing English historian Simon Taylor in *The Rise of Hitler: Revolution and Counter-revolution in Germany, 1919–1933* (New York: St. Martin's Press, 1985) has a different conception from that of Gordon Craig. His interpretation of the success of the Nazis is, however, no less familiar. In his splendidly illustrated and well-written little book he concentrates on the struggle between Social Democrats and Communists and also on the impoverishment and despair of the middle class caused by the war and inflation. While discontented Germans were numerous, Taylor explains, the economic polarization that grew out of the formation of financial and industrial cartels and the consequent weakening of free competition, provided an ideal base for Nazi recruitment among farmers, small merchants, and the lower rank of civil servants. By 1930, the center and right parties, representing the middle class, had been duped by Hitler into believing that only the Nazis could stop the rise of Bolshevism. Ultimately, then, it was disunity on the left, the fears of the middle class, and the ambitions of German capitalists that brought about the triumph of Hitler. Hence, according to Taylor, the Nazi assumption of power was dictated by interest politics, a thesis somewhat at odds not only with Craig's but also with the pluralistic argument of Childers and Kater.

In *Modern Germany: Society, Economy and Politics in the Twentieth Century* (New York: Cambridge University Press, 1982; second edition, 1987), V. R. Berghahn takes a position similar to Taylor's. The welfare reforms adopted by the Weimar Republic were valuable, Berghahn writes, but they did little to placate the growing trade unions. Like Taylor, he emphasizes that Germany's industry underwent a process of cartelization that squeezed out small producers. "Soon heavy industry and the working-class movement were locked in their old irreconcilable battles." It was toward these workers—according to Berghahn—that Hitler directed his early socialist propaganda. However, to his surprise, the group that responded most favorably to him was not the workers but people living in rural areas, especially the Protestant farmers of the north, who had been hard hit by rising industrial prices. From there, Hitler's appointment as chancellor, achieved through convoluted party politics, was virtually inevitable. He came to power as a result of intrigue, but he also enjoyed a broad popular base.

In the revised edition of his classic *The Nazi Seizure of Power: The Experience of a Single German Town, 1922–1945* (New York: Franklin Watts, 1984), a study of Northeim in the province of Hanover-Brunswick, the American historian W. S. Allen offers yet another interpretation compatible with studies that find the Nazi electorate principally among the middle and upper classes. He demonstrates that the desire of the middle class to control the urban lower class and their political arm, the Social Democratic Party, facilitated the coming to power of the Nazis. More than anything else, he argues, the politics of Northeim became more radical in the early 1930s because of the effects of the Depression. Many then voted for the NSDAP, the party that promised everything to everyone and topped off its generous promises with an enormous dose of extreme nationalism and revanchism.

And so the debate over the causes of Hitler's triumph continues, with the different participants emphasizing aspects of social experience—romantic tendencies, religious affiliations, voting behavior, class struggle—that resist being combined into a single view or even being critically compared. The final answers still evade us. It seems unlikely we will find them unless we understand the extent of the social chaos in Germany during the early 1930s. Although it was perhaps not unlike that in many other countries, then or now, the turmoil its people suffered must have seemed all the more painful precisely because the breakdown of the social order took place in such a highly developed country.

Eve Rosenhaft's interesting but turgidly written study, *Beating the Fascists? The German Communists and Political Violence, 1929–1933* (New York: Cambridge University Press, 1983), describes the turbulent Berlin scene, one in which the Nazi Storm troopers (SA) deliberately placed its eating and sleeping quarters in the "Red" districts of the capital and there fought its deadly battles with the communist paramilitary units whose own brutality and violence matched that of the Nazis. "Beating the fascists" may have been an exhilarating pastime for unemployed young Berlin workers, but surely it contributed to the already widespread conviction in Germany that the Republic was powerless. Rosenhaft displays much sympathy both for the communist street-fighters and their bosses. Yet she fails to recognize that the real targets of the communist assault teams were not the Nazis but the Weimar Republic and the democratic parties. Meanwhile, the Communist Party prepared its own suicide by applauding the blows delivered to the "fascist" Republic, while neglecting to prepare for the genuine crisis. The party spoke grandiosely of the coming underground struggle against "fascism without a parliamentary mask," that is, Hitlerism, but in fact when Hitler came to power the communists proved defenseless.

This might have had something to do with Stalin's insistence that the Social Democrats were far worse than the Nazis and the Western powers were more dangerous to Soviet Russia than Germany under any leader. Since Rosenhaft herself disapproves of the communists' policy of concentrating their venom on the "social fascists," in other words on the Social Democrats, it is not quite clear why she also approves of the political violence that helped put an end to the parliamentary system in Germany. For example, she inserts inverted commas around the word "plundering" when referring to the ransacking of shops in Berlin by communist street-fighter units. Such actions were, in her opinion, merely "sporadic impulses towards direct collective action for the immediate relief of material hardship." For her, the communist leadership only attempted "to assimilate such impulses, and to direct them so that they developed a mass political character." The effects on the shopkeepers and the other German citizens who had their own "impulses" to protect their property are simply ignored.

Anti-Semitism

Hitlerism's greatest crime was the slaughter of millions of Europeans, chief among whom were the Jews, an infamous act matched only by the orgiastic massacre of other millions by Stalin, Mao, and the Khmer Rouge. How much did the people of these countries know about the massacres? Could they have done anything to stop them? It is difficult to gauge the responsibility of the civilian population in any of these countries, including that of the Germans. There were not many Jews in Germany in 1933, perhaps 500,000 in a population of some 65 million. Of them, about 300,000 emigrated after 1933, so that only about 200,000 were left by the time the war broke out in September 1939. During the war 130,000 of the Jews who had remained in Germany, and another 30,000 who had emigrated to other countries, were killed. The rest may have survived the Holocaust in the concentration camps, in hiding, or in mixed marriages.[1]

All in all, then, we are dealing with a relatively limited number of German-Jewish victims when compared with the more than five million other Jewish victims of Nazi persecution who were citizens of Poland, the Soviet Union, Hungary, and other foreign countries. Moreover, the great majority of Jews, whether German or non-German, were put to death outside the old Reich in the SS death camps of the East. Furthermore, even though many atrocities took place in Germany in 1933, and more during the official pogrom of 1938, the entire German population was not exposed to the spectacle of brutal persecution before the war, although most people were aware that persecution of the Jews and of anti-Nazis was taking place. Then too, during the war, the concentration camps in Germany were both widely dispersed and well isolated from the population. Much historical confusion therefore exists over the extent of the Germans' responsibility.

Ian Kershaw points out in his excellent regional study *Popular Opinion and Political Dissent in the Third Reich: Bavaria, 1933–1945* (New York: Oxford University Press, 1983) that historical opinion on the question of responsibility ranges all the way from the view that the persecution of the Jews was the work of Hitler and the gangsters around him in the face of a disapproving German population to the view that the German people themselves waged a war of extermination against the Jews. Kershaw shows that the public of Bavaria, his test case, included a small percentage of "dynamic" Jew-haters, a much larger proportion of old-fashioned and thus relatively moderate anti-Semites influenced by the Catholic Church, and an even larger proportion of those who were indifferent or mildly sympathetic to the Jews. Kershaw writes of the failure of the Nazi propaganda machine to inspire hatred of Jews among the Germans. "Except on isolated occasions when the Jewish Question directly confronted them, most obviously following the 1938 pogrom [which was organized by the authorities], Germans seldom had Jews on their mind. The constant barrage of propaganda failed to make the Jews the prime target of hatred for most Germans, simply because the issue seemed largely abstract, academic, and unrelated to their own problems. The result was, for the most part, widespread disinterest in the Jewish Question."

This sounds convincing, but are we to interpret it as an acquittal or an indictment? It is true that in Nazi Germany there were no spontaneous pogroms and that Jewish survivors of the Third Reich who had been hiding in Berlin and other German cities tell us of at least as many acts of humanity toward them as of baseness. It is quite likely that proportionally no more Jews in hiding were denounced in Nazi Germany than, for instance, in France or some Eastern European countries.

Conditions in German-occupied Europe, however, were wholly different from those in Germany. Moreover, the German Jews were much better assimilated than their Eastern European counterparts. What condemns the German population, in my opinion, is not that they volunteered to kill, because they generally did not, but that they were indifferent. Ukrainian and Baltic militiamen clubbed thousands of Jews to death in devastated countries that were under ruthless German occupation. The German people lived, until 1945, in an orderly society, and yet they failed to inquire about the fate of their Jewish fellow citizens. With several honorable exceptions, even the German resistance gave low priority to the question. Finally, in Eastern Europe, where the members of the German SS and their Eastern auxiliaries were doing the killing, thousands of ordinary German soldiers readily participated in the Final Solution.

Kershaw puts his finger on something painfully true when he writes that "the Nazis were most successful in the depersonalization of the Jew." The Berlin Jew in hiding had a human face; he appeared as an ordinary neighbor to others—consequently he was often not denounced to the authorities. The Jewish slave laborers from Eastern Europe, whom the SS dragged across Germany, were emaciated, louse-ridden, and dressed in convicts' garb. They looked like criminals and were the object of public contempt. As Johnpeter Horst Grill notes in his interesting regional study *The Nazi Movement in Baden, 1920–1945*

(Chapel Hill: University of North Carolina Press, 1983), "Jews [in Germany] were regarded as an expendable alien race." This was, indeed, the key to the tragedy of Jews in Germany—and, unfortunately, in most other parts of Europe.

Among the many modern studies on the Final Solution, Sarah Gordon's *Hitler, Germans, and the "Jewish Question"* (Princeton NJ: Princeton University Press, 1984) is one of the most challenging. She, too, makes use of dozens of statistical tables, ranging from the "Percentage Distribution of Jews and Non-Jews in Selected Parties of the Reichstag, 1867-1916," through the "Occupational Distribution of Independents Who Opposed Persecution," to "Attitudes of Nazis Toward Racial Persecution." This last table is also the most ironic. It is based on the work of Michael Müller-Claudius, a German researcher who interviewed forty-one members of the Nazi party in 1938, after *Kristallnacht*, and sixty-five in 1942. He found that in 1938 a clear majority of the Nazi party members expressed "extreme indignation" at the treatment of Jews. By 1942 only 26 percent of the Nazi party members were "extremely indignant." Still, both in 1938 and 1942, only 5 percent of the Nazis interviewed approved of racial persecution.

All this sounds incredible, and it would be easy to reproach Gordon for taking such statistics seriously. Nevertheless, both she and Kershaw, who has also made use of Müller-Claudius's findings, buttress this argument with a formidable pile of documents that seem indeed to prove that most of the Germans, and even many Nazi party members, did not wish to see the Jews brutalized or killed. Kershaw, who disdains statistics and charts but who has examined thousands of documents in Bavaria, argues consistently that the persecution of Jews was conducted mostly in secret precisely because the German masses did not approve of the brutality and the killings. Gordon, whose research concentrates on the Government District of Düsseldorf, a major part of the Rhineland, demonstrates that many Nazi party members continued to have sexual relations with Jews even after the adoption of savage laws against such relationships. She states again and again that people voted for Hitler in 1932 and 1933 less because of the Party's extreme anti-Semitism than because of the Depression, fear of communism, the desire to avenge the Versailles Treaty, and sundry other reasons.

The trouble, Gordon argues, was that the German people were indifferent to the fate of the Jews. They simply let Hitler and his radically anti-Semitic cronies determine Jewish policy.

In Gordon's lengthy final chapter she concludes that by 1933 Jews had been well integrated into German society. Still, some significant differences remained between Jews and non-Jews, and it was easy for the Nazis to stereotype the Jews as aliens. Gordon places the main responsibility for German anti-Semitism on Hitler's world view, which interpreted human history as a mortal struggle among nations for living space and for world domination. Hitler saw the Jews as a nation bent on world domination; they posed a racial threat to all other nations. In his paranoid mind, the extermination of the Jews was an absolute and urgent necessity because they were simultaneously much more and much less than human. As a superman, the Jew was already in control of most of the world; as a nonhuman parasite, he was eating away at the body of the healthy races, particularly the Germans.

The people of Germany, according to Gordon, did not go along with the ethnic theories of Hitler, but because he appealed to them in many other ways, they did not question his racist ideology. In any case, she argues, it was extremely difficult for a German to resist the Nazi persecution of Jews. Still, there were Germans who did so, mostly male white-collar workers and independent professionals. The least active opponents of Nazi anti-Semitism, she points out, were women and blue-collar workers. Finally, those who helped Jews were more often than not political conservatives or devout Catholics or both. Gordon rejects all the existing views on the causes of Nazi anti-Semitism, including the Marxist theory of anti-Semitism as a result of psychological scapegoating. She concludes that there is no satisfactory explanation why anti-Semitism was an integral part of Nazism. After all, Gordon writes, had Hitler ignored the Jews in Germany, his popularity would not have suffered significantly. But Hitler, far from ignoring the Jews, found in them the explanation for the tragic history of the human race. For him, they were the Original Sin of mankind. "Hitler came as close as any man in history to playing God. And when the millions of Jewish and other victims pondered their own imminent deaths and wondered 'Why must I die, since I have done nothing to deserve it?' probably the simplest answer would have been that power was concentrated in one man, and that man happened to hate their 'race.'"

Suggestive as this is, one must add two warnings. The first is that while it was truly dangerous for a German to oppose the Nazi regime, it was not at all dangerous to refuse participation in the acts of terror. Moreover, one cannot quite agree with Kershaw and Gordon that only a small minority of Germans were aware of the mass extermination programs. Granted that the true extent of the "Final Solution of the Jewish Question" remained a secret to most Germans until after the war, they must have known at least of the mass murder of non-Jews in Eastern Europe. For example, virtually every German soldier in the Eastern theater of operations must have been aware that the Russian prisoners of war were simply not fed. This awareness must have been communicated to the Germans at home. After all, as Sarah Gordon points out, the Nazis starved to death or otherwise murdered millions of non-Jewish Poles and 3,300,000 Russian prisoners of war.

The second caveat is that, as George Orwell told us in *1984*, it is in the nature of the totalitarian regimes to postulate the existence of an enemy. Had Hitler ignored the Jews (and the Slavs), he would have had to select other victims. And yet Gordon is right: by giving absolute power to one man and regarding him as their savior, the Germans did sell their soul to the Devil. Here lies their responsibility for the death of the Jews and millions of Russians, Poles, and other East Europeans. And it is no consolation to reflect that in Mao's China, Stalin's Soviet Union, and smaller tyrannical countries of the world other peoples have likewise sold their souls.

Indoctrination

Let us put aside the many sophisticated theories of totalitarianism and raise only a few simple questions. Did the Germans embrace triumphant Hitlerism, did they identify with their leader, and did they obey him gladly? To these questions, the authors answer with an almost categorical denial. Kershaw and Allen, the two scholars who have examined most closely popular attitudes in the Third Reich, one within a single town, the other within a single province, agree that under Hitler social life went on more or less as usual, at least until 1939. The inhabitants of W. S. Allen's sample town generally resisted Nazi influences, if only passively. Kershaw writes of a dissent in Bavaria that, if overwhelmingly verbal, was nonetheless widespread. "Seldom has a government placed so much store on the control and manipulation of opinion as did the Nazi regime. Yet, despite some notable propaganda successes, steerage was incomplete."

Who, then, committed the crimes? Who in the Third Reich participated in the totalitarian experiment? The ready answer used to be: the SS more than any other institution. Hitler's army of political soldiers has come to be the ultimate symbol of ruthless efficiency and total devotion to a cause. Yet Robert Lewis Koehl of the University of Wisconsin now tells us in his book *The Black Corps: The Structure and Power Struggles of the Nazi SS* (Madison: University of Wisconsin Press, 1983) that not even the SS was ideologically consistent, nor were its members completely devoted to the Führer.

Koehl describes, with admirable restraint, how the SS grew out of a perceived need for a cadre of loyal guardians of the German nation. This function determined its complex structure, impelled the SS to deal with all aspects of life, and caused it to assume unlimited authority. Having done so, the SS became completely fragmented.

The SS was, in fact, an astonishingly vast, complex, and irrational organization. Created after World War I as a minuscule force of political soldiers to protect Nazi meetings, it came to absorb the entire German police organization. In addition, it assumed or duplicated the work of several ministries and set up its own armed forces. The SS spied on foreign countries, on Germans abroad, on the population at home, on Nazi Party members, and on its own members. It devised, organized, and carried out the "Final Solution of the Jewish Question," the resettlement of millions of ethnic Germans and other people in Eastern Europe, the improvement of the Germanic race, and the protection of racially desirable unwed mothers and illegitimate children. SS members set up and guarded concentration camps; they arrested, tried, and executed the politically, socially, and physically undesirable part of the population; and they engaged in unspeakable torture and insane medical experiments. The SS was an economic empire, a training school for future leaders, and a recruiting office for non-German Nazi sympathizers. In the first year of its existence, the SS stood for racial purity; during the war it took as recruits for the Waffen SS (its fighting branch) ethnic Germans from Eastern and Southeastern Europe, Northern European volunteers, non-German auxiliaries from the East, and ordinary German draftees.

The SS was a state within a state, yet its members infiltrated every other party and state institution; in turn, the SS was infiltrated by rival party and state organizations. It included thousands of people who were not party members; many SS members were not even convinced National Socialists. Some of its crack fighting units were made up not of Germans or even Europeans but of Tatars, Uzbeks, and other Asiatics. The SS engaged in virtually every conceivable kind of political, economic, and military activity, and yet it rarely acted completely on its own. It did not initiate the Final Solution, Koehl writes, nor was it the group that took the largest share of material benefits from it, even though "the SS in all its branches took a conscious hand in the process and sought to enrich itself collectively and individually." According to Koehl, the SS carried out the Final Solution not as a carefully planned process but as a chaotic act of thievery, exploitation, and murder. The SS police courts probably executed more SS criminals than did the Allied courts after the war, though not for their chief crime, murder, but for stealing. Finally, SS chief Heinrich Himmler was Hitler's most loyal servant, and yet he conspired against his master during the last year of the war.

It is difficult to exaggerate the chaos of this most organized of all totalitarian organizations. The SS randomly killed millions of able-bodied slave laborers, yet it allowed other millions to stay alive. In the occupied East, the SS treated some Slavs as subhumans but treated others, including some but far from all Ukrainians as valuable Aryan stock to be won over. The SS deplored the mass killing of Orthodox Serbs by the Catholic Croats and the unorganized massacre of the Bessarabian Jews by the Romanians, only to carry out, in turn, its own more orderly massacre. Koehl's conclusion is categorical: there never was a specific SS phenomenon. While not apologizing for the SS, he still argues that "the SS of wartime became an alibi of a nation. The real SS was more multiform. . . . Certainly for the Holocaust the SS deserves all the blame it has gotten, if not the *exclusive* blame sometimes bestowed. The Waffen-SS undoubtedly prolonged the war; it bought the Nazis time they did not know how to use. . . . It was their [the SS's] tragedy that they had previously surrendered these choices to such masters as Hitler and Himmler. As sorcerers' apprentices, they found themselves in the ruins of the sorcerer's workshop—Germany."

One must agree with Koehl that in Nazi Germany not even the SS was completely indoctrinated or totally committed. Yet it was an organization whose main "achievement" was mass murder. For that not only the SS is to blame but all those people who, in 1933, casually discarded the notion of *Rechtsstaat*, a state based on the rule of law. The German people in 1933 did not unanimously choose Hitler, nor did they, as a whole, obey him gladly and voluntarily. Most of them, however, did give up the values of skepticism and freedom for the sake of immediate material benefits, revenge for Versailles, and national greatness. Even worse, they became or were casual, indifferent, and callous toward persecution. They became, as many of us might become one day if we are not on guard, the apprentices of a mad and wicked sorcerer.

WHO WERE THE FASCISTS?

Perhaps someone will one day formulate a universally acceptable definition of fascism and will clearly identify the fascists; that day still seems far off. *Who Were the Fascists,* edited by Stein Ugelvik Larsen and others (Oslo: Universitetsforlaget, distributed by New York: Columbia University Press, 1980) and containing contributions by some of the world's foremost specialists on fascism, shows—if it still needs to be demonstrated—that fascism was not a monolith. But Larsen and his colleagues also show that a few characteristics were shared by the many varieties of fascism and that we can speak of typically fascist tendencies. Moreover, even if we are unable to tell precisely who the fascists were, we can state with some confidence who was not fascist. To do the latter, we must rid ourselves, at last, of the communist-inspired habit of characterizing as a fascist anyone who is to our right and, occasionally, even to the far left.

Among other general conclusions, *Who Were the Fascists* succeeds in identifying those social groups and occupations that were most likely to support the European fascist movements of the interwar period. For example, small farm-

---

The full version of this somewhat abbreviated essay appeared in the March 3, 1983, issue of the *New York Review of Books,* under the title "What Was Fascism?" A flurry of letters followed, two of which were printed together with my reply in the June 2, 1983, issue of the *New York Review.* One letter defended the Catholic Church and the Franciscan Order in Croatia against charges of guilt during the wartime persecution of the Eastern Orthodox, the Serbs, and the Jews. In my reply I argued that both the Church and the Order needed to deal, at last, with uncomfortable issues in their past. The other letter, by Professor Yosef Yerushalmi, raised the very justifiable questions of whether there was such a phenomenon as left-wing fascism, whether the term totalitarianism covers both phenomena, and why I did not go further in developing a theory of fascism.

ers and civil servants were consistently overrepresented; the participation of workers, on the other hand, varied from country to country, though in some places, such as Eastern Europe, it was enormous. The lower-middle class, composed of petty shopkeepers, craftsmen, clerks, and middle-level farmers, the authors demonstrate, was far less important in the development of fascism than is commonly assumed. Fascism was not simply the political manifestation of petty bourgeois discontent.

The study also concludes that the social composition of fascist membership changed over time, generally moving from a lower-class constituency to all social classes. Fascism was a movement of young people, but only in its early stages, and one wonders whether the fascist systems would not have eventually followed the pattern of communist regimes in becoming gerontocracies. Fascists were not the willing tools of monopoly capital, but rather acted on the whole autonomously. Finally, Larsen's collection of essays shows that fascism had extraordinary regional variations: in Eastern Europe it tended to be both radical socially and murderously anti-Semitic; in Italy and the Iberian peninsula it tended to be neither.

Richard Hamilton's *Who Voted for Hitler?* (Princeton NJ: Princeton University Press, 1982) confirms, with a vast amount of data, what the perceptive essays in Larsen's book suggest; namely, that research on fascism has, after innumerable false starts, reached a point where some categorical statements can be made. Hamilton shows, for instance, that those who voted for Hitler were not necessarily Nazis. In fact only a small proportion of those who cast their votes for the Führer, even those who wore Nazi uniforms, cared to know what National Socialism was all about. Hamilton's findings support the conclusions of the essays in Larsen's collection that careful distinctions must be made among fascist party leaders, members, sympathizers, and electoral supporters.

But Hamilton's excellent book also confirms that it is extremely difficult to make more than a few basic statements regarding fascism. What, for instance, does the social composition of the Hitler electorate tell us about the fascist vote in Europe as a whole? Very little, since those who voted for the Nazi ticket in Germany might not have voted for a fascist leader elsewhere. After reading Hamilton's voluminous work and learning about voting patterns in nearly every conceivable German rural, semirural, and large-town setting, one must conclude that the Nazi voter could be one of many persons—an industrial worker, a peasant, a bureaucrat, someone rich, educated, and cosmopolitan, or a petty bourgeois.[1] We can say confidently, however, that the average Nazi voter in the early 1930s was a Lutheran. Indeed, if anything is characteristic of Germany at the end of the Weimar period, it is that in those years the Protestant north and center embraced the cause of Hitler, while the Catholic Rhineland and south did not. So much for the accepted view of Bavaria as the homeland of National Socialism.

Yet all of the information is of little help in understanding fascist voting patterns in the rest of Europe. There were very few Protestants in Italy, Spain, or Romania, all centers of fascist activity, while fascism failed dismally in the almost exclusively Lutheran Scandinavian countries. The right-wing political radicalism of Protestant Germany and the relative moderation and conservatism of German Catholics must therefore be seen as a peculiarly German phenomenon. The steadfastness of the German Catholic minority in opposing the Protestant majority may even help to explain why the political boundaries run approximately along the same lines today, although now the Protestant north and center tend to vote for the Social Democrats and the Catholic provinces to vote for Christian Democrats and Christian Socialists.

Hamilton's fundamental distinction between the Protestant vote and the Catholic vote is not new, but his minute examination of voting data proves it valid. Far more controversial is his argument that, in the major cities, the upper and upper-middle classes gave more support to Hitler than the lower bourgeoisie. As other critics of Hamilton have pointed out, he does not always take into account the fact that in well-to-do German suburbs lower-class servants as well as other lower-class people often lived at the same address as people with higher social status, the poor being relegated to the drabber sections of the buildings. So it is difficult to know exactly who voted for the Nazis in those districts. Domestic servants did—they were among Hitler's most fervent followers.

Both of the books under review suggest many other conclusions, both firm and tentative, and they raise countless controversial issues. In fact *Who Were the Fascists* is almost unmanageable because of its size and the abundance of material it contains. Originating from papers presented at an international conference on comparative European fascism held in Bergen, Norway, in June 1974, Larsen's book contains some fifty essays by forty-four contributors. They deal with fascism in Austria, Germany, Italy, Slovakia, Croatia, Romania, Hungary, Spain, Portugal, Switzerland, France, Belgium, the Netherlands, Great Britain, Ireland, Greece, Norway, Finland, Denmark, Sweden, and even Iceland. We find essays about the triumph of fascism, fascism as a major but not dominant force, and fascism as a refuge for lunatics and outcasts. Each movement and party is treated with the same solemnity and scholarly detachment. There is no outrage or moralizing but much analysis of social class, age cohorts, peer groups, occupational categories, and status. Virtually every fascist movement is carefully dissected by the methods of modern social science.

Wisely, the contributors concentrate on the less well-known fascist movements: the generally minuscule Scandinavian parties receive 165 pages, Germany and Italy together only 91. Five articles deal with the Nasjonal Samling, the Norwegian Nazi Party. The result of the latter is to make the reader familiar, or so it seems, with practically every regional and professional subgroup in a party that consisted of only a few thousand Norwegians.

Ideologically and methodologically, the contributions range from the modified neo-Marxism of Reinhard Kühnl (from Marburg, West Germany) to the broad multicausal analysis of Juan J. Linz of Yale. Two Norwegian scholars have contributed a "geoeconomic-geopolitical model for the explanation of violent breakdowns of competitive mass politics," but if this contains an explanation of fascism, it is hard to find it among the authors' schematic charts and tables on "semi-peripheralized territories," "seaward empire-nations" (as distinct from "seaward peripheries" and "landward empire-nations"), "consociational formations," and "frustrated empire-building."

The first general essay, "The Concept of Fascism" by Stanley G. Payne of the University of Wisconsin, is one of the most interesting. It begins with an analytical list of the main theories of fascism, from the classical Marxist theory of "fascism as a violent, dictatorial agent of bourgeois capitalism," to the view of Benedetto Croce and Friedrich Meinecke that fascism was a "product of a cultural and moral breakdown." Erich Fromm, Wilhelm Reich, and Theodor Adorno believed that fascism was "the result of neurotic or pathological psychosocial impulses." Payne also considers Hannah Arendt's view that fascism was "a typical manifestation of twentieth-century totalitarianism" as well as theories holding that fascism represented "resistance to modernization" or that it was "a unique radicalism of the middle class." To these Payne adds the views of such authors as Renzo de Felice and Karl D. Bracher who deny any fundamental coherence to the concept of fascism.

Payne argues that a systematic definition of generic fascism is both necessary and possible, and he proposes a rather complex system of classification made up of both positive and negative characteristics. True fascism, he explains, is in opposition to liberalism, communism, and—less violently—conservatism. It advocates the creation of a new, nationalist, authoritarian state, an integrated social structure, and the building of an empire. Fascism, he writes, espouses an idealist creed calling on its followers to participate by an act of will. More importantly, it develops a very special style and organization characterized by an emphasis on patriotic symbols and visible political "choreography," romantic and mystical rhetoric, attempts at mass mobilization, the cult and practice of violence, heavy emphasis on the masculine principle and male dominance, an organic view of society, an exaltation of youth, an emphasis on the conflict of generations, and of course, a charismatic, personal style of leadership. Does Payne leave anything out? He could, in my view, have said more about imperialistic expansion and war, about the militarization of society, and about the fascists' mania for demonstrations and marching.

Payne, like Juan J. Linz, another perceptive analyst of fascism, maintains that true fascism must be distinguished from right-wing authoritarianism—which tended to be monarchist rather than dictatorial, rationalist and religious rather than irrationalist. The conservative "new right" forces in Europe after World War I were based on traditional elites rather than on newly formed groups or organizations; they affirmed the existing social hierarchy, and most important, they relied on the army. The right-wing authoritarians, Payne notes, rejected the fascist principles of party militia and mass party militarization.

Payne leaves it to the reader to decide who among the interwar right-wing political leaders was a fascist and who was merely a right-wing authoritarian. Yet no sooner does one agree to play this game than one is assailed by doubts. If, according to his definition, Franco, Perón, Antonescu of Romania, or Father Tiso of Slovakia qualify as new rightists, and not as fascists, then why not put Mussolini himself in this category? The Duce, after all, failed to abolish the monarchy, and his social and political radicalism was largely posturing. And why not Hitler himself, who, on June 30, 1934, in the Great Blood Purge, annihilated his own party militia at the bidding of the German Army?

Finally, the most vexing question: if fascism implies an integrated social structure, nationalism, violence, mass mobilization, charismatic leadership, quasi-religious political symbols, and the elaborate staging of political events, accompanied by incessant demonstrations and marching, then why not consider such systems as those of Stalin, Mao, Kim Il Sung, Pol Pot, Idi Amin, or other modern dictatorships to be fascist as well?

Payne and the other writers do not even mention the possibility of left-wing fascism, nor do they discuss the possibility that a "totalitarian" model could apply to both left and right regimes. This is a wise decision on their part, for if they imposed their definition of fascism on groups that proclaimed themselves antifascist, they would be guilty of the sort of obfuscation that they correctly impute to the dogmatic Marxists who described social democrats, for example, as "objectively" social-fascist. But the question remains: does the use of antifascist slogans rule out racist characteristics? Stalin and Hitler, after all, share something fundamental, which we do not know how to name but that brings the two dictators closer to each other than Hitler is to, let us say, Hungary's Admiral Horthy, or than Stalin is to Hungary's János Kádár.

For all of its references to fundamental characteristics, Payne's definition cannot tell us everything about fascism, as becomes evident from Stanislav Andreski's disturbing essay "Fascists as Moderates." Andreski, a historian at the University of Reading, is of Polish origin, and hence one of several contributors who were driven into emigration by East European tyranny. Andreski's point is that fascism, rather than being "the extremism of the center," as S. M. Lipset wants us to believe, was "the centrism of the extremists." The fascists, Andreski writes, strutted about in military costume and pretended to be radical in every respect, but in reality they inhabited a kind of halfway house between laissez-faire capitalism and Bolshevism. On this view, fascism, or at least fascist economic policy, foreshadowed Western European developments after World War II. Heavy bureaucratic control without wholesale expropriation, a strong dose of nationalization, price and wage controls, and huge state investment: all this would place the fascists slightly to the left of the British Labour party, according to Andreski. Why to the left? Because fascist, particularly German fascist, centralism was far more efficient than the centralism of the British Labour Party, which is constantly undermined by the anarchism of the unions. This sounds less plausible when we remember the accounts by Speer and others describing the Nazi regime not as centralized but as composed of bitterly conflicting and often inefficient fiefdoms.

It is a relief, after all this comparative theorizing, to move on to the discussion of particular fascist movements. Here there is much new data, and a lot to learn. In Austria between the wars Nazism won followers mainly from among the anticlerical urban petty bourgeoisie, but it was only one of several fascist movements. The fascist Heimwehr drew its followers from among the traditionalist rural Catholic population. Eastern European fascism was truly unique: very popular yet rarely successful. In such Eastern European countries as Romania, Bulgaria, Hungary, and Poland the established authoritarian regimes effectively preempted the platform of the genuine fascists and for the most part also won favor with Italy or Nazi Germany or both. Because the Eastern European fascists were rebellious, radical, and anarchic, Hitler favored the authoritarian right-wing governments and allowed the latter to crush local fascists movements.

Slovakia and Croatia, especially Croatia, provide us with the horrifying example of Catholic clergy gone mad with missionary fervor. The Slovak priests did not shed blood—they let the state take care of that—but the Croat priests who took part in the fascist Ustasha, especially the Franciscans, did so. Their victims, as the careful study by Yeshayahu Jelinek shows, numbered thousands among the Orthodox, communists, and Jews. In Romania the fascism of the Iron Guard group was rural, mystical, socially rebellious, and mainly xenophobic. The Iron Guard, or Legion of the Archangel Michael, murdered in a sort of religious frenzy—at one point four Iron Guardists fired 120 bullets into a renegade who was lying sick in a hospital bed; they then chopped up his body, danced, sang, and kissed each other. But more Iron Guardists were murdered by the Romanian royal dictatorship than any other group. In Hungary the Arrow Cross was both a substitute for a left-wing radical party (the communists were an insignificant underground movement of mostly Jewish intellectuals) and a home for discontented members of the petty bourgeoisie, the urban middle class, the gentry, the officer corps, and the aristocracy. Arrow Cross membership fluctuated wildly, but working-class participation in it remained consistently high.

The collection concludes with an ambitious comparative analysis by Peter H. Merkl of the preconditions for the growth of fascism—cultural despair, social malaise, demobilized soldiers, civil war, the Red threat, the Great Depression, religious decline, and so forth. Merkl provides the most coherent explanation of the youthful character of the fascist movements, at least when they began, and of the importance of civil servants in them, for he connects the rise of fascist groups with the deep feelings of resentment against the old elites among young people and lower bureaucrats during the 1920s. But his conclusion that there were left-wing, center, and right-wing fascist movements, depending on the proportion of working-class members, assumes that workers are always socially progressive—a debatable view.

These are valuable books, serious, reliable, and objective, qualities that their subject did not share. Cast in the abstractions of social science, neither study can adequately reflect the color and excitement that made fascism attractive to millions of Europeans. Nor do the books fully convey its viciousness and horror. Further, because they are all-encompassing, they cannot make clear the fundamental difference between German National Socialism and the other fascist ideologies. Nazism was undoubtedly the most monstrous form of fascism. Unlike the others, the National Socialist system alone would not, and probably could not, have existed without mass murder and war.

PERPETRATORS

1

In 1989, in an article entitled "The Incomprehensible Holocaust" (see the chapter under the same title in this volume), I discussed sixteen books selected from the vast Holocaust literature published during the 1980s. Since then, hundreds more books and articles have appeared on the subject, so that writing about the Holocaust has become an industry in itself, one with a terrible and never-ending fascination. A change is taking place, however, in the general character of such works. While survivors' memoirs and historical accounts as well as philosophical, theological, and psychological studies continue to appear, interest has been growing in previously neglected subjects. One such subject is the experience of ordinary non-Jews who were involved in the Holocaust, whether as murderers, collaborators, bystanders, or saviors. Then, too, more writers have felt the need to discuss the fate of millions of non-Jewish victims of Nazism and to make at least passing references to other cases of genocide. It is not the uniqueness of the Jewish Holocaust that is being challenged but the tendency of earlier writers to remain strictly within the confines of the Jewish tragedy.

More and more studies discuss the adventures of Jews who survived by "passing" and who, as a consequence, lived simultaneously in two worlds. The best known examples of this recent trend are Louis Begley's *Wartime Lies* (New York: Knopf, 1991), a chilling, witty novel about a Jewish boy and his aunt who survive the Nazi years in Poland by acquiring false Aryan papers, and Agnieszka Holland's more recent film, *Europa, Europa*, about a Jewish boy who

---

This essay appeared under the title "Strategies of Hell" in the October 8, 1992, issue of the *New York Review of Books*.

survived by becoming a member of the Hitler youth organization. But while Begley's novel, however much it may be based on experience, does not claim to be other than fiction, the appeal of *Europa, Europa* as an exciting adventure story is marred, at least in my opinion, by its claim to be entirely true. I simply do not believe that a circumcised Jewish boy could have avoided, year after year, the rigorous medical inspections and the male-bonding nudity that were regular features of the Hitler Jugend training camps. It is also a bit too much to have a long lost brother turn up in a concentration camp uniform not a second too late before the young Jewish hero, captured by the Red Army as a Nazi soldier, is about to be shot dead.

Some of the new books tell no less unlikely sounding stories, yet they are thoroughly documented and so must be believed. Jews in hiding often had no choice but to share the fate of the ethnic group within which they had found shelter. Jewish women who were passing as non-Jewish Germans were raped by the liberating Soviet soldiers who claimed to be avenging Nazi atrocities. Jews pretending to be Polish Christians were persecuted and in some cases murdered by Germans, Ukrainians, and Lithuanians, and by Soviet soldiers eager to kill Poles. Jewish refugees serving in Soviet partisan units were in danger of being shot by Polish, Ukrainian, or Lithuanian partisans fighting both Nazis and Communists. If they joined other resistance groups, they risked being executed by Soviet partisans as suspected German or Polish agents. As he assumed one role after another, the hero of Nechama Tec's *In the Lion's Den* (New York: Oxford University Press, 1990) (see the chapter titled "In Disguise" in this volume), the young Galician Jew Oswald Rufeisen, was in danger as a Jew, a Pole, a German policeman, a nun, a Soviet partisan, and a Bolshevik commissar.

Jews in disguise invariably confronted the moral dilemma of having to identify, at least outwardly, with gentile spectators of the Holocaust and sometimes even with the Jew-killers. The more effective their disguise, the more some were in doubt about their own identity. Success in passing often hinged, after all, on the degree of one's past familiarity with non-Jewish cultures. The Berlin Jewish girl hiding with Christian friends and shielded by her "Aryan" looks and manners felt she was primarily German. For some young Jews who survived the war in a Polish monastery or convent, a hastily acquired Christian piety became a genuine commitment. Other Jews survived by assisting their oppressors: the young woman described in Peter Wyden's *Stella: One Woman's True Tale of Evil, Betrayal, and Survival in Hitler's Germany* (New York: Simon and Schuster, 1992) hunted down Jews in Berlin on behalf of the Gestapo.

Recent Holocaust literature pays more attention than previously to the question of how widespread was the desire among Europeans to see an end to a large Jewish presence in their midst. All the evidence indicates that millions upon millions of Europeans, not only the Germans, were keen for this to happen. No doubt, most of these people hoped for a nonviolent solution of the Jewish question; they were even prepared to absorb a small number of Jews into gentile society. Yet without a widespread consensus that it was desirable to be rid of most Jews, the Nazi extermination program would have been far less successful. Nor would the Final Solution have succeeded to the degree it did without the callousness and even, in some cases, the anti-Semitism of the British and American political leaders, foreign services, professional associations, trade unions, press, and public.[1]

One question still to be adequately addressed is whether the rejection of the Jews was a special phenomenon that can be explained by many centuries of anti-Semitism or whether it was a particularly odious phase in a continuous process of ethnic purification that had been taking place for years in many parts of Europe. A case can be made for both propositions. That millions of European children were brought up thinking that the Jews were responsible for killing Christ, for example, surely would have affected popular attitudes at the time of the Holocaust. The general trend toward ethnic purification has not only been neglected, however, but seems to bear a particularly heavy share of responsibility.

The desire of the European nations to rid their lands of all types of minorities was given a major impetus by the French Revolution, but the movement became infinitely more vociferous and violent in our century. The French Jacobins and their nineteenth-century nationalist imitators in Europe aimed at assimilating such ethnic minorities as the Bretons and the Jews in France, or the Romanians, Slavs, Germans, and Jews in Hungary; they would punish only those among the minorities who openly resisted assimilation. After World War I, the aim of the groups in power changed increasingly to forcible absorption, expulsion, or annihilation. The campaigns for ethnic purification undertaken during and immediately after World War II affected the lives of more than a hundred million people. Examples include Poles and other Slavs killed, persecuted, or displaced by the Germans; Germans killed by East Europeans; Ukrainians and others killed by the Soviets and Soviets killed by Ukrainians; Serbs killed by Croats and Croats killed by Serbs—to name only some of the most terrible cases. Among them the Jews, being both wholly defenseless and the object of an official Nazi policy obsessively bent on eliminating them, were the most unfortunate group of victims, but the fate of the others deserves more attention than it has had so far.

Particularly informative among the more recent studies discussing the personal lives and character of the murderers is *"The Good Old Days": The Holocaust as Seen by Its Perpetrators and Bystanders* (translated by Deborah Burnstone, foreword by Hugh Trevor-Roper; New York: Free Press, 1991). The study is based on letters, diaries, and other documents that have been intelligently selected by three German compilers: Ernst Klee, a filmmaker and writer; Willi Dressen, a jurist deeply involved in the investigation of National Socialist crimes; and Volker Riess, a historian.

The photographs in the book tell even more about the behavior of the German soldiers than the documents. Wartime hangings with the executioners grinning under the gallows have long been a favorite photographic subject, but never was there more demand for such snapshots than during World War II. Scores of amateurish photographs depict SS and Wehrmacht soldiers posing beneath people hanging from a rope, or they record, in monotonously repetitive sequences, the mowing down of rows upon rows of shivering, half-clad women and children. The pictures were taken in spite of official orders not to do so or talk about what had taken place. It is true, as the records in *"The Good Old Days"* show, that the German murder squads sometimes delegated the job of execution to local East Europeans, but more often they did the work themselves.

In the accounts of mass murder, satisfaction over a job well done often mingles with self-pity over having had to perform such a demanding and unappreciated task. In fact, the murder assignments were unrewarding: policemen complained of not having received the cigarettes, schnapps, and sausages given the SS men following a successful joint massacre. Many members of the *Einsatzgruppen,* or murder squads, were not from the SS but were professional police and other middle-aged men drafted into the police forces. They were generally neither well paid nor well fed; not all had the opportunity to rob their victims. Few among them belonged to the Nazi Party and not all were convinced National Socialists.

As the documents show, these men killed to please their superiors, because they knew that there were plenty of volunteers in regular army units ready to take their places, or because they feared to appear as weaklings. The SS man or policeman who did not like the idea of machine-gunning defenseless adults and smashing the heads of infants found it was easy to say no. The worst that could happen to such recalcitrants was to be transferred to another unit. Others were sent home for being soft (*"wegen zu grosser Weichheit"*). In none of the vast literature on the Holocaust is there, so far as I know, the record of a single case of a German policeman or member of the SS having been severely reprimanded, imprisoned, or sent to the front—much less shot—for his refusal to participate in mass murder.

"Today gypsies, tomorrow partisans, Jews and suchlike riff-raff," notes one diarist. What both murderers and German military onlookers often objected to was not the killing itself but the methods used. Hence the gradual progression from pogrom-like clubbings and axings, which were usually left to Latvian, Lithuanian, or Ukrainian civilians, to machine-gunning by Germans and their uniformed auxiliaries, and, finally, to the setting up of death camps where efficient industrial killing could be carried out.

During the first months of the war in the East, when killings still took place in public, German sailors from the Baltic ports and soldiers from far away garrisons indulged in what *"The Good Old Days"* describes as execution tourism. These visitors raised objections to the officers in charge only when they observed that arms and legs, some of them still moving, were sticking out of the makeshift graves. The ground above the graves, some of the spectators noticed, continued to heave for several hours after the executions.

In perhaps the most distressing account in *"The Good Old Days,"* two German divisional chaplains, one Catholic, the other Protestant, report on their investigation undertaken at the request of two lower-ranking military chaplains, again one a Catholic and the other Protestant, who were themselves acting upon the request of some soldiers, into the case of ninety Jewish orphans in a Ukrainian village in August 1941. The children's parents had been killed by the SS at the request of the local army command only a day or two earlier. The two divisional chaplains, like the two other clerics before them, visited the house in which the starving and thirsty children were locked up but left without offering them even a cup of water. They were scandalized by the atrocious conditions in which the children were held but were bothered even more by the fact that the incessant wailing of the children could be heard by both soldiers and civilians. In their separate reports to the chief of staff of the 295th Infantry Division, the divisional chaplains insisted that locals not be allowed to enter the house "in order to avoid the conditions there being talked about further," and "I consider it highly undesirable that such things should take place in full view of the public eye."

Because two army divisional chaplains, that is, high-ranking officers, were involved in the affair, there was a thorough investigation by the divisional general staff. Finally, the commander of the Sixth Army himself, Field Marshal von Reichenau, ruled that the execution of the children should be carried out as planned, although of course in an orderly manner. In a remarkable act of interservice cooperation, the Wehrmacht dug the grave, the SS arranged the executions, and the local militia were ordered to do the shooting. "The Ukrainians were standing round trembling," noted the SS lieutenant supervising the affair ("I had nothing to do with this technical procedure"), and when they finally fired, they did so poorly. "Many children were hit four or five times before they died," reported the lieutenant.

What strikes one is the full cooperation offered by regular army units, the high proportion of Austrians in the murder squads, and how lightly, if at all, the murderers and their accomplices were punished after the war.[2] The two Catholic chaplains who reported on the Jewish orphans were both ordained as bishops in the German Federal Republic.

Members of the SS and police murder squads were recruited from every sort of occupation. Several unit commanders were doctors of law; others had risen through the ranks. Many officers and men suffered acutely under the stress of their assignment: "The wailing was indescribable. I shall never forget the scene throughout my life. . . . I particularly remember a small fair-haired girl who took me by the hand. She too was shot later," complained the SS lieutenant supervising the execution of the children in the Ukrainian village. Others, however, remained steadfast: "Strange, *I am completely unmoved. No pity, nothing.* That's the way it is and then it's all over," wrote the Austrian Felix Landau in his diary on July 12, 1941. He was more worried, however, about his "Trudchen" cheating on him during his absence.

The Germans in *"The Good Old Days"* were generally low in the Nazi hierarchy. This is not so for Rudolph Höss, the commander of Auschwitz, whose memoirs have now been issued, the publisher tells us, in their first complete translation into English. It would have been useful, however, had Steven Paskuly, the editor of *Death Dealer: The Memoirs of the SS Kommandant at Auschwitz* (translated by Andrew Pollinger; Buffalo NY: Prometheus Books, 1992) pointed out precisely in what way his version differs from that of the 1959 English-language edition. Still, this edition is usefully supplemented by diagrams, a detailed chronology of the events at Auschwitz-Birkenau, and the minutes of the January 1942 Wannsee Conference, at which representatives of the major German ministries and other services were told about the progress of the Final Solution.

Höss was sentenced to death by a Polish court and hanged, in 1947, in Auschwitz. He was similar to the murderers included in *"The Good Old Days"* in his limited intelligence, his desperate efforts to please his superiors, his determination not to appear weak, and his many prejudices. He was different because, unlike the average SS man and policeman, he was an "Old Combatant" and a dedicated National Socialist. Next to Adolf Eichmann, whose police and court hearings have filled thousands of pages, Höss is the best-documented Nazi killer. He wrote his lengthy autobiography, which is supplemented by detailed portraits of fellow SS leaders and, among other things, a report on the confusing rank order of the various SS service branches, while in a Polish prison. A Polish psychologist and the prosecuting attorney both suggested that he give an account of himself, but unlike Eichmann, who basically answered questions, Höss was free to put down whatever he wished. The result combines a considerable amount of accurate information and some genuine insights into his past with remarkable historical distortions. Like many other Nazi leaders, Höss had little sense of statistical reality, especially in connection with the Jews, whose numbers he vastly overestimated. He and Eichmann expected the arrival in Auschwitz of 4 million Jews from Romania, 2.5 million from Bulgaria, and 3 million from Hungary. In fact, there were no more than 1.5 million Jews in the three countries.

Höss was born into a devout Catholic middle-class family in Baden-Baden. He soon became "disgusted" with the Church, he writes, but remained forever a believer of sorts. Having distinguished himself as a front-line soldier in World War I, he joined the Free Corps of right-wing veterans after the war and began the typical career of a Nazi leader. He took part in the fighting in the Baltic countries between 1918 and 1921, which he describes correctly as one of the most brutal and vicious wars in modern history, a *bellum omnium contra omnes* involving Russian Whites and Reds, German Free Corps, Poles, Latvians, and other local forces. Later, because he took part in the murder of a man who had allegedly betrayed the Nazi terrorist Leo Schlageter to the French authorities in the Ruhr, he spent six years in Weimar Germany's prisons, an experience that taught him, he says, to respect the rights of prisoners.

A party member since 1922, Höss joined the SS in 1934 and was soon sent by Himmler to help set up one of the first concentration camps in Germany. In 1940 he was made commander of the new camp at Auschwitz where, Höss writes, his "children could live free and easy," and where his wife "had her flower paradise." As for himself, he was never really happy. He resented the conflicting instructions he received: one day he was ordered to exterminate all the Jews, and the next day he was told to select for slave labor all persons strong enough to work. He complains constantly about the greed, sloth, corruption, and intrigues of his underlings, and his memoirs largely consist of criticism of the inefficiency and brutality of the SS and the Kapos, the prisoners who were put in charge of the others. There is no evidence to show that he ever tried to alleviate the atrocious camp conditions, and he himself invented new methods of torture. Still, an imprisoned Polish artist assigned to work in the Höss household told the editor of this book that the family had treated him as a guest and that he was invited to dine with the commander.

As Höss tells it, he felt sorry for all his victims: the Russian POWs and Polish political prisoners whom he had gassed as a rehearsal for the gassing of the Jews; the Gypsies, for whom he had much sympathy but whom he sent to the gas chambers nevertheless; the prisoners in the Women's Camp who were worse off even than the men ("I have always had a great respect for women in general"); and even the Jews whom he alternately admired and despised. True contempt and dislike he supposedly reserved for his fellow SS officers.

In his farewell letters to his family and in his "Final Thoughts," Höss declared himself a National Socialist and had this to say about the Holocaust: "Today I realize that the extermination of the Jews was wrong, absolutely wrong. It was exactly because of this mass extermination that Germany caused itself the hatred of the entire world. The cause of anti-Semitism was not served by this act at all, in fact, just the opposite. The Jews have come much closer to their final goal." Standing on the gallows, he apologized to the Polish people. As Steve Paskuly, the editor of the memoirs, notes in his epilogue, Höss, who greatly admired the Jehovah's Witnesses for their courage in the camp, thought of himself as a soldier of faith, a true believer whose religion was National Socialism.

2

An impressive work exclusively devoted to Holocaust bystanders is Gordon J. Horwitz's *In the Shadow of Death: Living Outside the Gates of Mauthausen* (New York: Free Press, 1990). His subjects are the Austrians in and around Mauthausen, a town located close to a notorious Nazi concentration camp, although not one primarily for Jews. Only 40,000 of the 119,000 people who died there between 1938 and 1945 were Jews, and therefore the people who lived near the camp (or camps, since Mauthausen had many subsidiary establishments) did not necessarily think of the camp inmates as Jews.

Set up in 1938, soon after the Anschluss of Austria, the Mauthausen camp housed German and Austrian criminals, "asocials," political prisoners, homosexuals, Jehovah's Witnesses, and later, Poles, Spanish republican refugees handed over to the Germans by Vichy France, Soviet and other POWs, as well as, of course, Jews. With a large stone quarry at its center, the Mauthausen camp was a thriving business enterprise for the SS but it was also a particularly brutal place. One form of punishment consisted of having to run up the 186 steps of the quarry shouldering a heavy slab of stone. The SS called those who fell, were pushed, or leaped into the pit "Parachute Troops" (*Fallschirmjäger*).

In 1940 a gas chamber was set up in nearby Castle Hartheim, at first to kill only mentally ill and retarded Germans and Austrians but later camp inmates as well. Subsequently, a gas chamber was set up in the Mauthausen camp itself, with Soviet POWs as its first victims.

The center of Mauthausen, a small town of about 1,800 almost exclusively Catholic inhabitants (there had been no Jews there before the war), was three miles away from the camp. The local people, as Horwitz's interviews and documents show, regularly witnessed atrocities being committed whenever new arrivals were driven across the town or whenever local farmers and workers had to go near the quarry. A public road led directly across the camp, and although those using it were forbidden to linger, they heard and saw enough for the atrocities to become widely known and often discussed. Even in the early years of the camp, inmates were shot in full view of the peasants and left to die on the roadside. Eleanore Gusenbauer, a farmer, filed a complaint in 1941 about the tortures and the random shootings: "I am anyway sickly and such a sight makes such a demand on my nerves that in the long run I cannot bear this. I request that it be arranged that such inhuman deeds be discontinued, or else be done where one does not see it."

Complaining was not without its risks: some who protested what they saw happening were sentenced to a stay in a concentration camp. For example, when a man called Winklehner threw bread and cigarettes to the inmates, he was taken to the Dachau camp, where he later died. All in all, however, the locals learned to live with the camp. They resented the rowdiness of the SS but profited from the business the SS brought to the town. The civilians employed at Castle Hartheim soothed their consciences with the knowledge that they were not directly involved in the gassings. Near Hartheim, parts of human bodies littered the countryside and tufts of hair flew out of the chimney onto the street, but neither this nor the smell of burning flesh prevented the staging of popular candlelight festivals at the castle. Even the monks at the famous Benedictine monastery nearby at Melk accepted the sight and stench of the local subsidiary camp and crematorium.

On February 2, 1945, when hundreds of Soviet officers escaped from the camp, townspeople joined in the hunt. Only a dozen made it to freedom, their escape thanks in part to a couple of brave local inhabitants who thus helped persons who were clearly seen as the enemy. During World War I, Mauthausen had served as a giant POW camp; it must have been difficult for the townspeople to distinguish between prisoners of war, common criminals, political prisoners, and innocent victims. Still, the passivity and silence of most of the population is disheartening and so is the wave of acute anti-Semitism that swept the region after 1945, as it did throughout Europe from the Netherlands to Poland. Today, despite some efforts by the Austrian government to preserve the memory of the camp, no one really wants to talk about what happened in Mauthausen. Horwitz, who managed, after much effort, to find revealing sources, concludes: "The efforts [to address the past] are minimal compared to the enormity of the deliberate silences, evasions, and distortions of a generation that slowly, mutely fades into the grave."

3

In the extensive literature on collaboration, a special place has always been reserved for Jewish collaborators. Perhaps the most dreadful accounts to appear on this subject are not about the Jewish Councils or the concentration camp Kapos but about the Jewish retrievers (*Abholer*), raiders (*Ordner*), stool pigeons (*Spitzel*), and catchers (*Greifer*) in Berlin who brought other Jews to the collection centers and prevented escapes. The most trusted among them did the work of the Gestapo by detecting and arresting Jews who tried to pass as non-Jews. The "catchers" included the blonde, blue-eyed Stella Goldschlag, the subject of Peter Wyden's *Stella*. Wyden is himself from Berlin; his family came to New York just before the outbreak of the war, and Stella, for whom he had a secret passion, was one of his friends and classmates in the luxurious private high school that Jewish upper-class youngsters attended after the Nazis had dismissed them from the state schools.

The picture drawn by Wyden of Berlin's Jewish upper class is not flattering, but he candidly admits that he doesn't know how he himself would have behaved had he been left in Berlin to face the Nazis. The Jewish elite had been too successful for their own good, Wyden argues, and too certain of their niche in German society. They were contemptuous of the Jewish refugees from the East, and many among them were anti-Semitic.

Assimilated Jews, in Berlin or elsewhere, had enormous difficulties coping with their sudden decline to the level of the most downtrodden of East European Jews. How was a person called Siegfried to react to the Nazi order adding the middle name Israel to his first name? How was the decorated veteran of the First World War to behave when kicked in the behind, in public, by young SA louts who had never even been soldiers? Those who could emigrated; others became Zionists; still others kept affirming their devotion to the fatherland that had deserted them; some tried to join their persecutors.

At first, young Stella Goldschlag lived a semi-illegal life: during the day she wore the yellow star while working in a factory, but at night she was a free and immensely attractive German woman who went to parties using an assumed name. Later, when she tried to live entirely as an Aryan German, she was arrested, tortured to reveal the names of those who had provided her with false papers, and at last talked into helping the Gestapo. Soon she was out in the streets, dressed elegantly, haunting the cafés and other places where Jews attempting to pass for gentiles tended to gather. Together with other upper-class Jews in her team, she caught and delivered to the Gestapo people who had often been her friends and former classmates. What makes the story particularly harrowing is that Stella and her friends carried revolvers, probably the only Jews in the world so equipped by the Nazis. They needed the guns not only to make arrests but also to defend themselves.

Today it may seem almost inconceivable that these catchers never even thought of turning the guns on their masters, yet for them, the notion of shooting German policemen would have been no less inconceivable. Like so many other victims, they also admired and desperately tried to imitate their oppressors. For other, worse-off victims of totalitarianism, they felt only contempt. After the war, Stella claimed that she had only tried to protect her parents. Yet, as Wyden shows, she continued in her job and became more active than ever after her parents had been sent to Theresienstadt. Stella and her friends enjoyed what they were doing because it gave them power and allowed them to identify with the dashing Nazis.

A surprising number of Jews survived the war in Berlin, the city that Hitler most wanted to be *judenfrei*. At least 1,400 managed to stay in hiding; several thousand others remained relatively unharmed because they were married to Christians; thousands survived in camps in and near the capital; and hundreds got through the war in a Jewish hospital that was oddly allowed to exist. Immediately after the end of fighting, Stella was arrested and tried by the Soviet occupation authorities; she spent ten years in various East German camps and prisons. Following her release, she was tried twice by a West Berlin court and was sentenced each time to ten years. However, because she had already spent ten years in Soviet custody, she was not imprisoned again. Wyden visited her repeatedly in her comfortable West German apartment in 1990 and 1991: still attractive, mendacious, a professed "victim of the Jews," but very much isolated. Her daughter is a public health nurse in Israel; she says she hates her mother and has fantasies about killing her.

Those who migrated from Germany and Austria before the war tended to have money, the right connections, and relatives abroad who were both devoted to them and well-to-do. People like Stella's family, who had less money and no foreign friends, usually stayed put and were mostly killed. The unfairness of it all was one reason for Stella's bitterness and hatred. In Wyden's account Berlin gentiles applauded when Stella and the Gestapo were catching Jews. This is quite different from the picture that emerges from Inge Deutschkron's simple and charming memoir, *Outcast: A Jewish Girl in Wartime Berlin* (translated by Jean Steinberg. New York: Fromm International, 1989).

The teenaged daughter of a teacher, Inge Deutschkron found a job in a workshop for the blind in 1941. Then and later, she writes, she was met with almost invariable kindness on the part of non-Jewish Berliners. Upon seeing her wearing a yellow star, a man insisted that she take his place in the subway, which she was, of course, not allowed to do. People slipped apples and meat stamps into her pocket. After the deportations of the East had begun, in October 1941, Inge and her mother went into hiding. Scores of gentile acquaintances and people she did not know at all took enormous risks in giving work to the two women and in feeding and sheltering them. They were forced to change residences repeatedly, for no one could take the risk of keeping them for more than a few months, but the two women always found volunteers to take them in. If there is any bitterness in Inge Deutschkron's account, it is mostly directed against the Jewish communal authorities, whom she accuses of having helped the authorities organize the deportations.

Toward the end of the war, the bombings and the influx of German refugees from the East made the situation for the mother and daughter not very different from that of the other Germans, and when the Red Army arrived, they, too, were roughed up by Soviet soldiers. Unsentimental, resilient, and aware that luck can make all the difference, Inge Deutschkron, who now lives in Israel, has remained a true Berliner.[3]

THE NAZI PAST
IN THE TWO GERMANYS

How did the leaders of postwar Germany deal with the crushing memory of the Holocaust? Did they own up to it? Some did, while others tried to suppress or to marginalize it; but those who triumphed politically were the ones who dared to face the problem. Gradually, too, the German people have come to grips with their responsibility. This is the fundamental message of Jeffrey Herf's stimulating and original *Divided Memory: The Nazi Past in the Two Germanys* (Cambridge MA: Harvard University Press, 1997).

Germany is an ideal place to study the links between the Holocaust and the politics of memory, not only because the Nazis of Germany were the initiators and the chief executors of the satanic plan to kill the Jews but also because the relevant documents are available—and because the country was divided for forty years after the war. The French have had to cope with the memory of their shared guilt in collaboration and in the Holocaust within an undivided country. Since every French government has felt responsible for protecting the prestige and the dignity of the entire nation, they have generally preferred to remain silent about the issue. In Germany, by contrast, two separate and mutually hostile regimes worked to turn the memory of the Holocaust and other Nazi crimes to their own advantage, while also wielding it as a weapon in the global cold war.

It is one of the great ironies of our time that the Communist regime in East Germany, which claimed to be free of guilt with regard to the genocide of Jews, came to spout anti-Semitic slogans and to act as one of the bitterest enemies of Israel, while West Germany, governed at least on the middle level by former

---

This article first appeared in the March 20, 1998, issue of the *New Republic* under the title "After the End."

Nazis and quite reluctant to prosecute war criminals, became a genuine friend of Israel and the Jews. Moreover, while East Germany (and Communists everywhere) tried to ignore the memory of the Holocaust, West Germany, which the East Germans regularly described as fascistic, led the rest of the world in making restitutions to the Jews and in inviting a national self-examination.

All of this is persuasively, often brilliantly, demonstrated by Herf (though a shorter book with fewer repetitions would have been just as persuasive). Herf does not propose to write a study of the German public. The people figure in his book mainly as the subjects of occasional opinion polls. Herf's heroes and antiheroes are, rather, the political elite, especially those wielding the most power in the decade or two after World War II. The list of these notables includes, on the Communist side, Paul Merker, a dedicated Stalinist in the East German Politburo who nevertheless championed restitution to the Jews, thereby inviting his own ruin, as well as such intrepid followers of the ever-twisting Moscow party line as Walter Ulbricht, Wilhelm Pieck, Otto Grotewohl, and Alexander Abusch. On the West German side, the principal characters are Federal Chancellor Konrad Adenauer, Federal President Theodor Heuss, and the Social Democrats Kurt Schumacher and Ernst Reuter.

What bound all these men together, aside from the burden of guilt that they shared with the rest of the German nation, was that none of them ever tried to deny the horrors that had been visited on the Jews and other victims of Nazi rule. Of course, total defeat by the Allied powers, as well as Allied prompting (especially at the Nuremberg trials), helped the German leaders along the road to honesty. Still, with this major concession to truth the consensus of the German leadership came to an end. Subsequently, they disagreed among themselves on such things as whether Nazi crimes had been committed in the name of, or by, the German nation; whether the capitalists and the landowners of Germany, or the Nazi rabble, were to blame; whether only a small group of criminals or many Germans were involved in the killings (and who among the Germans ought to be punished); and whether, and at what price, the forgiveness of Jewry ought to be sought.

How fortunate is Herf's generation of historians! Earlier specialists who wished to learn about political decision-making in East Germany had to be satisfied with interviewing disgruntled refugees from the Communist leadership and reading excruciatingly dull speeches by Communist bosses as well as the even more exasperating articles in East German newspapers and journals. But now, archival documents are widely available in the unified Germany, more so than in most other democratic countries. Herf has made full use of them. His main sources are the state archives in West and East Germany, the

STASI (East German secret police) files as well as the secret and top-secret notes, diaries, and letters of the political elite. Other historians, though they might want to interpret those documents somewhat differently, will probably not find many more sources than those Herf has uncovered.

Herf's dramatis personae were all born in the last quarter of the nineteenth century, which means that they had recollections of the old Empire and especially of World War I. None ever belonged to the Nazi party. Quite the contrary. As Herf explains, they brought into the post-Nazi era the memory of their sufferings, or at least of their unpleasant personal experiences, under Nazi rule. They also brought with them their political and intellectual baggage from the pre-Hitler years.

The Communists looked back to the struggles in the late Weimar republic when, at Stalin's orders, they branded the Social Democrats as "social fascists," or greater enemies of the proletariat than Hitler and the Nazis. In Communist analysis Hitler was only a tool of monopoly capital in its final, dictatorial, terroristic, and imperialist phase, but the Social Democrats were really dangerous because they deliberately misled the proletariat in order to delay the inevitable collapse of the decrepit capitalist system. Even after the SA and the Gestapo had smashed the German Communist Party, masses of Party members had joined the Nazis, and thousands of Communist functionaries were in exile or in concentration camps, the Party leadership confidently expected the revolt of the German workers and the victory of Communism.

In 1935, to be sure, Stalin reversed the suicidal ultraleftist policy announced in 1928 at the Sixth Comintern Congress in Moscow. He now encouraged the formation of antifascist Popular Fronts, into which even the Social Democrats were admitted. But Walter Ulbricht and his ilk were never enthusiastic about this volte-face, though they obeyed Moscow's orders, of course. After World War II, the Communist leadership needed little inspiration to rekindle their hatred of the Social Democrats or at least of those Social Democrats who would not submit to Communist dictates. But the Communists also carried with them the memory of World War II, when German workers in field gray uniforms casually massacred masses of Soviet men and women. Since it was impossible to reconcile these conflicting memories, most Communists chose not to think at all. Instead, they parroted the Party line. This changed from a bitter condemnation of the German people to their gradual exculpation and from regret about the fate of the Jews as well as support for the creation of Israel to denunciation of Israel, and of many Jews, as cosmopolitan, capitalist enemies.

The intellectual baggage that the new West German leaders brought with them to the postwar world, as Herf indicates, was no less complex. Such conservatives as Adenauer suffered only relatively minor indignities under the Nazis but he and others were disgusted by the nihilism, the terror, the racism, the vulgarity, and the extreme nationalism of the National Socialists. In fact, the intellectual and moral chasm separating Adenauer and the Nazis was far wider than the chasm separating Ulbricht and the Nazis. Other West Germans, such as the liberal Theodor Heuss, abhorred the ruthlessness and the anti-Semitism of the Nazis yet he could not help but remember that he himself, as well as his party, had voted in parliament on March 23, 1933, to give dictatorial powers to Adolf Hitler.

As for the Social Democrats, they alone among the deputies in the Reichstag on that day (the Communist Party had already been outlawed) did not vote to make Hitler dictator. Many Social Democrats, their postwar leader Kurt Schumacher included, went through hell in Nazi concentration camps. Yet Schumacher also brought with him the memory of the frustrating late Weimar days, when he and a few other militant Social Democrats advocated the creation of a common national front against the Nazis, only to see themselves rebuffed by the bourgeois parties, most Social Democrats, the trade unions, and the Communists. Of course, the Social Democrats also brought with them their prewar vision of a state-owned economy and a Marxist society. Only in 1959, at the Godesberg conference, did the Social Democratic Party abandon this dream.

All in all, as Herf points out, the postwar leadership of both Germanys, while confronting an entirely new situation, displayed elements of continuity. Herf investigates the two Germanys systematically, in separate chapters. Though developments in West Germany in the late 1940s and the 1950s held the key to what German-Jewish relations are today, the disastrous developments taking place in the Soviet Zone at that time are even more interesting, in part because we used to know so little about them.

Theoretically, as Herf insists, there should have been common ground in the post–World War II era between Jewish victims and Communist victims. Jewish survivors naturally belonged to the KPD, the German Communist Party. After all, the Soviet Union supported the creation of Israel; the Red Army had played a crucial role in the defeat of Hitler; and democratic institutions seemed very dangerous in German hands. At first, it looked as if such common ground could be achieved. Denying their traditional belief that only a small coterie of landowners and capitalists and their Social Democratic stooges were responsible for Germany's ills, the Communist exiles in Moscow recognized that many other Germans shared the guilt. The Party's first manifesto, of June 13, 1945, spoke of "millions and millions" who had supported the fascist criminals.

Even later, during what Herf calls "the Nuremberg interregnum" of 1945–1946, when the International Military Tribunal sat in judgment on the major German war criminals, the Communists were still driven by ambivalence. On the one hand, they advocated the expropriation of the landowners and the capitalists, a move judged sufficient to eliminate the roots of fascism; on the other hand, Ulbricht, Pieck, and the others distrusted the German people to the point of arguing that what the Germans needed was dictatorial rule. (No matter what the situation, of course, the Communists would still have wanted to set up a dictatorship.) More ominously, the KPD attributed its limited prewar popular appeal to insufficient nationalism, which meant that sooner or later the Party would begin to operate with slogans not very dissimilar from those once used by the Nazis and the nationalists. Needless to say, the Communists also insisted on their exclusive right to interpret the past.

Actually, it took some time for a monolithic Communist point of view to be established, given the existence, alongside the so-called Muscovites and former Nazi concentration camp inmates, of another significant group of Communists: the survivors of the war in Mexican exile. Suspicious of, and sometimes excluded from, the United States, German Communist refugees had gone to Mexico, where they were embraced by leftist comrades from the Spanish Civil War. Subjected to Western propaganda and cultural influences, the Mexican exiles, most of whom were Jewish, tended to see things differently from the Moscow contingent. Perhaps Herf should have emphasized that the Muscovites did not really have an opinion of their own. After all, they, too, were survivors, not of Nazi but of Soviet terror. Those who had escaped arrest by the NKVD were a thoroughly intimidated lot who, while not losing their mind-boggling admiration for Stalin and the Soviet Union, knew just how lucky they were to be alive.

The Mexico group was different, especially Paul Merker, a non-Jew with a Jewish wife. Merker was an old-time Communist, an ultraleftist, and the only member of the KPD Politburo not in Moscow or in a German prison. Between 1931 and 1933, Merker had operated in the United States as a secret Comintern agent. Later Moscow sent him back to Berlin and then to Paris, from where he fled to Casablanca in 1940. He arrived in Mexico City in 1942 where, in the words of Herf, he "joined other German Communist émigrés to bring the issue of Jewish suffering from the periphery to the center of the narratives of Communist antifascism for the first—and only—time in its history."

In Mexico, and back in Berlin after 1946, Merker argued in favor of *Wiedergutmachung* or restitution and stated repeatedly that the Communists shared in the responsibility for the German tragedy. In 1948 he wrote the introduction to the Communist Party's statement concerning Israel. It expressed full support for the "progressive struggle of the Jewish workers in Palestine" and insisted that this struggle was "supported by the Soviet Union and by all of progressive humanity." Late in the same year, however, when Stalin dropped his pro-Israel policy and veered over to the Arab side, Merker's days in the KPD Politburo were numbered. Two years later he was pushed out of the Politburo. By that time, East Germany was branding Israel and world Jewry as enemies of the Arab workers and as agents of American imperialism.

At the time of the Korean War, the East German media compared American policy in Europe and Korea to Hitler's aggression. The spokesman of the nationalist campaign was the Jewish Communist Albert Norden, who identified Israel and the United States with capitalism in terms that were nearly verbatim repetitions of Nazi propaganda. East German monuments dedicated to "The Victims of War and Fascism" did not mention the Jews and attacked the United States as the enemy of peace and the wartime destroyer of German cities. During the East German campaign against "cosmopolitanism," 150,000 former Social Democrats were expelled from the SED, the unified Socialist Party under Communist control. As for the small Jewish community in East Germany, a large part of it fled to the West, together with 2.6 million other East Germans, before the erection of the Wall in 1961.

Paul Merker was arrested in December 1952. At his hearings, the political police attempted to link him to the American Communist Noel Field, then in prison in Hungary, who served as a government witness against the Communist defendants at the Stalinist show trials in Hungary and Czechoslovakia. But Merker refused to confess to imaginary crimes, and for some reason East Germany never mounted the sort of show trials that were characteristic of the period. At a secret trial held in 1955, he was sentenced to eight years for having been "an agent of Jewish capitalists." Merker was released in January 1956 but he never again held an important political office.

Despite Herf's enthusiasm for Merker, his tragedy must be judged a minor episode in the history of the German Democratic Republic. There was never a chance that the Communists would shoulder moral and fiscal responsibility for the Holocaust; this was forbidden by Moscow's dictates and by Communist ideology, which held that the Jews were not a nation and that the issue of anti-Semitism had no autonomous political significance.

While the East German Communists were engaged in their inhuman and ultimately suicidal policies, the West Germans were going through the birth pangs of democracy. Many things did not turn out well in the Western zones either. As Herf and other historians have demonstrated, Germans after World War II tended to feel so sorry for themselves—as victims of the war, of the bombings, of rape by Soviet soldiers, of the massacre and expulsion of millions of Germans in Eastern Europe, of hunger, even of Nazism—as to ignore the sufferings of others. At best, they felt that Jews and Germans were equally victims. The German people generally approved of the Nuremberg trials of the major war criminals, if for no other reason than because they seemed to exculpate the other Germans. All the greater was the popular resentment when German courts attempted to continue where the International Court had left off. Those in the West utterly disliked the Allied effort and especially the massive American effort, at denazification, in which hundreds of thousands were interned or lost their jobs. True, after a year or two of arduous investigation, there still remained a huge number of unfinished cases—but there were, in 1945, eight million Nazi Party members.

Interestingly, the West Germans did not resist the Allied attempt at democratization. Quite the contrary. Sensing that this was to be their future, they became superb disciples. The German statesman who best showed the way in this direction was Adenauer, whom Herf admires, though he seems to like him less than Paul Merker or Kurt Schumacher. The oldest of the great postwar leaders, Adenauer had been mayor of Cologne as far back as 1917. He opposed the Nazis and suffered many indignities at their hands. He emerged from the war firmly intent on fundamentally changing Germany and its people. Adenauer was, I think, modern Germany's greatest revolutionary.

This Catholic Rhineland conservative, as Herf explains, despised the Prussian celebration of the authoritarian state and Herder's and Hegel's ranking of the nation and the state above the individual. He abhorred German idealism and romanticism. Seeing both Communists and Nazis as nihilists and materialists, Adenauer hoped to re-Christianize Germany. As Chancellor between 1949 and 1963, he helped turn West Germany into a liberal parliamentary system no different from, say, the Netherlands. He helped bring about Franco-German reconciliation, fostered European integration, and made Germany—the quintessential mid-European power—a part of the Atlantic Community. While the East Germans were experiencing their second terroristic and militaristic dictatorship, the West Germans successfully developed democratic institutions.

The drawbacks of the Adenauer revolution were not insignificant, but in the long run they could be overcome. Convinced that democratization and justice could not go together and that the German people would accept the former but not the latter, Adenauer relentlessly strove for an end to denazification and for the freeing of war criminals. In this he was eminently successful. By the late 1950s, there was hardly a Nazi criminal still in prison.

It is one of the greatest ironies of our time that political purges and judicial retributions were more severe in the countries once occupied by, or allied to, the Third Reich than in Germany itself. In Norway or in Hungary a murderer of Jews or even just a Nazi sympathizer was much more likely to be punished after the war than in either of the two Germanys. Curiously, the situation regarding Nazi crimes was not very different in East Germany compared to the situation in the Western zones. Herf's statistical data illustrate that the rate of release of war criminals was about the same in both Germanys. He goes so far as to state that "despite its antifascist legitimations, the German Democratic Republic was, if anything, even less aggressive in prosecuting crimes of the Nazi era than was the Federal Republic."

It is true that East German prisons and a few former Nazi concentration camps remained chock full of inmates, though these were not Nazis but mainly members of the former social elite. Still, it is also true that the proportion of former Nazi party members in the East German administration was much smaller than in the West. Hans Globke, the head of the Federal Chancellery under Adenauer and once an important Nazi functionary, was only one among the thousands of National Socialist bureaucrats, judges, university professors, generals, and medical doctors, some of them guilty of the vilest crimes, who continued to advance their careers in West Germany. While West Germany denied assistance to the widows and the children of those executed for desertion from the Wehrmacht during the war, it awarded even the most notorious SS commander his pension as a "police general." (Herf makes clear, incidentally, that the effect of the cold war on the release and the rehabilitation of Nazi war criminals in either of the two Germanys was not as crucial as is commonly assumed.)

Many West German statesmen rejected Adenauer's two-faced policy. Theodor Heuss demanded a more steadfast moral stand against the Nazi crimes, and Kurt Schumacher raged at the sight of his former tormentors occupying important positions. But the influence of Heuss and Schumacher on the course of events was limited. Caught between his unconditional anti-Communism, his Marxist economics, his resentment of American capitalism and imperialism, and his strong patriotism, Schumacher cut a heroic but anachronistic figure. He died in 1952, in part as a consequence of his wartime miseries in the Dachau concentration camp. What the Social Democrats of the early postwar years did best was to educate the German workers and to cultivate good relations with western Social Democrats as well as with Jewish labor circles. Adenauer realized that, whereas the German people had no wish to see justice done, they were quite willing to make amends and to pay restitution to the Jews. The result was the consistently pro-Israeli policy of the West German regime and a total of 110 billion German marks paid out to the survivors.

Herf's excellent book concludes with a reflection on memory and *Vergangenheitsbewältigung*, the attempt to overcome the past, since the 1960s. He makes it clear that the 1960s provoked genuine soul-searching among younger Germans. Add to this the crucial role of Chancellor Willy Brandt between 1969 and 1974, symbolized by his visit to Warsaw, where he went down on his knees at the memorials for Jews killed in the Warsaw Ghetto uprising in 1943 and for Poles killed in the great Warsaw Uprising in 1944. While the Americans, Adenauer, and many others taught the German people how to live and act as democrats, the younger generation of Germans are teaching themselves and their older compatriots how to look back at the past, not with rose-tinted glasses, but with the awareness that during the war millions of Germans, together with millions of other Europeans, committed abominable and unpardonable crimes. In the final analysis, then, this is an encouraging story.

2

JEWS AMONG

"ARYANS"

IN DISGUISE

Of the thousands of Jews who survived the Holocaust by disguising themselves as gentiles, Oswald Rufeisen, the subject of Nechama Tec's *In the Lion's Den* (New York: Oxford University Press, 1990), may have been the most resourceful. I first heard of him in the early 1960s, when the Israeli Supreme Court debated the request of Father Daniel, a Carmelite monk at the Stella Maris monastery on Mount Carmel in Haifa, to be given Israeli citizenship on the basis of the Law of Return. If this were granted, Father Daniel—formerly Oswald Rufeisen—would be identified on his Israeli passport as a Jew. One of the five judges was in favor of accepting Father Daniel's claim, but the others turned him down, arguing that "a Jew who changed his religion cannot be counted as a Jew in the sense and the spirit that the Knesset (Parliament) meant in the Law of Return and as it is accepted among our people today."

Several years later I met a historian, a specialist in East European affairs at the University of Haifa, who told me how at the time of the Supreme Court case he had been asked to interview Father Daniel. He did not find him at the monastery—Nechama Tec tells us in *The Lion's Den* that Father Daniel spends very little time there—so the historian talked to another monk, originally from Germany. "I don't know why Father Daniel is creating such a commotion," the monk said. "After all, I was born a Jew myself, but I didn't mind petitioning the Israelis for Israeli citizenship and I don't insist on my so-called rights." "What kind of a person is Father Daniel?" the historian asked. *Ein typischer Galizianer* (a typical Galician), answered the monk—one of the nastier insults that a Western or Central European Jew might direct at an East European Jew.

The original of this essay appeared as part of an article entitled "Witnesses to Evil" in the October 22, 1992, issue of the *New York Review of Books*.

In fact, Father Daniel did not fit the stereotype of the Galician Jew: he was not dirt poor, barely literate, and arrogant. As Nechama Tec, a professor of sociology at the University of Connecticut, who herself once "passed" as a Catholic in wartime Poland with the help of non-Jewish Poles,[1] shows in her fascinating and conscientiously researched account, Oswald Rufeisen came from a very modest West Galician family that had adopted the German-Austrian culture of the Habsburg monarchy of which Galicia was a part before 1918; at home the family spoke High German. This, more than anything else, later helped to save Rufeisen's life. His father had served in the Habsburg army during World War I; he was wounded and became a *Zugsführer,* or buck sergeant (a far more modest rank than that of the position of platoon commander, which is usually held by a lieutenant, ascribed to him by Tec).[2]

In 1922, when Oswald Rufeisen was born, Galicia was already part of the Poland that had been re-created following World War I. Rather typically for the region and for its integrated families, Oswald first attended a Polish school where he was the only Jew and where he learned to recite Catholic prayers (which also helped him to survive later on); he then went to a Jewish school in which instruction was in High German; and finally to a Polish high school. He did not, he told Tec, suffer any discrimination in the Polish schools, and he had just graduated from high school when the Germans attacked in September 1939. The family fled east but only Oswald and his brother Arieh made it to Lithuania, at that time still a neutral and independent state. Vilna (Wilno, Vilnius) was under Polish rule in the years between the two world wars but Stalin had recently turned it over to Lithuania, knowing well that the latter country would soon be part of the Soviet Union. In Vilna, Oswald worked for a shoemaker and learned the trade, another turn of good fortune that would soon save his life.

In June 1940 the Red Army occupied Lithuania and, among its many crimes, deported to Siberia a number of Zionists and Bundists. Most Jews now tried to get out of Lithuania; Oswald's brother Arieh and other members of their Zionist group Akiva received certificates to emigrate to Palestine; 2,400 other Lithuanian Jews made it to Japan, thanks to help from a warm-hearted Japanese consul. Yet when the Germans came, at the end of June 1941, Oswald was still in Vilna. Shortly thereafter, a Lithuanian policeman arrested him and his friends in the street for speaking Polish in public and for walking on the sidewalk rather than in the middle of the street. Thus they suffered doubly as Poles and as Jews.

Life for Oswald now became a series of narrow escapes. The Germans killed all the Jews in the prison except for four they needed as shoemakers. Oswald,

In Disguise 49

who was briefly able to go outside the prison, made the acquaintance of a local farmer who hid him and sent him to a relative in Belorussia. By then, Oswald had decided that for the rest of the war he would not admit to being a Jew. Again and again on his wanderings, he was recognized by Germans and Belorussians as a Jew; again and again, he persuaded them otherwise. Because he spoke perfect Polish and German, he did not, despite his looks, fit the local stereotype of a Jew. Also, he shrewdly claimed to be half-Polish and half-German, which meant that he could neither be elevated to the rank of a *Volksdeutscher*, too daring a gamble, nor be reduced to the status of a Pole, an equally dangerous position, although not for the same reason.

Oswald was recruited to work for the German gendarmerie in the Belorussian town of Mir, where he advanced from interpreter to being in charge of dealing with the locals. By then he had learned to speak Belorussian. He was given a modified SS uniform and a gun, as well as a horse, which he could ride very well, for he had learned to ride as a boy: further proof in the eyes of onlookers that he could not possibly be a Jew.

Oswald's superior in the town of Mir was *Polizeimeister* (Master Sergeant) Hein, a true police professional. Serious, efficient, taciturn, fair, strict about the rules, kind, and fatherly toward Oswald, Hein never hit or killed anyone. He obeyed the rules, of course, which in Belorussia decreed that all the Jews should be liquidated wherever they happened to live. So Hein organized the appropriate *Aktionen* and sent his more bloodthirsty underlings to do the job. He made sure, however, that the Jewish families about to be killed were properly informed that they had been sentenced to death.

It was Oswald's task to translate the death sentences into Belorussian (he spoke no Yiddish; not that he would have volunteered to use the language). He told Nechama Tec, and eyewitness accounts cited by Tec seem to bear Oswald out, that by forging papers and by other evasive tactics he had saved as many lives as he possibly could. When once asked to shoot Jews himself, he politely declined. This was accepted because he was one of the German squad; the Germans did not allow the Belorussian police to refuse.

How was Oswald able to get away with it all when so many people suspected him of being a Jew? Why did no one ask him to drop his trousers, a surefire method of inquiry that is mentioned in Louis Begley's *Wartime Lies* (New York: Knopf, 1991); made much of in the film *Europa, Europa,* and was widely practiced, in my experience, in Hungary under Arrow Cross fascist rule? (In Budapest this method of investigation, in the open street, was the specialty of a notorious deaf-mute squad.) He says that there was only one occasion, at a public bath, when he could have been discovered but then Hein paid no attention to him. It all sounds rather unlikely, almost theatrically contrived. Still, there are the many Jewish survivors from Mir whose lives he saved and who testify to having seen him on horseback in German uniform brandishing a gun.

The most difficult moment came when Oswald learned that the complete liquidation of the Mir ghetto was planned for August 13, 1942. He immediately alerted some fellow Zionists in the ghetto and supplied them with a small arsenal of guns, grenades, and bullets. A breakout was organized and three hundred people escaped, quite a few of whom actually survived. The five hundred who remained were all killed. But Oswald himself was betrayed by someone who still remains unidentified; he confessed the gun smuggling and later even his Jewishness to *Polizeimeister* Hein. He was arrested, although only formally, for he continued to work for Hein and to take his meals with the gendarmes. When Hein later let him run away, he fled to a nearby Polish convent at which he knew the mother superior. The nuns sheltered him for sixteen long months; occasionally he had to be dressed as a nun. Meanwhile, he learned Christian rituals and was even baptized.

When the situation became untenable for the nuns themselves, Oswald escaped to the forest and then joined the partisans before he was liberated by the advancing Soviet army in August 1944. Oswald worked briefly for the Soviet NKVD but then moved to Cracow in Poland, where he first became a monk and then, in 1952, an ordained priest. In 1956 his order agreed to send him to Israel.

Today, Father Daniel leads a small group of persons who hope for the reunification of Jews and Christians. He holds that Christianity and Judaism were originally one, and he advocates the creation of a Hebrew Church. People whom he had saved in Mir and elsewhere gather regularly in Israel and celebrate him as a hero.

COLD BRAVE HEART

On February 13 and 14, 1945, the baroque city of Dresden went up in flames under the impact of massive British and American air raids. Among the thousands scrambling over the ruins in an attempt to escape the firestorm was an elderly couple; he with a star of David on his chest, she without. At first Victor Klemperer and his wife Eva lost sight of one another, and to make matters worse, he was nearly blinded by the flying debris. When they met again, Eva, on the advice of a Jewish friend, tore off the star that her husband had been wearing for three and a half years.

From that moment on, he was no longer a Jew precariously protected from deportation by his marriage to an "Aryan." They were now homeless refugees, two among millions of other Germans, prisoners of war, foreign laborers, and the East European allies of the Nazis fleeing from the Red Army. Although he was worried that he would be unmasked as a Jew, Klemperer had in reality little to fear. The Gestapo building had been destroyed in the air raid together with the documentation on the few Jews who were still in Dresden. In any case, people had more important things to worry about than whether there was a Jew among those eating the soup that was ladled out by young women of the National Socialist Welfare.

Victor Klemperer, born a Jew, had converted to Protestantism more than three decades earlier. Although Hitler now remade him a Jew, he felt no loyalty to Jewishness or to the Jewish tradition. He had been a German before the persecution began and now that there was no record of his being a Jew he was

---

This is the full reprint of my review of Victor Klemperer's *I Will Bear Witness: A Diary of Nazi Years, 1942–1945* (translated from the German by Martin Chalmers; New York: Random House, 1999), which appeared under the title "Cold Brave Heart" in the April 17–April 24, 2000, issue of the *New Republic*.

a German again—not a fanatical one, but a German humanist in the cosmopolitan tradition of Lessing and Goethe. Since 1920 Klemperer had been a professor of Romance literature at the Dresden Technical Academy, and although he was sent into retirement in 1935, he received his state pension almost to the end of the Nazi regime. A few months after the end of the war, he would again be teaching at the Academy, and when he finally retired, in 1954, he would do so as a respected university professor in East Berlin. During this long career, Klemperer left his homeland only for professional reasons and brief vacations; he never seriously contemplated emigration. We, too, must regard Klemperer as a German whom Nazi perversity condemned to a pariah existence for a few years. It is true that, unlike his own brothers, he had never tried to "pass," nor did he feel, like many assimilated Jews, that fate was treating him unfairly. In his reckoning he was not really one of "them." Klemperer was both a victim and a cool observer; an individualist with a critical view of himself and of those around him. It is these qualities that make his diaries of such immense value: they present an unprejudiced picture of everyday life in Germany, of Jews and non-Jews.

Klemperer's massive journals encompass the years between 1918 and 1959. They were first published, in German, between 1994 and 1999, in several thousand pages. All the volumes are abbreviated versions of the handwritten or typed manuscript. An English version covering the years 1933–1941 appeared in 1998; the present volume covers the years 1942–1945. They can be complemented by two other works, produced while Klemperer was writing his diaries: *Curriculum Vitae,* the reminiscences of his younger years, and *LTI,* or *Lingua Tertii Imperii,* which analyzes the Third Reich's perversion of the German language.

LTI (1947) was published in East Germany, and since then it has appeared in many new editions, even an edition enriched with copious notes in English. Most of *LTI*'s contents had originally formed a part of Klemperer's diaries; these sections are understandably missing from the diaries' English translation. *LTI* explains, often brilliantly, the Nazis' use of the German language as well as their invention of archaic-sounding terms, all with an aggressive, combative content. The title is itself a spoof of the Nazi bureaucratic and military predilection for anagrams. Among many other things, the book successfully explains the effect that totalitarian ideology had on language as well as on language's unique power to determine the behavior of individuals and the moral norms of society.

Unlike *LTI*, Klemperer's diaries did not see print until long after his death in 1960 and only after the collapse of the German Democratic Republic. The GDR made him a university professor, a member of the Academy of Sciences, and a deputy in its rubber-stamp parliament; however it would not publish the diaries, presumably because of the drastic hostility of the pre-1945 text to Marxism and communism and the barely concealed contempt for East German Communist practices expressed in the post-1945 diaries. (This, despite the fact that Klemperer had been a Party member since 1945.)

Why did Klemperer keep on writing his diaries, in that minuscule handwriting of his, when even the possession of a few sheets of blank writing paper could have landed him in a concentration camp? He himself did not expect to survive Nazi rule; his wife as well as Annemarie, their brave German friend (of whom more in a moment), exposed themselves to mortal danger by transporting and hiding Klemperer's outpourings on paper. In the early 1940s Klemperer made clear that he was writing not merely in order to have something to do and not even because "it is my duty to write . . . it is my life's task, my calling," as he noted on February 8, 1942. He was writing because he wanted the diaries to appear in print.

Klemperer hoped to become famous by his chronicling of extraordinary events, and he also wanted to make those around him famous: for instance the others in the "Jew-House" he inhabited. But if this was the case and if he was writing for the public, then why did he not attempt, at least minimally, to put the best foot forward? He had scarcely a good word to say about his brother George, a professor of medicine at Harvard, whose money transfers helped to keep the couple alive. Nor did he show much respect for his relatives and colleagues, whether Jewish or non-Jewish. He did esteem the Aryan Helmut Richter, the real-estate agent who acted as the trustee of their house and protected it from confiscation. Richter, a dedicated anti-Nazi, provided Klemperer with money, bread coupons, and razor blades; he even offered to hide Klemperer when the massacre of Jews threatened, and himself ended up disappearing forever into a Nazi concentration camp. Yet once Richter was gone, the diaries barely mention his name.

Then there was Dr. Annemarie Köhler, a surgeon in Pirna, near Dresden, who was codirector of a private clinic. Annemarie was an old friend; she undertook the risky task of hiding Klemperer's journals and other manuscripts as well as the couple's furniture, silver, stamp collection, and everything else of value. She sent Klemperer books, cigars, meat, and bread ration coupons. Annemarie and her entire family were religious Christians and outspoken anti-Nazis. Political conversations with her brought enormous relief to Klemperer; he was angry when he did not hear from her. Yet the diaries show no affection or gratitude to her.

If the diaries were meant for publication, why did Klemperer admit on its pages that he regularly stole bits of food from a fellow tenant in the Jewish house? Why did he compare Theodor Herzl and the Zionists to Hitler and the Nazis? And why the innumerable obscure, abbreviated entries, mixed with frequent insights and exciting information? Here is an unusual diarist who was both passionate and indifferent to the outcome of his outpourings. The telling was all.

Victor Klemperer was born, in 1881, in a small country place. He grew up in Berlin, the younger son of a well-known reform rabbi. For a while he alternated between university study and an attempt at a career as a journalist and a writer. As a result, only in 1913 did he receive his doctoral degree, and in the following year he garnered his *Habilitation,* the second doctorate that is indispensable for teaching at a German university. Meanwhile he married Eva Schlemmer, a pianist and a musicologist from a Christian family. The subject of his *Habilitationsschrift* was Montesquieu; Klemperer remained forever an admirer of Montesquieu, Corneille, and Voltaire. He published widely on French literary figures and cultural developments of the early modern period.

There is hardly a page in his diaries on which Klemperer does not mention his wife. They had no children. Both of them were cantankerous, incurable hypochondriacs and chain smokers. (The Nazi ban on Jewish smoking during the war may ironically have prolonged Klemperer's life.) He complained endlessly about Eva's migraines and hysteria, about having to do the household chores while she was in bed. Yet hidden behind the bickering and the bitter remarks are expressions of genuine devotion: "And Eva's nerves are deteriorating very badly. But it was a great joy to come home and to love each other very much," he wrote on October 18, 1936. Their main delight was his reading aloud to her. In any case, the complaints diminished after 1941. After World War II, when Eva was nearing death, he once wrote that his greatest happiness was to see her feeling somewhat better. Judging from the diaries, Eva was the only person close to Klemperer's heart.

In 1915 Klemperer volunteered for the war and served in a Bavarian artillery unit, and for a short period he saw action on the Western front. This guaranteed that he was not fired immediately from his academic post after 1933. At the technical academy where he was teaching, Romance literature was of secondary importance. When his position was abolished in 1935, he could not be sure whether it was an economic measure (he had attracted very few students) or whether it was directed at him as a Jew.

The diaries for the years 1933-1941 recount how the Klemperers at first improved their style of life under Nazi rule. They bought an expensive car and built a comfortable villa in Dölzschen, a suburb of Dresden. All this gave him little pleasure, for he expected his imminent demise from an imagined heart condition or his eventual demise at the hands of the Nazis. The diaries note the growing terror of anti-Semitic demonstrations and governmental repression, yet often they make also for nearly comic reading. Klemperer was hopelessly clumsy; he had great trouble learning how to drive, and he wrecked the car before it could have been confiscated as an anti-Semitic measure. He refused to learn English, in part because he disliked the British and the Americans. He so worried about his spoken and written French that he never seriously tried to find a teaching position in that country. Although also a professor of Italian literature, he spoke no Italian. In any case, the door to emigration closed soon after the outbreak of the war.

By January 1942, when the second volume of the diaries opens, Klemperer had long lost the right to use the university library and sometime after that any library at all. The pair had been forced to give up their cleaning woman, even though she was over forty-five and thus past the age when her blood could have been polluted. He now had to sign his name as Victor Israel, and he and his wife had been obliged to sublet their house and to move into a so-called Jew-House, in which they rented two large rooms. They had given up their telephone before it could be confiscated. After September 19, 1941, Klemperer had been obliged to wear a canary-yellow Jewish Star; this was, without any doubt, the most humiliating experience of his life. For a long time he would not go into the street and later only after dark. But there were even worse things to face in 1942, the nadir of their Nazi experience.

Neither historiography nor the Klemperer diaries explain why 1942 was such a nightmarish year or why the harassment of those Jews who had been permitted to remain in Germany eased thereafter. While the deportation and the extermination of the German Jews proceeded apace, two categories of Jews were allowed to stay behind. The first category were men married to Aryan women; the plan to deport them had been dropped following the famous protest of their Aryan wives, in March 1943, in front of Gestapo headquarters on the Rosenstrasse in Berlin. But Jewish husbands, such as Klemperer, had to wear the star. The second category comprised the so-called privileged: Jewish women married to Christians, Jewish men whose wives and children were Christian, those who had earned the Iron Cross First Class during World War I, and a few others. The privileged did not have to wear the star, and they could theoretically live a relatively free life. Yet neither group was really safe. The slightest infringement of mostly unannounced Nazi regulations could land one in a concentration camp.

In January 1942 Klemperer was arrested by a Gestapo man for using the streetcar, even though such a thing was not yet forbidden to Jews. To be sure, he was released on the same day. In February the searches of Jew-Houses began, accompanied by increasingly brutal beatings, the confiscation of the meager food reserves, and general devastation. In the same month Klemperer was put to work shoveling snow, along with other older Jews. In March, Jews were forbidden by law to buy flowers, and their food allotment was reduced, more so even than that of the Aryan population. In May the Klemperers were ordered to kill their cat, which had been the main consolation of Eva's life.

Eventually the Gestapo came after them: two young men beat him up at their home and spat in Eva's face, calling her a "Jew's whore." (This is recorded on May 23, 1942.) Another time, when he was plowing through Alfred Rosenberg's tedious *The Myth of The Twentieth Century*, a Gestapo officer entered his room and slammed the book on his head. Eva now had to take the finished manuscript to Annemarie almost page by page. He wrote, on May 27, 1942: "I shall go on writing. That is my heroism. I will bear witness, precise witness!"

By now Jews had no more radios; they had been barred from the theaters, the cinemas, the concert halls, the restaurants, and all but the local shops. They were allowed no smoking materials, woolen blankets, shaving soap, deck chairs, chocolate, fruit, milk, hair clippers, unused hair scissors, and combs. In the summer heat, old Jews were paraded around in their winter coats and were publicly beaten by Gestapo men. Two brutes appear again and again in Klemperer's diaries hurling epithets: "pig," "Jewish pig," "sow," and "piece of dung." His ears were boxed; the Gestapo men spat between his eyes. On June 11, 1942, Klemperer records that Eva, too, was kicked around viciously: "You, traitor to your race!"

But Klemperer went on reading and writing, with the manuscript pages being hidden, before transportation, in his Greek dictionary. He received his pension and his money from his brother's blocked account as well as food packets from a friend in Sweden. Once, the tax office returned some money to him. In the waiting room of Dr. Katz, a "privileged" Jewish physician and the only doctor whom the Jews were allowed to see, there hung World War I photographs of Katz: a dashing officer on horseback, sporting a monocle, and on his chest, the Iron Cross First Class. On July 5, 1942, Klemperer noted in his diary that Dr. Katz "attributes much of the blame—and here we are in agreement—to Zionism; much blame also to the unchecked influx of the money-hungry eastern Jews," and yet Katz vehemently opposed baptism.

Actually, the Jews were not the worst off in the city. At the Zeiss-Ikon optical factory, where many of the remaining Jews were employed, Russian women were forced laborers. The starving Russian women raided garbage cans and were secretly fed by Jews. Klemperer noticed Soviet POWs rummaging through the Jewish community center's rubbish bins. The year 1942 was bad, in fact, for all Dresdeners; the Klemperers were near-starving but Christians also suffered grave hardships. Eva tried to eat in restaurants, but there was next to nothing to eat there either. So she begged for food from friends. (We tend to think of the Germans as well supplied with food and goods from the loot in occupied countries.) In 1943 the food situation improved for all, and it continued improving for a while thereafter.

In September 1942 Victor and Eva were forced to move again—incredibly, to more agreeable and more elegant quarters. Eva's piano went with them as a matter of course. In December, Eva attended a tango concert and even danced afterwards. The insane contradictions of their lives thus continued. In the first half of 1943 the majority of the remaining Jews were taken away either to be shot in the Baltics or to the model ghetto at Theresienstadt, in Bohemia. From there the majority of them were shipped to Auschwitz.

From April 1943 to June 1944 Klemperer was on labor duty, first in a plant where his job was to pour herbs into tea bags with a tin scoop, and later in a place where he had to fold envelopes. He was paid the wages of an unskilled laborer, but such work bored him to desperation. Since he worried about not having enough time for his diaries, he prevailed on Dr. Katz to release him from service. He later mused: "Aryans and Jews with serious heart problems are doing labor duty... why was I let go? Does he [Katz] consider me at death's door, am I at death's door?" He had no more duties until early in February 1945, when he was ordered to deliver letters calling up all the remaining able-bodied Jews for labor service outside the city. He felt that he was delivering death sentences, but he himself had still not been called up. In any case, the Allied bombers put an end to the new labor project.

One of the most fascinating questions posed by the Klemperer diaries is how the German people behaved toward the Jews. The journal entries for the years 1933-1941 make clear that more were sympathetic than hostile. The trend continued in 1942 when expressions of sympathy became more and more frequent. From time to time strangers walked up, smiled, and shook Klemperer's hands: "You know why!" When he was shoveling snow, passersby complained aloud about the indignity of old and meritorious people having to do such backbreaking work. Klemperer records in February 1942 that the foremen of the snow shoveling detail were invariably friendly: "You must not overexert yourself, the state does not require it." And a few days later: "Look, I can't tell you, 'Work more slowly,' you have to know that yourself."

Klemperer states repeatedly that in neither of the two factories was he experiencing even a flicker of anti-Semitism. The foreman at the second factory occasionally yelled at him but only because he was so clumsy and slow. Christian fellow-workers voluntarily made up his quota. Workers in the plants were forbidden to talk to Jews, but they did so nevertheless. On June 4, 1943, he notes: "Again and again I observe the comradely, easygoing, often really warm behavior of the male and female workers toward the Jews." Shopkeepers secretly passed forbidden food to him; an old lady tried to pay his bill in the shop; Christian acquaintances brought them food and other gifts.

In 1943 as news from the front was getting worse—or getting better, from the victims' point of view—Klemperer heard more and more often from Christian strangers: "Chin up, it won't last ... they can't last another winter in Russia." On April 12, 1944, an optician with a Nazi Party badge on his lapel: "Have you heard anything from Arndt, the jeweler, in [the ghetto of] Theresienstadt? ... The swine! ... But it can't last much longer." And in August, again: "Chin up! The scoundrels will soon be finished!" No doubt these were individual incidents that Klemperer fastidiously recorded, but he recorded the nasty events as well. There was the older worker who called from his bicycle, "You damned Jew!" (April 28, 1942), and the blond young man in a sports car who said, "You wretch, why are you still alive?" (April 18, 1942). Still, the city policemen were invariably courteous and addressed him as "Herr" or "Herr Professor" in clear violation of their instructions.

In 1943 the Gestapo raids ceased or became perfunctory. When called in to the Gestapo on what turned out to be a minor matter, Klemperer was correctly treated. In October 1944 the Gestapo allowed a Dresden Jew with intestinal cancer to travel to Berlin for an operation in the Jewish hospital. Meanwhile Dr. Katz was not allowed to take care of the gravely ill Frau Cohn, because she was an Aryan; Aryan doctors were even harder to find, however. It is perfectly possible that some of the compassionate people whom Klemperer met committed or would soon commit horrible crimes as soldiers and policemen in the East. Somebody, after all, had to do the killing of millions of Jews, Poles, Russians, and others. But in Dresden, in their hometown, "ordinary" Germans tended to behave decently toward the frail, bent, old professor. Klemperer had become a local curiosity, one of the less than a hundred star-wearers left in the city in a population of six hundred thousand. Unlike the minority of radical anti-Semites, the majority of Europeans did not want all Jews to disappear from their midst; they only wanted there to be fewer Jews. Klemperer and his fellows would probably have been welcome to stay.

Who, then, was the enemy? The Gestapo thugs, the authorities, the Party bosses, and the venom-spitting Nazi journalists. Klemperer alternated between the belief that the Germans were generally good people and that he alone was a decent German. The diaries make clear, however, that ordinary Germans also lived under severe terror.

Klemperer was amazingly well informed about international and national events. He learned of the death camps soon after they had been set up, and on October 24, 1944, he wrote that "six to seven million Jews . . . have been slaughtered (more exactly shot and gassed)." Yet his correct information was often complemented by false news and wishful thinking. He hesitated between expecting an immediate German collapse and the realization that the regime would last for quite a while.

As refugees from the destruction of Dresden, Eva and Victor traveled by train, on foot, or in horse-drawn wagon from Dresden to Bavaria. Like other refugees, they were sustained on the way by acquaintances and the local authorities. Their liberation in Bavaria, early in May, was nearly unnoticeable. In the small village where they were staying, one heard about the Americans being in the neighborhood. Having been freed from the Nazi yoke, Klemperer expressed no elation whatsoever. Instead, he took up his lamentations about everyday problems. Soon he decided that the Americans were arrogant, uncultured, and unruly, and that the situation was unacceptably messy. The Americans, he observed on May 22, 1945, "drive quickly and nonchalantly, and the Germans run along humbly on foot, the victors spit out the abundance of their cigarette stubs everywhere, and the Germans pick up the stubs. The Germans? We, the liberated, creep along on foot, we stoop down for cigarette ends, we, who only yesterday were the oppressed, and who today are called the liberated, are ultimately likewise imprisoned and humiliated. . . . I find it dreadful now to see the victors and avengers racing through the city [Munich], which they have so hellishly wrecked."

At that moment, though, the Klemperers profited from his Jewish origins, for otherwise they would not have been able to travel home so quickly from the American to the Soviet zone. Their return journey, again partly on foot, proved their inner strength, courage, and determination. On June 10 they arrived in Dresden. The crisp diary entry, "In the late afternoon we walked up to Dölzschen," concludes the book.

The same Aufbau-Verlag in Berlin that published Klemperer's diaries up to the end of World War II printed his postwar diaries in 1999, which came to about 1,800 pages. According to these later journals, Klemperer was extremely busy during the last fifteen years of his life, teaching, lecturing, serving on committees, meeting important people, traveling, writing books, articles, and his diary. Specialists in German politics, history, and culture can find many a golden nugget here, but unlike the highly readable and exciting diaries written in Nazi times, these pages are much too crowded with obscure references, names, and data.

The post-1945 diaries are politically and morally disappointing. The undaunted resister, who had daily defied the Nazis with his writings, left the Protestant church soon after the liberation, and in November, 1945, he joined the Communist Party. This allowed him to take back his house and to get rid of the tenant, while keeping the tenant's furniture and other belongings. Thanks to the Party he regained his post at the technical academy and was given a chair professorship, successively at Greifswald, Halle, and Berlin.

All this would be nearly normal had Klemperer not railed, in Nazi times, against the opportunism of his colleagues. Before 1945, Klemperer unhappily noted the promotion of mediocrities in his field and the concessions that his colleagues were making to those in power. One reason why he joined the KPD in 1945, he claimed, was to enable him to seek punishment for the academic prostitutes who, in his opinion, should be hanged even higher than others. But when former Nazi colleagues were allowed to return to their posts as though nothing had happened, Klemperer kept quiet.

Klemperer had once converted to Protestantism because this was likely to help him in his career, and for the same reason he now became a Communist. No doubt he bore both religious affiliations lightly; his post-1945 diaries are replete with scathing criticism of Soviet barbarism and the stupidity of the German party leadership. At one point he planned to write a "Language of the Fourth Reich," analyzing the Nazi-sounding vocabulary of the Communist regime. But unlike in the years before 1945, when Klemperer's critical voice about his totalitarian surroundings stayed sharp, his criticism of communism did not go very deep. The Soviet tanks were, after all, the guarantors of peace and of his own safety.

Dreams of genuine liberalism and democracy had to yield to practical considerations. Klemperer barely learned the rudiments of dialectical materialism; however, this was not really expected from him in the political examination for his Berlin post in 1951. At no time did he contemplate moving to West Germany, which he disliked, as he did the Americans whom he considered worse than the Soviets. He wrote in his diaries that he was sitting on a hard bench between two comfortable chairs. But it was a comfortable bench indeed.

Adjustment to changing times was quite natural; one had to make a living and in any case Klemperer was the first to confess to his egoism. What is disturbing is his indifference—more, his callousness—toward those who had risked their lives for him and for his writings. He did remain loyal to his wife, who had risked and suffered so much for him. When Eva died in 1951, he confessed to feeling a terrible loneliness. He was fortunate to have a student, Hadwig Kirchner, fall in love with him shortly thereafter. The two married within a year, when he was seventy-one and she twenty-six. Hadwig came from a religious family and was herself a believing Catholic. While both disliked the communist system, both dutifully participated in communist activities.

But then there is Annemarie Köhler. Like Helmut Richter, she remains barely identified in the English translation of the pre-1945 diaries, even though Klemperer wrote about her many times. The inadequacy of the book's notes is, in fact, the great weakness of Martin Chalmers's superb translation. Historical events are identified, but many people who played an important role in Klemperer's life are not given the attention that they deserve. One must turn to the endnotes of the German edition of the postwar diaries to learn the facts of Dr. Köhler.

Annemarie was born in 1892 and died in 1948. She kept Klemperer's diaries hidden in a suitcase at the clinic. After the war, she returned everything to the Klemperers, even the suitcase that Red Army soldiers used for target practice. Yet Klemperer now treated Annemarie very poorly. While he was rising in the social and political hierarchy, Annemarie felt isolated and again in opposition.

Klemperer was decent enough to write a *Persilschein*, an affidavit testifying that Dr. Dressel, Annemarie's partner at the clinic, had helped him during the war at the risk of his life. But he does not seem to have lifted a finger on behalf of Annemarie's brother, who had been a member of the conservative nationalist Stahlhelm but also (according to Klemperer himself) a dedicated anti-Nazi. The brother was thrown into an East German communist concentration camp, from which he never returned.

Embittered, starving, and mortally ill, Annemarie complained that it was now Klemperer's turn to be "the PG" (*Parteigenosse*, or Party member) and that he and his fellows "were now acting as once the Nazis had acted." On November 6, 1946, Klemperer noted that in Pirna he was now "among political enemies," and when Annemarie died, of lung cancer in 1948, he wrote in his diary, on September 23, that "for us, she had long been ossified and actually quite dead." Somehow I cannot forgive Klemperer for this bit of brutal honesty.

Klemperer's indifference toward the dying Annemarie was just one instance of his continuous disregard for the interests, and even the lives, of others. No reviewer seems to have raised the vexing question of why Klemperer identified in the diaries all those who were making anti-Nazi statements or engage in anti-Nazi activities. Consider only the cases of Annemarie Köhler and Helmut Richter.

On April 15, 1937, Klemperer wrote that "Dr. Dressel [Annemarie's medical partner] practices passive resistance and Annemarie active resistance"; on February 8, 1941, that "her welcome was very friendly ... her conversation was very anti-Nazi and very defeatist"; and on June 24, 1942, that "this afternoon ... these pages go to Pirna [Annemarie's clinic]. My latest fear is that they are not absolutely safe there either. Annemarie is notorious after all." Annemarie Köhler must have known that she was hiding diary pages, but one wonders whether she ever looked into any of them, and if she did, whether she read the following entry for February 14, 1943: "Eva must take the diary to Annemarie soon again. The guillotine at Münchner Platz goes to work for less cause."

The Gestapo tolerated a great deal of grumbling in Germany, especially if it was done by members of the social and cultural elite. While lower-class people often landed in prison for a few drunken remarks about the Führer, the upper classes could take many more liberties. Perhaps Klemperer assumed that Annemarie Köhler would enjoy the benefit of this consideration. But how is one to interpret his entries on Helmut Richter, the protector of their house in Dölzschen? Klemperer understood that Richter was engaged in conspiratorial anti-Nazi activities, and yet he wrote on February 14, 1943: "The man's whole behavior made it obvious to me that he knew *more* than just a rumor, that something *must* be underway involving the moderate working class, the bourgeoisie, and the army." And on May 1, 1943, Klemperer added: "He had heard from two reliable and informed sources that a military coup was anticipated as early as mid-May."

A few weeks later Richter was arrested. Here are Klemperer's comments of June 27, 1943: "My very first reaction [to Richter's arrest] was to be almost quietly pleased or amused, that my protector and guardian was now worse off than myself, that Aryans, too, were personally experiencing the hand of the tyranny.... But then I was tormented by what his arrest meant for us. Loss of bread coupons, loss of extra money ... the house in great danger, for who will be the next trustee? On top of that the overlapping anxiety: If they were to arrest Annemarie and carry out a house search!" Richter was held first in a prison and then disappeared into the Buchenwald concentration camp. Klemperer wrote on September 27, 1944: "My diaries and notes! I tell myself again and again: They will not only cost my life, if they are discovered, but also Eva's and that of several others, whom I have mentioned by name, had to mention, if I wanted them to have documentary worth. Am I entitled, perhaps even obliged to do so, or is it criminal vanity?"

Klemperer's arguments do not persuade. The diary's documentary worth would not have suffered had he chosen to use pseudonyms in the riskiest cases. Why spell out precise and revealing details even in the year 1942, when the Gestapo repeatedly turned all things upside down in the house so that, afterwards, it took the Klemperers many days to clean up the mess? I cannot explain Klemperer's behavior, but I am certain that Annemarie Köhler and Helmut Richter amply deserve to be honored as "Righteous Gentiles" at Yad Vashem in Jerusalem.

During the last several decades of his life, Klemperer repeatedly predicted a fatal heart attack; in 1960, when he was seventy-eight, his heart finally succumbed. His new wife remained with him to the end and later she undertook the arduous task of deciphering and typing the diaries for publication. Some critics believe that Victor Klemperer was a hero and a great man. I cannot share such a view. He was courageous, to be sure; however, he was also cynical, selfish, and an opportunist. What makes his diaries valuable is his faltering, neurotic, nonideological voice.

The picture that Klemperer draws of the German people does not fit the images at we all carry in our minds: Germans throwing themselves at the feet of the Führer; Germans supremely confident of victory; Germans hounding Jews out of German towns and villages without waiting for orders; Germans massacring Jews and others in the East. Those are all true pictures, of course, but there were millions of other Germans as well, along with changing situations that turned beasts into decent human beings, or decent human beings into beasts. Not once between 1933 and 1945 did Klemperer describe surging masses in the thralls of pro-Hitler hysteria, and not once did he report on spontaneous anti-Jewish mass action.

Still, he wrote about individual Germans who hated Jews, about Germans who were not anti-Semitic but were confirmed National Socialists, about those who hated Hitler but hoped for a German military victory, and about Germans who were anti-Hitler and hoped for their own country's defeat. When reading Klemperer's diaries, one is tempted to conclude that there were proportionally no more "willing executioners" among the Germans than there would be among other peoples, Americans included. But this cannot be the end of the matter. The raw fact is that Germans systematically murdered millions of people. So do the Klemperer diaries help us to pierce the incomprehensibility of this demonic turn of events? Not really.

3
VICTIMS

THE INCOMPREHENSIBLE HOLOCAUST

According to the historian Raul Hilberg, the United States alone captured forty thousand linear feet of documents on the murder of European Jews. Add to this other captured documents, police and court records, memoirs, oral histories, film documentaries, interviews, and two thousand books in many languages (there are over ten thousand publications of varying size on Auschwitz alone), and we can say that the Holocaust is a uniquely well-documented historical event. Yet a host of unanswered questions remain, and we have not even agreed on a name for the terrible thing that happened. The term "The Final Solution" has passed into common usage, but fortunately, this obscene Nazi euphemism does not correspond to fact because nearly half of the European Jews survived. "Holocaust" is the choice of Jewish organizations, but as Arno Mayer points out in *Why Did the Heavens Not Darken? The "Final Solution" in*

This essay first appeared, under the same title, in the September 28, 1989, issue of the *New York Review of Books*.

The essay led to an extraordinarily long series of exchanges, which were printed in the December 21, 1989; February 1, March 29, September 27, 1990; and the April 25, 1991, issues. Because in the article I reviewed sixteen diverse books, the letters also dealt with the most diverse questions. The most often discussed topics were the role of Popes Pius XI and Pius XII in Nazism and the Holocaust; the extent of East Europeans' assistance to the Nazis in the genocide of the Jews; the privileged treatment accorded to some inmates, especially to British POWs, at Auschwitz and the devastating effect it had on the vast majority of the underprivileged, as well as Denmark and Vichy France under Nazi occupation.

Rereading the essay, I now feel that I was wrong to charge the Catholic Church with only the sin of omission during the Holocaust; the historic Church as a whole was responsible for creating an anti-Judaic atmosphere that facilitated the work of the Nazis. This, Pope John Paul II recently all but admitted. Finally, today I would hesitate to call the Holocaust "the only true genocide." At least, in some of my more recent articles I have argued quite differently.

History (New York: Pantheon, 1990), Holocaust is a "religiously freighted word concept, . . . a term whose standard meaning is a sacrificial offering wholly consumed by fire in exaltation of God." In truth, why should one find sacrificial offering or exaltation of God in the involuntary agony of the Jewish millions, many of whom were converts to Christianity or unbelievers?

Others resent the Hebrew "Shoah," which, in the words of Philip Lopate, shares "the same self-dramatizing theological ambition to portray the historic suffering of the Jews during World War II as a sort of cosmic storm rending the heavens."[1] Arno Mayer prefers "Judeocide," arguably an apt term but one unlikely to win any more followers than his careful distinctions between "anti-Semitism" as the institutionalized form of prejudice, "Judeophobia" as a personal prejudice, and "anti-Judaism" as hostile feelings or actions directed against the Jewish religion and its adherents.

Clearly, finding the right name is not our gravest concern (I shall be using all these terms freely) regarding the worst mass murder—or one of the worst mass murders—in history, even though by choosing a name we are inevitably making a religious and political statement. Moreover, by hedging the question—writing "the worst," as opposed to "one of the worst"—I have already opened a hornet's nest in the Holocaust controversy. After all, did not Stalin and Mao kill many more people than Hitler? Did not the Turks murder proportionately more Armenians? Conversely, was not the Holocaust a unique event, aiming as it did at the extermination of an entire people, something neither Stalin, nor Mao, nor Enver Pasha sought to achieve?

Some of the writers under review have raised these questions, risking accusations of disseminating cold war propaganda, attempting to rewarm the theory of totalitarianism, or of exhibiting either Jewish ethnocentrism or German apologetics. At least, no serious historian would agree with those on the far right and the far left who try to compare the Final Solution to Hiroshima, My-Lai, or the bombing of Dresden. Nor need anyone pay heed to those who claim that the Holocaust never took place. (Note, however, that the foremost promoters of this persistent fantasy are not SS men but such pseudoscholars as the French university professor Robert Faurisson and the socialist Paul Rassinier, himself a former inmate of Buchenwald.)[2]

While elaborate critical discussions of the Holocaust have been taking place, we are still debating precisely who decided to proceed with the "Final Solution of the Jewish Question," when or why they did so, or what in fact they had in mind. It seems possible that no such clear-cut decision was ever taken, that the program of destruction, although it carried out general aims clearly announced by Hitler, evolved gradually, as an ad hoc affair. Was there a blueprint for murder from the very beginning, and if so, why did the Nazis foster a vigorous program of forced Jewish emigration during the first eight years of their rule? Why was emigration suddenly forbidden in 1941, after it had become nearly impossible anyway? When did the Holocaust actually begin? Immediately after the German attack on the Soviet Union in June 1941, or only after effective Soviet military resistance had been met, or only after things had begun to go badly for the German army on the Eastern front? What was Hitler's part in the entire affair, and what were the activities of Himmler, the Waffen SS, the army, the bureaucrats, the capitalists, the German public, the satellite governments, and the authorities in subjugated countries? What is one to make of the Reich railroad officials, who charged tourist group passenger fares for the Jews deported to the death camps (children paid only half fare) and then crammed them into cattle cars?

What share do the Poles or other non-German peoples have in responsibility for the Holocaust? Why did the Jews not resist more vigorously, and how guilty were their leaders and their ghetto police? How about the Catholic and the other churches, the Pope, the antifascist resistance, the German conservatives, the European bourgeoisie, the working-class movement, the non-Jewish concentration camp inmates, the Kapos and other *Prominenten* in the camps, the Foreign Office, the State Department, Anthony Eden, President Roosevelt, and Stalin? Why did proportionately more Jews survive in Fascist Italy and within the borders of Germany's allies such as Bulgaria, Romania, Finland, and Hungary than in the anti-Nazi and democratic Netherlands, anti-Nazi and undemocratic Poland, or in the occupied Soviet territories? Why did almost all the Jewish citizens of the Danish puppet state survive but only a few of the Jews in Norway, which had resisted the German invasion? Why was it possible to spirit Jews across the sea from Denmark to neutral Sweden but not across the thousand miles of the common Swedish-Norwegian border?

Was the German fury rooted in the country's peculiar social and political development, in the traumas of World War I and the Versailles Treaty, or in the fear of Bolshevism? What made the mass killings possible: German centralization and bureaucratic efficiency, or conversely, the anarchic disorganization of the Nazi state? Is it true that Nazi anti-Semitism had only a modest appeal for the German people, and if so, why did Germans do the Nazis' bidding in carrying out the Final Solution? Or was the killing chiefly the work of Nazi political troops? The debate continues, and Arno Mayer sounds most convincing when he writes in the preface of his work that "at bottom the Judeocide remains as incomprehensible to me today as five years ago, when I set out to study and rethink it." But why, then, is he so sure of his numerous provocative theses on the remaining 450 pages of his book?

Testimonies

A great many of the works reviewed here are personal reminiscences, and it is decidedly easier to comment on them than on the convoluted scholarly histories, which I shall deal with later. Admittedly, most of these memoirs lack the intellectual depth and brutal honesty of such classics of the Holocaust as Primo Levi's *Survival in Auschwitz*.[3] Admittedly also, the reminiscences under review seem to follow a well-established pattern: a happy and secure middle-class existence interrupted by a lightning bolt of terror and followed by unspeakable agonies; quiet heroism; survival through self-respect and a desire to tell the world about it; liberation; a painful search for a new place in the world; a modest career and a contented family life, although one marred by terrible dreams. Lately the number of such published reminiscences has increased dramatically, perhaps because most of the survivors are now retired and have time to document their lives; perhaps, too, because old age compels them to look back with some longing even to a homeland that proved treacherous and cruel.

Most survivor stories begin in Eastern Europe, meaning that their authors have had to cope not only with German but also with native anti-Semitism. Malvina Graf (*The Kraków Ghetto and the Plaszów Camp Remembered*; foreword and notes by George M. Kren; Tallahassee: Florida State University Press, 1989), Frieda Frome (*Some Dare to Dream*; foreword by Robert Abzug; Ames: Iowa State University Press, 1988), and Zofia S. Kubar (*Double Identity: A Memoir*; New York: Hill and Wang, 1989) all came from educated middle-class families in Poland and Lithuania, which may well have been the key to their survival: they had some money as well as friends in the local population.

Graf and Frome had a taste not only of German but also of Soviet rule and have little good to say about the latter. Malvina Graf escaped from the German to the Soviet zone in occupied Poland in 1939, but she found conditions so bad there that she and her brothers registered for repatriation to German-held territory. The USSR and Nazi Germany were allies at that time; still, the Grafs' attempt to go home was interpreted as disloyalty to the Soviet Union. Malvina, her relatives, and her friends were rounded up for deportation into the Soviet interior. She managed to go into hiding, however, only to fall into the hands of the Germans in 1941. Subsequently, she landed at the Plaszów concentration camp and was finally liberated, in Bavaria, by the Americans.

Frieda Frome experienced the Soviet occupation of Lithuania from 1940 to June 1941, when the Red Army was forced to withdraw from the country. This allowed the right-wing nationalist Lithuanian "Partisans" to emerge from prison and to begin massacring the Jews. The arriving Germans needed only to coordinate and expand this activity. Most of Frome's family—and 90 percent of all Lithuanian Jews—perished in the Final Solution but Frome and her sister survived by escaping from the Kaunas (Kovno) ghetto in 1944 and by hiding with warmhearted Lithuanian peasants. Liberated by the Red Army, she found life in Soviet Lithuania unbearable and fled again in 1945, the beginning of a long odyssey that ultimately led her to the United States. Frome sympathizes with the plight of Lithuanians, a tiny nation caught between German and Russian imperialism. Still, her account makes clear that, even without the German occupation, Lithuania and the other East European nation-states would have done their best, if by more peaceful means, to diminish the number of Jews and other ethnic minorities in their midst.

The university student Zofia S. Kubar was one of the approximately 18,000 Jews who hid in Warsaw during the war. She escaped from the ghetto in 1943 and succeeded in leading a new life on the Aryan side of the wall by looking less than conspicuously Jewish and by proving herself cool and resourceful. She was constantly in danger from blackmailers, often hordes of young boys who spied on Jews in hiding, squeezed them dry, and then denounced them to the Gestapo for yet another monetary reward. But she was also helped along by many decent Poles, sometimes complete strangers, who risked their lives on her behalf.

The penalty for assisting or even trading with a Jew in German-occupied Poland was death, a fact that makes all comparisons between wartime Polish-Jewish relations and, say, Danish-Jewish relations blatantly unfair. Yet such comparisons are made again and again in Western histories—and virtually always to the detriment of Poles, with scarce notice taken of the fifty thousand to one hundred thousand Jews said to have been saved by the efforts of Poles to hide or otherwise help them.[4] This is not to say that Polish anti-Semitism was not a strongly and widely felt prejudice, for it certainly was, or that life was not hard for most Jews in prewar Poland. It is to say only that one must not ignore the crucial differences between wartime conditions in Eastern and Western Europe.

The Czech Jewish novelist Jiří Weil lived in Prague in 1939, during the Nazi invasion. He pretended to kill himself and then went into hiding in the city, which enabled him to survive the occupation. A longstanding Communist, Weil was nevertheless critical of Stalinism in both his prewar and postwar novels, which led to his expulsion from the Party and an isolated existence in Prague until his death in 1959. The title of his *Life with a Star* (translated by Ruzena Kovarikova with Roslyn Schloss, preface by Philip Roth; New York: Farrar, Strauss and Giroux, 1989) is an allusion to the Star of David that the Jews were forced to wear during the Nazi occupation. It is a partly autobiographical novel. Its hero, Josef Roubicek, a modest bank clerk, submits at first to the Jewish community set up under the Nazis, which exposes him to heartless bureaucratic treatment in the purest Kafkaesque tradition and prepares him, inexorably, for the day of his deportation. But after losing his Christian mistress, who is hanged by the Nazis, his meager belongings, and even his cat—his sole remaining companion—Roubicek finally becomes a rebel. He hides out by joining a small resistance group of Communist workers. "It was then," Weil writes, "when the last sheets of my scribblings were burning in the stove, annulling the name of Josef Roubicek, that I understood that the Josef Roubicek who wanted to make excuses, to evade, and to dodge, only to avoid freedom, no longer existed and would never exist again." Melancholy, subdued (the Germans figure in the novel invariably as "they"), this is undoubtedly the best product of the socialist realist literary movement of the 1950s, if not the only good one.

Lucy S. Dawidowicz's *From That Place and Time: A Memoir, 1938–1947* (New York: Norton, 1989) does not quite fit into the category of survivor reminiscences because this well-known historian of the Holocaust was in the United States during the war. Nonetheless, she spent a year between 1938 and 1939 as an American research student in Vilna (what was then Polish Wilno and is today Lithuanian Vilnius).

Dawidowicz is most informative and entertaining on the often glorious history of Jewish Vilna, Yiddish culture, the rabbinical tradition, the YIVO Institute for Jewish Research (which she later helped to transplant to New York City), the anti-religious Jewish socialist Bund, and the local Jewish artists, scholars, and writers. But she overstates the extent of official Polish anti-Semitism before World War II. I doubt that Jewish political representations in the interwar Polish parliament or the vigorous Jewish trade union movement was tolerated by the government only because of foreign political considerations, as she implies; the Polish regime was far too cantankerous and conceited for that. And what of the fact, which she does not mention, that the mobilized Polish army in 1939 included several thousand Jewish reserve officers or that hundreds of Jews were among the masses of captive Polish reserve officers murdered by the Soviets at Katyn?

When Poland was about to be attacked, Dawidowicz returned to New York

The Incomprehensible Holocaust

by traveling across Nazi Germany, ironically the only safe exit route for a U.S. citizen at that time. In fact most Jews holding a U.S. or British passport, whether in Germany or in occupied Europe, survived the Holocaust. Jewish citizens of states relatively friendly to Germany, such as Turkey, were generally not so fortunate if caught in occupied Europe.

The late Stefan Korbonski, who was head of civilian resistance in German-occupied Poland and who was awarded the Yad Vashem Medal of Honor for "Righteous Gentiles" in 1980, writes in *The Jews and the Poles in World War II* (New York: Hippocrene, 1989) that the Germans executed about 2,500 Poles for their actions on behalf of Jews. In his short book Korbonski argues somewhat tendentiously that a workable symbiosis took place between the Polish and Jewish cultures, yet his complaints of an anti-Polish bias on the part of the Western, especially the Jewish, public are not unjustified. When will it finally be recognized that the presence of 3.3 million Jews in prewar Poland was not an accident but the consequence of the Polish kings' and nobles' having welcomed the Jews expelled from Western Europe? When will publicists cease to compare the situation in Denmark, where there were a few thousand assimilated Jews, with that in Poland, where Jews made up 10 percent of the population?

Even though many Poles were guilty of anti-Semitism, as they surely were, it ought not to be forgotten that according to the Nazi scheme the entire leadership of the Polish nation was to be destroyed, beginning with the systematic extermination of officers, professionals, teachers, and priests. The Soviets seemed determined to achieve much the same goal, murdering thousands of members of the Polish elite and deporting about 1.7 million Poles.

True, the Polish resistance offered only a very small amount of armed help to the fighters of the Warsaw ghetto in 1943; still, the SS commander suppressing the ghetto uprising wrote in his report that his soldiers "have been repeatedly shot at from outside the Ghetto.—i.e., from the Aryan part." I wonder whether anyone fired a shot elsewhere in Europe on behalf of persecuted Jews. (The Italian troops who protected Jews from being rounded up by German units in occupied France did not have to go that far.)[5] The Polish underground and the London-based Polish government-in-exile repeatedly alerted the world to the Final Solution, and it was not the fault of the Polish resistance that the West would not take these reports seriously.

Korbonski emphasizes that one-half of the nearly six million Polish citizens killed during World War II were Gentiles, and he rightly resents Claude Lanzmann's manipulative selection, in *Shoah,* of stupid sounding Polish witnesses to the Jewish Holocaust. Or what must Korbonski, a genuine hero, have felt when he was conspicuously not invited, in 1981, to the conference of the

United States Holocaust Memorial Council? But he makes himself unattractive by presenting a long list of Jews who presided over the Soviet terror in Poland and by remaining silent about the sickening pogroms against Jewish survivors that took place in a number of Polish towns and villages after World War II.

Polish-Jewish relations are plagued by one-sided, highly emotional interpretations. Heroes of the Polish resistance refuse to understand that for many Jews in pre–World War II nationalist Eastern Europe, communism seemed the only salvation, and that, after 1944, only a small minority of the Jews in Poland became murderous police chiefs and political commissars. In the other camp some Jewish publicists act as if the Poles themselves set up the gas chambers. No doubt the Germans would have had little difficulty in recruiting Poles as camp guards, just as they had no difficulty in recruiting Ukrainians, Russians, Lithuanians, and Latvians. The fact is, however, that the Germans judged the Poles unworthy of even such a task. The unholy competition for claiming primacy in suffering continues, and it may take another forty years before Jews and Poles begin talking reasonably with each other.

The dispute between Jews and Poles is closely tied to the continued controversy between Catholics and Jews, Poland being a mostly Catholic country and the Pope himself a Pole. There was the issue of the small Carmelite convent established, in 1984, within the Auschwitz camp and a twenty-three-foot cross erected near it. Jewish organizations objected to what appeared to them as an attempt to "Christianize" Auschwitz, and in 1987, at Geneva, four cardinals, led by the Cardinal of Lyon, reached an agreement with European Jewish leaders that by February 1989, the convent would be moved outside the camp, as part of a future interreligious center. The Cardinal of Lyon stated the case for moving the convent as follows: "It is the attempt to totally exterminate the Jews . . . of which Auschwitz is the symbol. Such affliction and suffering have conferred on the Jewish people through its martyrs a particular dignity that it quite properly its own. And to construct a convent at Auschwitz would, for me, impinge on that dignity." But when the convent and its dozen or so nuns stayed put, Jewish militants organized noisy demonstrations at the site this past summer, with some of the protesters reportedly being roughed up by Polish construction workers. Angered by the spectacle, the Cardinal Archbishop of Kraków, one of the original signers of the agreement, indicated that he would no longer honor his commitment. He was supported by the Primate of Poland, Cardinal Josef Glemp. The *Solidarity* newspaper criticized Glemp's statements for wounding the feelings of the families of Holocaust victims; however, the Cardinal of Lyon has said the agreement must be kept.

An underlying issue in all this vehemence is, quite obviously, the failure of the Church effectively to oppose the carrying out of the Final Solution. But why does the behavior of the Catholic Church during the Holocaust create so much more controversy than that of the German Protestants, the International Red Cross, or neutral Switzerland? The answer is that the Protestant churches, to take only one example, had always been acquiescent because of their nationalism and their traditional subservience to the state. With a few notable exceptions, Protestant clergymen, especially Lutherans, acted under the Nazis as executive arms of the German state. How different is the Catholic Church with its universalist ideology and its disciplined following!

Roman Catholicism represents a beautiful anachronism in our age of crazed nationalism; virtually every devout Catholic preserves in his heart some remnant of his denomination's transnational loyalty and the duty of Catholics to defy immoral laws. Indeed, no other institution produced a greater number of heroes in the years before and during the Holocaust: Polish, German, Italian, and French nuns, monks, and lay priests gave their lives or suffered imprisonment for the sake of Jews. But the Roman Church itself, although powerful enough to stop the Nazi euthanasia program for the extermination of Germans who were handicapped, retarded, "asocial," and gravely ill, did not undertake the same concerted effort on behalf of the Jews, the Gypsies, or the Soviet prisoners of war (some three million of the latter group alone perished in the Nazi camps). By speaking up in public against these horrors, the Church might just have created enough turmoil among German Catholics to stop or at least to slow down the Nazi program.

It really makes no difference whether Popes Pius XI and XII were prevented from confronting Hitler by the time-honored duty of the Church to survive even in the most inhospitable environment, by their personal sympathy for the German nation, by their justified fear of Bolshevism, or by their conviction that quiet, unobtrusive assistance to individuals, especially to converted Jews, would be more efficient. The fact remains that the Church could and should have done more, if for no other reason than to assert its institutional position in the face of the most abysmal neo-pagan attacks on its eternal values. Unfortunately, until this day [1989], the Vatican has not chosen to express its sorrow over that tragic historical shortcoming. Nor are many Jews willing to admit that the Catholic Church was guilty of no other crime but the unquestionably grave sin of omission.

If further proof is needed that the Nazis did not reserve their satanic cruelty for Jews alone, then Wanda Póltawska's *And I Am Afraid of My Dreams* (translated by Mary Craig; New York: Hippocrene, 1987) provides that evidence. The daughter of a Catholic post-office clerk in Lublin, she was only nineteen when she was arrested in 1941 for having served as a courier in the Polish resistance. Tortured mercilessly, she spent half a year in a Lublin prison and then three years in the Ravensbrück concentration camp near the German capital.

In the camp, scores of her fellow resistance fighters, all young women, were taken away periodically to be shot, while Póltawska and dozens of her companions were used as guinea pigs in a medical experiment whose sole purpose seems to have been to determine how much suffering human beings could sustain. Some died as a result of the operations. Few things show the uniqueness of Nazi brutality better than the insane procedures inflicted on these women, which consisted of removing their leg bones or injecting them with bacterial cultures, all under conditions of unspeakable filth and neglect that would have invalidated any conceivable scientific results. A good number of German doctors and nurses participated in the proceedings, and even though Póltawska's chief torturer, Professor Karl Gebhardt, was later hanged for his crimes, it is well known that many of the Nazi doctors involved continued to thrive in postwar Germany.[6]

Was there really no difference between the treatment of Jews and Catholic Poles at Ravensbrück? Not during the first years of the young Polish women's imprisonment, but later they began receiving Red Cross packages as well as letters from home and were occasionally helped by Polish prisoners of war. More important, these women were sustained by their youth, their ardent patriotism, and their knowledge of friends and family that awaited them in Poland. Unlike most Jews, Póltawska had a home to return to, where she now lives as a practicing psychiatrist and, perhaps understandably, a right-to-life activist.

Camp hierarchy was a complex affair, and not even those on top could feel secure. Violent death was an everyday possibility both for old-timers and for the *Prominenten,* or low-level bosses recruited from among the common criminals (green triangles) and political prisoners (red triangles), or, less frequently, the "asocials" (black triangles), homosexuals (pink triangles), Gypsies (brown triangles), and Jews. These people held the lives of others in their hands, yet even a slight mistake or the appearance of leniency could lead to their own execution.

As Louis J. Micheels explains in *Doctor #117641: A Holocaust Memoir* (foreword by Albert J. Solnit; New Haven CT: Yale University Press, 1989), rank and position were not the only sources of privilege: it was enough to own a good coat or to look well-fed. A less-than-haggard face inspired respect and could open the way to receiving food, which in turn, led to power and more privileges. Micheels's account makes one wonder whether he is truly describing life in the *anus mundi,* the Auschwitz concentration camp. While his parents were killed in another camp, Micheels, a Dutch Jewish medical student and a doctor-nurse in the Auschwitz main camp, slept in a real bed, moved about, read good books, played music, consorted with his Jewish fiancée, grew jealous of her flirtations, and once even made love to her, hidden in a closet. Here is how he describes one of his work assignments: "The laboratory was four miles from the camp, and it took us about an hour to walk there. But it was a pleasant walk . . . along the banks of the Sola River, past an agricultural station staffed by woman prisoners, to whom we waved enthusiastically in passing. . . . In the cold early morning the sky was sometimes a beautiful red, setting aglow the fields to the left across the river. To the right, in the distance, we could see the chimneys of the crematorium in Birkenau. It was a glaring and dramatic contrast. . . . My room [in the laboratory], spacious, neat, and clean, was on the first floor in the back; its large window looked to the fields beyond. . . . [SS] Untersturmführer Münch . . . was friendly, showed personal interest in people, never deliberately humiliated anybody." Only when Auschwitz was evacuated, toward the end of the war, did Micheels share in the misery of ordinary prisoners.

In a death camp like Treblinka practically no new arrival escaped annihilation: hence the horrendous losses among Polish and Lithuanian Jews, most of whom were transported directly from the ghetto to the death camps. Those, however, who were sent to Auschwitz, which was both a death camp and a labor camp, often escaped immediate selection for annihilation, provided that they looked relatively young and healthy. Eva Schloss, whose mother married Anne Frank's father after the war, arrived in Auschwitz from Holland only in May 1944. As she tells in *Eva's Story: A Survivor's Tale by the Step-Sister of Anna Frank* (written with Evelyn Julia Kent; New York: St Martin's, 1988), she passed the first selection and was detailed to the "Canada Commando," a privileged outfit charged with sorting out the confiscated belongings of the new arrivals. Her father and brother succumbed to hunger and exhaustion during the last days of the war, but Eva and her mother survived to be liberated in Auschwitz by the Red Army.

Unlike other survivors, she has only good things to say about the generosity and kindness of the Soviet soldiers she met. Of routine interest only (if any Auschwitz experience can be called routine), *Eva's Story* nevertheless confirms what has become evident from all the testimonies under review here, namely that a good social background, education, self-confidence, and familiarity with the German language were of immense help in the struggle for survival. Schloss's reminiscences also confirm what we have known for a long time, that whereas both her and Anne Frank's family were hidden by heroic Dutch Gentiles, they were also betrayed to the Gestapo by their Dutch neighbors and were questioned and guarded by the Dutch police under SS orders.

Who are the survivors? What price in self-respect did they have to pay for being able to dodge the continual selection process? As their testimonies show, even the most heroic and noble among them may not be free of a gnawing sense of guilt. In the criminal *univers concentrationnaire* none remained wholly innocent, if only because he once grabbed a piece of bread before the others.

(No sooner had I written the above lines on the tormented conscience of survivors than I recalled a bilingual—English and Hungarian—book of interviews published recently in Hungary, whose subject, a Hungarian peasant and former prisoner of war in the Soviet Union, told the author: "Eating human flesh, that happened sometimes. When there really isn't anything else, you have to eat that too. . . . I too ate human flesh." The book reports that Lajos M., a Hungarian peasant, suffered a nervous breakdown in old age.)[7]

Some survived thanks to their special skills; others were saved by belonging to a closely knit political group. Len Crome's *Unbroken: Resistance and Survival in the Concentration Camps* (New York: Schocken, 1988) tells of the struggle for survival and the resistance activity of a small team of brave young German Communists. They were *Das Rote Sprachrohr* (Red Megaphones), not all of them Jews. Few stories have appeared, in English, on the tragedy of German Communists in the Third Reich. This alone makes the book worth reading, despite its dogmatism and naiveté.

The author, Len Crome, served with the International Brigades in Spain and is the brother-in-law of Jonny Hüttner, whose story forms the major part of the book. A Jew and longstanding Communist, Hüttner was arrested in 1936 and escaped from the Dora camp in April 1945,[8] having already passed through several prisons and camps, including Auschwitz. His condition alternated between abject misery and—whenever Communists succeeded in seizing control of the camp's internal administration—relative comfort and security. Communists in power were greatly preferable to professional criminals in power, but even Communists protected mainly their own kind, which meant substituting other names for the names of Party comrades on the list of those destined to die.

Camp conditions varied not only for different categories of prisoners but also according to the degree of overcrowding, the urgency of reducing the number of inmates, or the mood of the commandants. None of the accounts of survivors under review tells a story of unrelieved suffering; none escaped unspeakable brutalities.

Most contributors to the illustrated documentary collection *Lódz Ghetto: Inside a Community Under Siege,* compiled and edited by Alan Adelson and Robert Lapides, with annotations and bibliographical notes by Marek Web (New York: Viking, 1989) perished in the death camps.[9] This makes their testimonies even harder to bear. These diarists, poets, and ghetto officials tell of heroes and scoundrels, of human dignity and utter debasement. Above all, the documents tell of ghetto leaders who sacrificed lives in the hope of saving other lives. The "Eldest of the Jews," Mordechai Chaim Rumkowski, the autocratic leader of the Jews at Lódz, caused many thousands of Polish Jews to board trains that would take them to the death camps. His ghetto police, assisted by the Germans, suppressed strikes and internal resistance. He handed over to the Gestapo members of the Jewish resistance as well as those who tried to go into hiding or hid others.

Alan Adelson and Robert Lapides calculate that only about ten thousand of the two hundred thousand people in the Lódz ghetto survived the war. They conclude that but for Rumkowski's deceitful or misinformed assurances of their safety, the Jews might not have willingly boarded the death trains. But even Adelson and Lapides are uncertain whether Rumkowski, who himself was killed in 1944, had been deliberately deceitful. And if the Jews had refused to board the trains, what then?

The Commandants

Very few works have dealt with the concentration camp commandants, although Claude Lanzmann and Gitta Sereny, among others, have interviewed former SS men involved in running the camps.[10] The Israeli historian Tom Segev makes a careful attempt to construct a collective portrait of the concentration camp commandants in his *The Soldiers of Evil: The Commandants of the Nazi Concentration Camps,* which was translated by Haim Waitzman (New York: McGraw-Hill, 1987). For the book he interviewed several of the commandants or talked to their families. The book would have benefited from some statistical data—for example, on the social and geographic origin of the commandants or on their education and training; still, one gathers that the commandants came from almost all social strata, except the aristocracy and upper bourgeoisie, and that many, but by no means all, were born into Austrian and South German Catholic families.

The large number of Austrians among the officers in charge of the Final Solution, such as Ernst Kaltenbrunner, Odilo Globocnik, Franz Stangl, Amon Göth, and Karl Fritsch, as well as Adolf Eichmann (the latter an Austrian by choice, however, not by birth), does not necessarily prove that the Austrians were more zealous Nazis than the Germans. Rather, as latecomers to the Reich, they may have been given the less desirable assignments. The camp commandants "were mediocre people," Segev writes, "without imagination, without courage, without initiative." They obeyed orders, but they were "not Germans like all the Germans and not even Nazis like all the Nazis." Almost without exception, they joined the Party and the SS very early; the SS was their family, with which they tended to identify fully. "More than anything else, they were soldiers—soldiers by choice. Political soldiers, in the service of evil. The military was more than employment for them, more than a career. It was a way of life."

No SS man was obliged to serve in a concentration camp, but most saw no reason to avoid it. Once there, they grew into the job and became more wicked daily, as had the woman I once saw in a German television documentary on the Majdanek trial. A Bavarian farmhand, she first became a prison guard and then a supervisor in a concentration camp, where one of her specialties was drowning "unruly" Jewish women in the latrine. After the war, she went back to being a farmhand until she was arrested and tried. During the trial she sat in the dock, an old peasant woman, knitting.

Historians

Scholars of the Final Solution have been called the skilled craftsmen of the "Holocaust enterprise," and to be sure, they earn rewards in fame, royalties, and endowed Holocaust Chairs. Understandably too, some critics worry about the possible ritualization and trivialization of a subject that cannot be treated like any other historical study. Can mass murder be dealt with as one more academic topic? Can it be submerged in a mass of footnotes? In the words of Nora Levin: "The world of Auschwitz was, in truth, another planet."[11] But as Michael Marrus argues in his excellent survey *The Holocaust in History* (New York: New American Library, 1987), "the alternative, silence, is surely a counsel of despair." In any case, the writings of a good many contemporary scholars make admirable efforts to understand something that is basically incomprehensible. I am thinking here in particular of the work of such scholars as Marrus, Uwe Dietrich Adam, Yehuda Bauer, Randolph L. Braham, Martin Broszat, Christopher R. Browning, Lucy S. Dawidowicz, Saul Friedländer, Martin Gilbert, Raul Hilberg, Michael H. Kater, Walter Laqueur, Robert J. Lifton, Charles S. Maier, George L. Mosse, Gerald Reitlinger, Karl A. Schleunes, and Shulamit Volkov. Most of these writers, and others as well, are cited in Marrus's work; several have contributed to or are discussed in François Furet, ed., *Unanswered Questions: Nazi Germany and the Genocide of the Jews* (New York: Schocken, 1989), also under review here.

A question addressed by all these historians concerns the centrality of anti-Semitism in Nazi ideology and in German public opinion. Most historians agree that anti-Semitism was not a predominant ideology in nineteenth-century Germany. Or are we to forget that anti-Semitism was more virulent in France and Russia at the turn of the century than in Germany and that during World War I German troops marching into Russian territory were received as liberators by the Jewish population? Nor was anti-Jewish ideology a constant preoccupation of the leaders of the Third Reich. Only a minority of the early Nazis were "paranoid anti-Semites," and anti-Jewish propaganda did not do much for the Party's popularity before 1930. It was, however, absolutely central to the thinking of Hitler, for in his perverted version of Darwinism, the Jews were the "antirace," a mortal threat to his plans, to the German nation, and to the human race.

As Saul Friedländer has explained, it was fanatical hatred of the Jews that distinguished Hitler's ideology from that of the other fascists, not his anti-Marxism, which was common to all of them. The Jews, not the Marxists or the Bolsheviks, were the targets of Hitler's first and last ideological statements. He could, and did, conclude an alliance with Stalin, whom he admired in many ways; an "arrangement" with the Jews was unthinkable for him. What remains unexplained, therefore, is why so many Germans willingly participated in the Final Solution. Some writers point to the demonic appeal of Hitler. Others repeat, although less categorically, Hannah Arendt's thesis on the banality of evil: the willingness of the faceless bureaucrats to do what they perceived to be their Führer's wish, especially because the incessant power struggle within the Nazi bureaucracy could be won only by gaining the approval of its supreme arbiter.

Historians also generally agree on the uniqueness of the Holocaust: unlike the other monsters of the twentieth century, the Nazis aimed at total success. As the German liberal historian Eberhard Jäckel has written: "Never before had a state . . . decided that a specific human group, including its aged, its women, its children and infants, would be killed as quickly as possible, and then carried through this regulation using every possible means of state power."[12]

In 1986 a number of German historians, Ernst Nolte and Andreas Hillgruber among them, raised the issue of the uniqueness of the Holocaust, arguing that it was only one of several cases of genocide and that the Nazis were merely imitating Stalin's "Asiatic" politics. The ensuing *Historikerstreit*, the "Dispute of Historians" over recent German history, aroused the educated German public, painfully bringing home such issues as German self-respect, national identity, and Germany's place among civilized nations. Nolte's and

Hillgruber's position was angrily rejected by the philosopher Jürgen Habermas and scores of liberal German historians. The emerging consensus seems to be that while there is little use in constantly worrying over German national identity, and even though it may have been excessively self-accusing on the part of some historians to try to turn the Holocaust into a (West) German national obsession, it would be far worse to attempt to forget it. The Holocaust was indeed unique: the only true genocide of our times.

Yet a disturbing dilemma remains for historians. At least two thousand learned books have been written on the murder of 5.1 million Jews and considerably fewer on the death, by artificially created famine, deportation, and outright murder, of 14.5 million Soviet "class enemies" (kulaks), or on the total number of victims of Stalinist terror, estimated at some 20 million.[13] Even less has appeared on the Communist massacres in China, Cambodia, and Tibet or, for example, on the murder of the Nigerian Ibos. Such a vast discrepancy cannot be explained away by the shortage of archival sources or by the argument that the Ukrainian kulaks, unlike the Jews, were determined enemies of their state. Why then were the children of kulaks also treated as class enemies, regardless of their social and economic condition? It appears that the preoccupation with the Jews and their killers reflects a tendency to concentrate on those who are "ours": the educated and civilized West Europeans. Not only has the history of the Holocaust been a central and necessary concern of the Jewish communities in the Western countries but historians generally have been overwhelmed by the spectacle of a nation once thought to be among the most "civilized" destroying one of the most civilized of peoples. They have been less concerned with the mass murder of peasants.[14]

How did the Holocaust take place? The question is the subject of a complex historical debate, separating "intentionalists" from "functionalists," and the extremists in each camp from the moderates. The intentionalists argue for a "straight path," meaning that Hitler's thinking from very early on followed a coherent line, calling implicitly and explicitly for the elimination of Jews. The question of just how early divides the extreme and more moderate intentionalists. Moreover, as Ernst Nolte sees it, because the Nazis hated modernity more than anything else and because, for them, Jews in Germany were the quintessential representatives of modernity, they never flinched in their early decision to do away with them. Hitler only awaited the favorable opportunity before issuing the orders to his underlings.

For their part, the functionalists uphold the theory of a "crooked path," arguing that the Third Reich was a maze of competing power groups, rival bureaucracies, and threatening personalities, and that the Final Solution occurred only as a result of these rivalries. It emerged "bit by bit," writes the Munich historian Martin Broszat, depending on local initiatives by such vicious and aggressive leaders as the SS General Reinhard Heydrich, the chief of the Nazi security system. In this setting the role of Hitler could only have been indirect. He gave no instructions that anyone has been able to document; rather, his underlings attempted to follow faithfully, as Hans Mommsen argues, the vision of an ideologically obsessed but essentially lazy leader. Still, no serious historian has argued that Hitler wold not have known what was happening.

Such a summary only hints at the range of issues discussed in *The Holocaust in History* and *Unanswered Questions*. Yet I am tempted to agree with Saul Friedländer, who writes that even though the functionalist argument fits better with the main tendencies of modern historical analysis, the evidence itself strengthens the traditional intentionalist position, chiefly because of Hitler's pathological hatred of the Jews. Hitler controlled the rhythm of the anti-Jewish measures, and while he was restrained between 1933 and 1939 by his conservative allies as well as by world opinion, and while between 1939 and 1941 he was groping for a new solution to the "Jewish Question," in 1941 he no longer had any grounds to hesitate. According to Friedländer's explanation, Hitler knew that the invasion of the Soviet Union would burden him with millions more Jews and therefore planned the massacres well in advance; he subsequently would have given direct orders for their execution. But Friedländer also writes, "The historian's paralysis arises from the simultaneity and the interaction of entirely heterogeneous phenomena: messianic fanaticism and bureaucratic structures, pathological impulses and administrative decrees, archaic attitudes within an advanced industrial society." Or as Martin Broszat has pointed out: any thesis concerning the Final Solution is a matter of probability, not certainty. No written order by Hitler to proceed with the Final Solution has ever been found, yet the justification for extermination was already spelled out in *Mein Kampf*.

The Dissenter

The Holocaust is not the primary concern of Arno Mayer's historical research. Nor, to be just, is it that of several other historians whose names I have listed above. But Mayer, who was born in Luxembourg and who in 1940 had to flee the Nazis, is deeply concerned with the subject and has grown impatient with what he perceives as a trivialization and fragmentation of Holocaust studies. Finally, as is shown by his numerous publications, Mayer's interest lies in the survival into the twentieth century of the "old order" in Central and Eastern Europe and in what he sees as the disastrous consequences of that survival. In

Why Did the Heavens Not Darken? he sets out to prove that the upper classes and powerful economic forces that dominated the old order were instrumental in Hitler's political triumph, in the anti-Bolshevik crusade against Soviet Russia and, albeit less directly, in the murder of the European Jews. I do not believe that Mayer has accomplished his purpose. For one reason, because of his excessive assurance, he invites the reader to become a believer without giving him the evidence on which to base a belief— his book lacks notes or footnotes, and only secondary sources are listed in the bibliography.

As Mayer clearly indicates at the outset, he wishes to look beyond the Holocaust to find the causes of the crisis of Western civilization during the first half of the twentieth century. Justly castigating the now fashionable fragmentation of the historical discipline, Mayer proposes to recall "the centrality of ideology, politics, and war in human affairs." First, he writes, we must abandon the vantage point of the cold war, for without discarding "the residual cold war blinkers" we cannot trace the interconnection of anticommunism and anti-Semitism; it was anticommunism, he asserts, that led Germany's old elite, whether in the army, the bureaucracy, or high industrial circles, to collaborate with the Nazi regime and support the military drive for unlimited living space in Eastern Europe, the precondition for the Final Solution.

Second, he argues, we must place the "Judeocide" in its pertinent historical setting, the great European upheavals of the first half of the twentieth century: World War I, the ensuing Bolshevik revolution, the Nazi counterrevolution, and World War II, which was in Mayer's view the inevitable outcome of the Nazi counterrevolution. Mayer proposes an inclusive interpretive model in order both to explain the horrors of our time and to show that both Germany's Eastern campaign and Judeocide were integral components of the Thirty Years' War of the twentieth century.

Mayer believes the Bolshevik Revolution was the great emancipatory event in Eastern Europe, especially for the Jews, and that, in its liberating effects, it can be compared to what the French Revolution accomplished for Western Europe and its Jews. Tragically, however, the "time-honored elites" in Germany and East Central Europe weathered the crises of 1917–1919 and remained determined to preserve the unstable old regimes in which they still held power. The Great Depression caused the "power elite of big business and agriculture, seconded by the old civil- and military-service nobility" to turn to Hitler "because he, unlike them, was adept at rallying popular support for the defense of the established but endangered economic, social, and cultural order."

Putting aside the question of how liberating was a revolution that systematically suppressed all competing revolutionary parties and dissenters of every kind, this sounds to me very much like the old Marxist adage about fascism being "the last bastion of capitalism." But Mayer himself subsequently contradicts this thesis: "While big business at critical moments encouraged the Nazi defiance, it was not its prime mover.... Fascism prevailed in Germany less because some sectors of big business used it as a stratagen to save capitalism than because the old elites resorted to it to preserve their superannuated positions of class, status, and power." Without a doubt the latter statement, not the first, is Mayer's true thesis, but no matter; both theses, in assuming that the historian must assign a dominant role to one group or the other, are open to the same question. How can anyone determine who were the prime movers and who were merely secondary when considering, on the one hand, the vast horde of German noblemen, officers, judges, imperial bureaucrats, professors, and land-owners and, on the other, the no less numerous capitalists, industrialists, businessmen, managers, and commercial farmers?

Mayer sees the Nazi takeover and the war as reactionary moves, inspired primarily by anti-Marxism; Nazi anti-Semitism was for him far less important. "There is no evidence to support the view that the destruction of the Jews was the primary motive and purpose of Hitler's pursuit of power and determination to go to war." Even after the attack on the Soviet Union, Mayer states categorically and repeatedly, the Jews were not to be annihilated, only "extruded." The invasion of Russia was "not to trap the Jews for a predetermined Judeocide. Rather, Operation Barbarossa was both a military campaign to conquer boundless living space in the east and a crusade to eradicate the Soviet regime and the Bolshevik ideology." As Mayer sees it, only after the military drive against the Soviets had taken a disastrous turn, during the winter of 1941–1942, did the Nazis vent their frustrated anger on the Jews. "Indeed, had the blitzkrieg succeeded in the east as it had in the west the year before, Europe might ironically have been spared the worst horrors of the twentieth century."

It is impossible to agree with this reasoning. As other critics have pointed out, Hitler's Judeocide was not merely a byproduct of Hitler's anticommunist crusade; it was one of Hitler's chief war aims. And Mayer seems to me factually wrong in tying the Judeocide to German setbacks on the Eastern front; there is ample evidence to show that the *Einsatzgruppen,* the specially formed police battalions of the SS, began the systematic liquidation of Eastern Jewry as soon as circumstances permitted, a few weeks after the invasion of the Soviet Union in June 1941.

Other questions arise about Mayer's analysis of the situation following World War I in Eastern Europe, the vast stretch of the continent lying between Germany, Italy, and the Soviet Union. In his view this region was generally characterized by the survival of a reactionary anti-Marxist, anti-Bolshevik old order, a point that is essential for his overall thesis. "Along with the countries of the Iberian Peninsula, the countries of this rimland remained prime bastions of Europe's fading old order, rooted in preindustrial economies. Their ruling classes were dominated by landed nobles and gentrified middle classes; their governing classes by civil and military service nobilities." The old ruling elite, Mayer continues, all but blocked land reform in Eastern Europe, leaving small holders and agricultural workers at the mercy of the landowners. But Mayer himself exempts Czechoslovakia, a democratic country dominated by bourgeois politicians and businessmen. And what of the others? The native Bulgarian nobility and the Serbian nobility had both disappeared under the Ottomans, and the Muslim landowners had left with the retreating Ottoman armies in the nineteenth century. Both independent Serbia and Bulgaria were essentially peasant societies. After World War I, the newly created Yugoslavia and Czechoslovakia as well as expanded Romania seized the properties of German-speaking and Hungarian landowners, that is, most of the large estates, and distributed the land among the peasants.

Unfortunately, the peasants of Romania and Yugoslavia, short of cash and farming know-how, benefited little from the land distribution. The political and administrative leaders of Bulgaria, prewar Serbia, and postwar Yugoslavia had largely peasant roots or were descendants of small merchants. Romania and newly independent Poland were characterized by often violent struggles for power between disparate social groups, among them noble landowners.

Only in Hungary between the wars can one talk of the partial survival of the old order: aristocratic landowners, petty nobles, civil- and military-service nobility, and Jewish capitalists, but even in Hungary social change came in the 1930s, with people from both the middle class and lower-middle class demanding and getting more and more jobs in the civil administration and Jewish-owned enterprises.

"The fall of the Romanov, Habsburg, and Hohenzollern empires," Mayer writes, "brought a distinct relaxation of both official and informal discrimination" against the Jews. In reality official discrimination before World War I had existed at most in the Russian empire, not in the German Reich or in Austria-Hungary. There was unofficial discrimination and prejudice everywhere, of course, but at least in the lands under Francis Joseph, which composed much of Central Eastern Europe, Jews had virtually unlimited opportunities for education and employment. They could, and did, become army generals, judges, civil servants, and cabinet members. They entered the hereditary nobility and sat in both houses of parliament. Never before and never since have the Jews of

Central and Eastern Europe enjoyed greater personal dignity than during the *ancien régime* of the Habsburg dynasty.

Here, then, is the crux of the matter. The dissolution of the Habsburg monarchy in 1918 marked the end, or the beginning of the end, of the old order of hereditary and service nobles, who had been tolerant of minority religions and ethnic groups to a degree unheard of since that time. The states that were carved out of the empire experienced grave economic crises and social upheavals. In Hungary, the only East European country where the old nobility had survived more or less intact, the nobles and the Jewish capitalists were pitted against people emerging from the middle and lower-middle classes who had an unquenchable appetite for political and economic power.

No doubt, in Hungary as elsewhere in Eastern Europe, both the old elite and the new social forces were anti-Marxist and anti-Bolshevik. But the new elite and their fascist and fascist-influenced parties—the Iron Guard in Romania and the Arrow Cross in Hungary were only two of many—were also statist, anticapitalist, antiaristocrat, antiliberal, and xenophobic. They were also radically anti-Semitic, for they associated the Jews with everything they hated: Bolshevism, the old order of noble landowners and capitalists, foreign domination, and the Habsburgs. Because their countries were nation-states in name only, the new East European elite clamored for the forcible assimilation or the oppression of alien minorities, among whom they counted the Jews. Unfortunately, Arno Mayer nearly ignores the populist, social revolutionary element in East European chauvinism and anti-Semitism.

The coming of World War II brought cataclysmic regional conflicts and civil wars to the Eastern European countries, causing some of them to fall victim to Nazi aggression and others to jump on the Nazi bandwagon. The war also hastened social revolution and suppression of the ethnic minorities. The Jews were the first victims slaughtered by the Germans with varying degrees of assistance from local administrations and peoples. All the Eastern European regimes (where they existed) repeatedly adjusted their policy toward Jews to the dictates of "national interest" and the changing lines of battle. No Eastern European government was consistently murderous toward Jews during the war years; none was without guilt. As Arno Mayer himself points out, of all Hungarian social classes, the aristocracy resisted the Final Solution most consistently.

After the war came the turn of the 12 million German settlers in Eastern Europe: those who had not fled with the retreating German army were by and large driven out, deported, or killed. Other minorities were treated similarly, under the motto of settling accounts with fascists and Nazi collaborators. The drive against minorities continues to our day, against the Hungarians in Romania, the Turks in Bulgaria, the Albanians in the Kosovo region. The few remaining Jews and Germans are also leaving.

The tragedy of the East European Jews must be seen against this background. They were murdered by the German Nazis and the East European fascists, not by the entire population. Yet we must ask: What would have become of the East European Jews without Hitler? No doubt thousands of them would have sought their fortune in the West as part of the great migration begun at the end of the nineteenth century. Others would have been completely assimilated into a new industrialized society; still others would have left because they found the radical nationalism in Eastern European countries intolerable.

As the Habsburg monarchy crumbled, it was only a matter of time before the old nobility, the imperial bureaucracy, and the German as well as Jewish bourgeoisie would give up their places to the sons and grandsons of native peasants. The new elite, unlike the old, has shown no patience for alien cultures. Such slogans of the interwar period as "Poland for the Poles" and "Romania for the Romanians" heralded the end of the multinational Eastern Europe. In the new national societies, there would have been little room left for Jewish life and culture.[15]

Why did it happen? Why did millions die and other millions survive? After plowing through many dozens of books and having recalled my own experiences as both a victim and a witness, I have no clear answers. Arno Mayer seems right when he asserts that Hitler's Judeocide remains incomprehensible. But perhaps there are lessons, as suggested by Zygmunt Bauman in *Modernity and the Holocaust* (Ithaca NY: Cornell University Press, 1989):

> The lesson of the Holocaust is the facility with which most people, put into a situation that does not contain a good choice . . . argue themselves away from the issue of moral duty . . . adopting instead the precepts of rational interest and self-preservation. *In a system where rationality and ethics point in opposite directions, humanity is the main loser.* . . . And there is another lesson of the Holocaust, of no lesser importance. . . . The second lesson tells us that putting self-preservation above moral duty is in no way predetermined, inevitable and inescapable. One can be pressed to do it, but one cannot be forced to do it, and thus one cannot really shift the responsibility for doing it on to those who exerted the pressure. *It does not matter how many people chose moral duty over the rationality of self-preservation—what does matter is that some did.*

A MOSAIC OF VICTIMS

There is a demand and a definite need for works that combine the study of the Jewish Holocaust with that of the Nazi persecution of non-Jews. *A Mosaic of Victims: Non-Jews Persecuted and Murdered by the Nazis* (New York: New York University Press, 1990) is one of the more successful attempts in this direction. The editor, Michael Berenbaum, is project director of the U.S. Holocaust Memorial Museum; the contributors of the twenty-three essays come from several countries and represent divergent opinions, especially on such controversial questions as Polish anti-Semitism and Jewish Polonophobia, or Ukrainian resistance to and collaboration with the Nazis.

The two central questions that emerge from the collection of essays are whether the Nazi policy toward the Jews was based on a European consensus and whether the Holocaust was a phase in a larger historic movement to achieve ethnic homogeneity. To both these questions Richard L. Rubenstein, the author of the first general essay, gives a resounding yes. He argues that genocide is an established historical practice, whether in North and South America or in Australia, and that the policy of Nazi Germany differed from that of European colonizing powers only insofar as German policy was based on deliberately formulated intentions. In other words, Hitler was less hypocritical and he had fewer illusions.

Rubenstein argues that the Europeans were virtually unanimous in wanting to exclude the Jews from the political communities in which they lived, and whether or not they admitted it to themselves, exclusion was tantamount to a demand for extermination. In Rubenstein's view the Holocaust was, paradoxi-

---

The original version of this essay appeared as part of an article entitled "Witnesses to Evil," in the October 22, 1992, issue of the *New York Review of Books*.

cally, an unintended consequence of the Jewish emancipation that had given the Jews a political voice. Church leaders, especially, "saw the denial of political rights to the Jews as a beneficial step toward the creation of a Europe that was culturally, intellectually, socially, and politically Christian." Hence their deliberate silence in face of the Final Solution. The critical fact according to Rubenstein is "that the overwhelming majority of Germans regarded even the most assimilated Jews as aliens whose elimination would be a positive benefit to the nation.... Unfortunately, one cannot even say that it is irrational to want an ethnically or religiously homogeneous community consisting of those with whom one shares a sense of common faith, kinship, and trust." Witness the case of Japan, Rubenstein contends, whose astounding success is owing, in large part, to its ethnic and cultural homogeneity.

These extreme and even desperate statements depend far too much on Rubenstein's tendency to ascribe deep, unacknowledged genocidal motives to entire social institutions. Whereas one must agree with him that ethnic homogeneity has been the primary aim of many modern political movements and that the elimination of minorities shows the popular appeal of these movements, no proof exists that ethnically homogeneous societies are more efficient than pluralistic societies, Japan's recent success notwithstanding. Moreover, Rubenstein attributes too much purposefulness and unity to the "churches," not limiting himself to the Catholic church, although even in the case of the latter one cannot demonstrate the existence of any unambiguous policy toward the Jews.

Indeed, Rubenstein may well exaggerate the importance of the churches in the Holocaust. As Raul Hilberg argues in *Perpetrators, Victims, Bystanders: The Jewish Catastrophe, 1933–1945* (New York: Harper Collins/Aaron Asher Books, 1992), "the churches, once a powerful presence on the European continent, had reached the nadir of their influence during the Second World War." The major reason for the Vatican's powerlessness, Hilberg says, was that the Pope could not speak out against fascism without alienating the Axis powers or against communism without alienating the Allies.

In his essay on Germany's forced labor program in *A Mosaic of Victims*, Edward Homze demonstrates that by August 1944 there were 7.6 million foreigners working within the Reich and that in their case, as in all other cases of German policy, one must distinguish between the Nazi treatment of West Europeans, which was relatively mild, and that of the East Europeans, which was brutal, with the most abominable treatment reserved for the Poles and Soviet citizens. Peter Black shows, in his essay on forced labor in the concentration camps, that beginning in 1942 the policy of the SS toward the camp inmates changed from annihilation through hard labor to an attempt to hold down the mortality rate so as to create a large labor pool for the war economy. However, stupidity, sloth, brutality, and the steady ability of the Gestapo to replenish the numbers of prisoners weakened this entrepreneurial scheme. The Nazis remained killers.

Writing on Nazi policies against the partisans in Serbia, Christopher Browning shows in *A Mosaic of Victims* that the German army's ferocious terror did not pacify the population; instead, it provoked unrelenting violence. One manifestation of this senseless behavior was the German killing of thousands of innocent people in Serbian regions unaffected by partisan activity. Most of the German troops in Serbia were from Austria and were led by Austrian officers who were supposedly familiar with the peculiarities of the local population. Yet these commanders could think of no better solution than to execute one hundred "Communists and Jews" for every German soldier killed.

It did not matter that the Jews—as well as the Gypsies, who were almost completely annihilated—were the least likely to have engaged in guerrilla activity. One of the most horrifying absurdities of the war occurred at a camp in Sabac when predominantly Austrian soldiers gunned down about a thousand Central European Jewish refugees, mostly from Vienna, in retaliation for Serbian attacks on the German army. Even after the extensive killing of Serbian civilians had been stopped, late in 1941, the army continued to murder the completely harmless Jews and Gypsies.

Controversies begin with the essays on Poland and the Ukraine. Richard C. Lukas, the author of *The Forgotten Holocaust: The Poles under German Occupation, 1939–1944* (Lexington: University Press of Kentucky, 1986), among other books, has made it his life's work to remind the Western public of Polish sacrifices and suffering. He argues that between 1939 and 1941, when the Jews were herded into ghettos and confined there, the Poles were the major victims of German racial policies. The first killing by poison gas at Auschwitz included three hundred Poles and seven hundred Russian prisoners of war. Nor did the Germans ever abandon their objective of exterminating the Poles, with the result that of the six million Polish citizens killed during the war, over 50 percent were not Jews.

Referring to a study by the American sociologist Jan T. Gross, Hilberg writes in *Perpetrators, Victims, Bystanders* that "in 1940 and 1941 there was a widespread belief among the Poles that they were more exposed and threatened than the Jews. The Jewish communities had a form of self-government in their councils, Jews were not shipped to Germany, and they were not arrested or tortured for political reasons. At the same time it was thought that Jews, unlike Poles, were docile and subservient to the Germans."

Wartime beliefs do not, however, necessarily reflect reality, and it is depressing to encounter in some Polish publications (but not in Lukas's writings) the argument that during the first two years of the war the Jews were indifferent to the Polish plight—as if Jews had had a choice between indifference and compassion. Admittedly, however, that argument is not as frequently heard as the quite paranoid accusation that the Poles were somehow responsible for the Nazi Holocaust or that the Germans chose to locate their death camps in Poland because of Polish anti-Semitism and not because most European Jews lived there and because the Poles had no government to oppose the existence of gas chambers in their own backyard. It was, after all, far easier to transport a few hundred thousand Western European Jews to Poland than to ship over three million Polish and at least a million other East European Jews to an imaginary Auschwitz or Treblinka, set up, let us say, near Paris.

Israel Gutman, another contributor to *A Mosaic of Victims,* does not dispute most of the Polish claims but points out that, whereas the Nazis wanted to eliminate the Jews, the extermination of the Poles was not a Nazi goal. For instance, the Nazis did not hunt down the numerous Poles or Polish intellectuals in France, Hungary, and Belgium. Gutman is undoubtedly right about the Nazis' not wanting to kill all the Poles, but when it comes to Nazi plans regarding the Polish intelligentsia, I am not so sure. Lukas writes in the introduction to *Out of the Inferno: Poles Remember the Holocaust* (Lexington: University Press of Kentucky, 1989) that during the war the Nazis wiped out 45 percent of Poland's physicians and dentists, 40 percent of the professors, 57 percent of the lawyers, 30 percent of the technicians, almost 20 percent of the clergy, and most of the leading journalists. If we add to this the thousands of Polish professionals deported or killed on the orders of Stalin, then we can get some idea of the catastrophe of the Polish elite.

The most heated debate in *A Mosaic of Victims* takes place over the Ukraine. Bohdan Vitvitsky points out that of "a total population of 36 million, 3 million Ukrainian Gentiles perished at the hands of the Nazis, another 2.4 million were pirated off for slave labor in Germany, additional hundreds of thousands were murdered as Soviet POWs, and last, 11,000 collaborated."

Aharon Weiss does not share this minimalist view of the Ukrainian collaboration. He strongly opposes the attempts of the Ukrainians to deny that they were anti-Semitic and points out that a remarkable proportion of the Ukrainian populations welcomed the German army as liberators. He quotes, as a typical example of Ukrainian prejudice, the slogan of a group of militantly anti-German, and thus not collaborationist, Ukrainians: "Long live a greater independent Ukraine without Jews, Poles, and Germans; Poles behind the river San, Germans to Berlin, and Jews to the gallows." I do not know how many Ukrainians subscribed to this slogan. I have little doubt that its underlying philosophy was that of millions of Europeans.

The suffering of the Ukrainians is relatively little known. Taras Hunczak writes in *A Mosaic of Victims* that at least five million Ukrainians were killed in World War II (including six hundred thousand Ukrainian Jews), which means that, proportionally, the Ukraine suffered the greatest loss of population (16.7 percent), after that of Poland (19.6 percent). Compare these figures with the losses of Great Britain, which were 0.7 percent, or those of France, which were 1.5 percent. If we add to this the perhaps five million Ukrainians killed in Stalin's collectivization drive in the early 1930s and the millions of Ukrainians permanently displaced as a result of the war, then we get an idea of what Nazi and Soviet brutality, combined with local civil wars, did to the peoples of Eastern Europe.

A Mosaic of Victims contains, among others, a remarkable essay by the German historian Christian Streit on the ghastly fate of the Soviet prisoners of war. Some 3.3 million perished, or about 57 percent of the total; the German death rate in the Soviet POW camps was about 36 percent. Sybil Milton shows that the fate of Polish, Gypsy, and other non-Jewish children in the Nazi camps was no less terrible; the book includes separate studies of the tragic and similar fates of non-Jewish adult prisoners, homosexuals, pacifists, Gypsies, and Jehovah's Witnesses. I doubt I am the only reader who felt a great numbness after moving from one horrifying statistical demonstration of evil to another in *A Mosaic of Victims*; however, it is partly because it brings together deadly statistics from so wide a range of victims that the book is so valuable.

MEMORIES OF HELL

In the vast literature of the Holocaust, scholars have disagreed on nearly every major issue. They have been unable to establish with any precision, for example, the respective guilt and responsibility for the Holocaust of the Führer, his immediate underlings, the SS, the Wehrmacht, the Gestapo, the Nazi Party, the German social elite, and the rest of the Germans. Nor do they know for certain when, and by whom precisely, the satanic plan called the "Final Solution of the Jewish Question" was conceived.

In his brilliant and highly ambitious book, *Facing the Extreme: Moral Life in the Concentration Camps* (translated by Arthur Denner and Abigail Pollak; New York: Metropolitan Books/Henry Holt, 1996), Tzvetan Todorov attempts to analyze how people behaved in both the German and Soviet concentration camps and to examine much of the literature of the Holocaust and of the Soviet Gulag. Todorov has written an intellectually honest, unpretentious, and deeply optimistic book, which is almost religious in its conviction that goodness existed in the midst of the worst atrocities and, in fact, arose in response to those atrocities.

The ultimate test of human dignity for Todorov is the emblem of the totalitarian regime, the concentration camp. Can there be moral life in such a place?

This essay appeared as part of an article, under the same name, in the June 26, 1997, issue of the *New York Review of Books*.

In the "Exchanges" printed in the September 25 issue of the journal, a Polish writer took me to task for calling the canonized martyr Father Maximilian Kolbe a "notorious anti-Semite." Kolbe stepped forward and took the place at Auschwitz of a Polish prisoner with a family who was to be executed. In my reply I tried to point out that Kolbe was, indeed, a well-known anti-Semitic propagandist and that his magnificent act of self-sacrifice and defiance of the Nazis only proves the complexity of human nature.

94

Some famous survivors like Jean Améry, Primo Levi, Tadeusz Borowski, and Eugenia Ginzburg (who spent twenty years at the Kolyma camp in the Soviet Union) argue that in the camps a moral position was impossible. "It was a Hobbesian life," Levi writes, "a continuous war of everyone against everyone." Richard Glazar horrifyingly corroborates this argument in his *Trap with a Green Fence: Survival in Treblinka* (translated by Roslyn Theobald, foreword by Wolfgang Benz; Evanston IL: Northwestern University Press, 1995). Glazar was among the few Jews arriving in the Treblinka camp who were enlisted as workers in the death factory. At Treblinka, near Warsaw, Glazar was assigned to sort and pack the goods confiscated from the gas chamber's victims. It was backbreaking labor but it brought extraordinary benefits. Valuable goods could be stolen and later exchanged with the Ukrainian and SS guards and the food and clothing the murdered Jews left behind allowed Glazar and his companions to be among the best-fed and best-dressed of the Jewish victims of Nazism.

Moreover, as Glazar explains, the welfare of the working prisoners depended directly on the number of death trains arriving at Treblinka. When the trains became less frequent, the inmate-workers starved; thus when the number of trains suddenly increased, they shouted "Hurrah, hurrah!" The same trains often disgorged the prisoners' own relatives and friends en route to the gas chambers. In other camps mothers sometimes pretended not to know their children in order to save their own lives.

Todorov, however, finds many exceptions to the law of the jungle in concentration camp literature and points out that Primo Levi and other pessimists themselves performed quiet acts of compassion and heroism. Not everybody became demoralized, and survival was often a question of mutual assistance and sympathy. Levi's survival, for example, would have been impossible without the help of such good friends as the Italian worker Lorenzo, who brought him soup every day. Todorov also writes about Margarete Buber-Neumann, the non-Jewish German Communist who fled to the Soviet Union. Once there, both she and her husband, the German Communist leader Heinz Neumann, were arrested. Heinz disappeared forever in the Gulag; Margaret spent two years in a camp in Kazakhstan, after which, in 1940, the Soviet police handed her over to the Gestapo. She spent the next five years in the Ravensbrück concentration camp, where she risked her life to save other women from being selected for the gas chamber. Or consider the non-Jewish French poet and resistance fighter Charlotte Delbo, who, although she suffered unspeakable agonies at Auschwitz, wrote that in her group of French women, "Everyone who returned knows that, without the others, she would not have come back."

Todorov carefully distinguishes between spontaneous acts of humanity and group solidarity. The latter was often the best guarantor of survival but was almost always possible only at a cost to outsiders. French Jews acted in solidarity against other Jews, Orthodox Jews against secular Jews; French political prisoners shared none of their Red Cross packages with Russian prisoners; Communists turned on non-Communists and were particularly vicious toward fellow Communists whom the Party had branded as Trotskyites. Where was the dividing line between group solidarity and murderous group egoism? Todorov cites admiringly the example of Maximilian Kolbe, the Polish priest, who at Auschwitz took the place of a political prisoner about to be executed who had a wife and children. But Kolbe, who has recently been canonized, sacrificed his life for a fellow Pole, not for a Jew or a Russian. In fact, he was a notorious anti-Semite.

In the concentration camp, Todorov argues, moral values inevitably conflict with the need to ensure one's own survival, and suffering can make some people better while it degrades others. *Facing the Extreme* also warns against uncritically admiring intellectual or creative activity simply because it took place under the camp's harrowing circumstances. Some intellectually energetic persons tended to make use of those around them—as did the Jewish music conductor at Auschwitz, who cared more for musical perfection in her orchestra than for her musicians. After all, the SS, too, loved music, and when she died, SS officers covered her coffin with white flowers: "With bowed heads, [they] wept over the remains of their Jewish prisoner."

There is a fundamental difference between the ways in which Daniel Goldhagen, author of *Hitler's Willing Executioners: Ordinary Germans and the Holocaust* (New York: Knopf, 1996), and Tzvetan Todorov perceive "ordinary Germans." Goldhagen's ordinary German policemen, soldiers, workers, and housewives had absorbed, through generations of anti-Semitic culture, a tendency to hate all Jews, while Todorov's ordinary German concentration camp guards were, more than anything else, obeying the orders of a totalitarian state. Totalitarian regimes, he argues, tried to inculcate the ideas that the enemy is an internal one, that the enemy must be killed, that all people do not have the same rights, and that the state is the custodian of society's ultimate aims. "The enemy is not a human being" was a belief that animated not only millions of Germans but, according to Todorov, members of the Soviet police as well.

Some readers might resent Todorov's decision to address the Nazi and the Soviet systems in the same breath. He quotes, for instance, the following lines by the Polish writer Gustaw Herling, a former inmate of the Soviet Gulag: "I think with horror and shame of a Europe divided into two parts by the line of the Bug [River], on one side of which millions of Soviet slaves prayed for liberation by the armies of Hitler, and on the other million of victims of German concentration camps awaited deliverance by the Red Army as their last hope."

Are the Soviet and German camps comparable? Those who dislike comparisons between the two regimes argue that Stalin never tried to wipe out an entire race and that his methods of killing were less modern and less industrialized than those of the Germans. In a television interview Goldhagen argued that the two terror regimes were fundamentally dissimilar because Soviet camp guards were ordinary men and women. This means, according to Goldhagen, that the brutality of Soviet camp guards, unlike that of their German equivalents, tells us little or nothing about Soviet society.

Others would say, however, and I tend to side with them, that when the Stalinist regime deported or shot the children of the so-called kulaks for no crime other than former ownership of land by their peasant parents, then it, too, judged people on the basis of biology. It is true that the Soviets did not use gas chambers, but they had in northern Russia and Siberia a vast natural freezing chamber in which huge numbers of political prisoners died of cold and malnutrition. Nor can there be any doubt that the Soviet regime was as determined to kill off entire groups of human beings—the Polish intelligentsia, for example—as was the Nazi regime. Finally, the training of Soviet camp guards was as cursory and primitive as that of the German police reservists. Ideological commitment was not really expected from the rank and file in either country. The Bosnian Serbs who guarded and killed Muslims in Bosnia-Herzegovina, to take a more recent example, were not highly trained for their jobs. Rather, they were ordinary people—often the victims' own neighbors, if not their relatives or former friends. The reasons why ordinary people torture and kill innocents must be sought elsewhere than in the simplistic argument of national tradition.

Privilege, rank, and power were important words in the camps. Todorov and others ought perhaps to have paid even more attention to this fact than they have. The concentration camp, whether at Auschwitz or in Siberia, fostered an immensely complex social hierarchy in which some thrived, others survived, and others died. Black market activities flourished everywhere; sometimes there was even a sort of stock market where shares were floated. A totalitarian state in miniature, the concentration camp nonetheless based its economy on free enterprise.

In his important study of the hierarchy of the concentration camp, *The Order of Terror: The Concentration Camp* (translated by William Templer; Princeton NJ: Princeton University Press, 1997), Wolfgang Sofsky shows how power in the camps was based on seniority, politics, and race. The aristocracy consisted of German political prisoners and criminals who were surrounded by vast coteries of servants and sycophants. Below them was an upper middle class of Jehovah's Witnesses, Czechs, Northern Europeans, and some, but not all, Spanish Republican refugees. The Nazis had quite different reasons for allowing these groups to have more privileges than others. The Northern Europeans were seen as racially more acceptable; the Jehovah's Witnesses showed remarkable cohesiveness and willingness to help one another, while at the same time remaining politically detached. The next level, the lower middle class, was made up of Belgians, Dutch, French, Poles, and Italians (the latter only after Italy surrendered to the Allies in 1943). Finally, the lowest class consisted of homosexuals, Soviet civilians, Soviet POWs, Gypsies, and Jews. However, the system of classification was not static. People moved up and down on the social scale; some Jehovah's Witnesses were treated abominably; the Spaniards were at first killed by the thousands. In this world of constant persecution of inmates by other inmates, Sofsky argues, the SS did not need to make much effort to maintain its control. Between twenty and forty SS officers and NCOs and between ninety and a hundred and twenty Ukrainian and ethnic German guards sufficed to supervise a death camp such as Treblinka, where nearly a million Jews were killed.

Privilege was the alpha and omega of survival in places where prisoners essentially ran the camps for their captors—as they did in both Germany and the Soviet Union. Those who never managed to secure some kind of privilege did not survive to tell what happened to them. Even if it meant no more than the cook dipping his ladle deeper into the pot or a few days' work in a heated laboratory—as in the case of Primo Levi—privilege prolonged life. The trouble was that privilege could be lost faster than it was gained.

Charlotte Delbo's finely written *Auschwitz and After* (translated by Rosette C. Lamont, with an introduction by Lawrence L. Langer; New Haven CT: Yale University Press, 1995), describes the friendships and sacrifices among women at Auschwitz and Ravensbrück. But she also describes the ranking woman prisoner, the kapo, who robs and beats the others and celebrates her "wedding" to a girlfriend in her luxuriously furnished quarters while the other prisoners lie prostrate from exhaustion and hunger in their bunks. Delbo survived because of the group solidarity, in the best sense of the word, among women who had been in the resistance. But she makes it clear that, after an initial period during which she was treated as badly as her Jewish counterparts, she and others derived some advantages from their status as French political prisoners.

From the perspective of Sofky's analysis, we can see that Richard Glazar was put in an immensely privileged position when he was assigned to sorting the clothes of deportees gassed at Treblinka. There were times when he put on a new shirt every day and lived mainly on chocolate, butter, and sugar. "Maybe my next pair of pajamas hasn't arrived in Treblinka yet," he recalls himself thinking. "Maybe it's still in transit. Maybe I won't need any pajamas tomorrow." At one point, a fellow inmate exults: "*Oy*, what a big, wealthy transport. *Oy*, what a transport!" When the inmates revolted, in August 1943, in one of the great acts of Jewish resistance, Glazar was among the few who managed to escape. He and a companion subsequently passed themselves off as Czech workers belonging to the Todt Organization. Liberation found them living the good life of free gentile workers.

Felicja Karay's *Death Comes in Yellow* (translated by Sara Kitai; Amsterdam: Harwood Academic Publishers, 1996), describes the slave labor camp at Skarzysko-Kamienna, another Polish town. It was home to the gigantic German Hasag munitions factory. It employed Germans, *Volksdeutsche* (i.e., ethnic Germans who were not from the Reich), Ukrainians, Poles, and Jews—and those five nationalities meant five distinct rungs on the ladder of privilege, with a world of difference between each group. As Polish workers were generally unreliable, the Germans shot hundreds of them until someone in management came up with the brilliant idea that Poles would be more interested in working if they were allowed to engage in black market activity with the starving Jews. The Germans and Poles who ran the bakeries stole the flour meant for the Jewish slave laborers, and the Polish workers sold the baked loaves to the Jews. The presence of Jews made the Poles feel privileged and thus production did not really suffer. Delighted with this arrangement, the plant managers regularly reminded the Polish workers that the Jews alone were responsible for Poland's terrible conditions.

Thousands upon thousands of Jews died in these monstrous factory units, whose history and economics Felicja Karay, an Israeli scholar, is the first to examine seriously. She concludes her superbly documented account: "In each camp there was a life and death struggle for any crumb of power which might ensure survival. Everywhere, there was blind obedience to the most demonic of orders. In all camps, prisoners helped to exterminate their brothers. Under this system, the prisoners were taught to despise the weak and revere the strong."

According to Karay, the German system was successful in its mission to brutalize and corrupt every group, yet, she acknowledges, the collective success did not mean success with every person. Some prisoners fought not only to preserve their lives but also to preserve their identities by seeming to conform while surreptitiously helping others. "Research into the Holocaust," Karay writes, "deals not only with a study of human evil, but also with a study of human courage, holding out the possibility of hope."

THE GOLDHAGEN CONTROVERSY IN RETROSPECT

Holocaust literature is one of the richest devoted to a single event; it is also one of the newest. In the 1950s and '60s one could count on one's fingers the monographs that dealt with the destruction of the Jews. Then came a surge of interest in the 1970s, perhaps due to the arrival of a European generation innocent of this heinous crime. Since then the production of books, articles, and films on the subject has continued unabated; in fact, it is growing. Yet the thousands of books and the tens of thousands of articles, many of them not only accurate and scholarly but also beautifully written, have not achieved their purpose. They may have persuaded other scholars but not the public. For when Daniel Goldhagen's *Hitler's Willing Executioners: Ordinary Germans and the Holocaust* was published by Knopf (1996), with new claims, it was as if the previous literature had never existed.

Few works have achieved greater success and have aroused more heated debate in recent memory than Daniel Goldhagen's work. To be sure, the publisher's aggressive marketing played a major role in popularizing the work. But that alone does not explain its public appeal in the United States, Germany, and other countries, in all of which it became a bestseller. A provocative interpretation of the Holocaust coupled with a passionate and angry prose did much to spark the controversy, sustain the media hype, and arouse public in-

---

The journal *Central European History,* vol. 30, no. 2 (1997), first published this essay with the title "Holocaust Views." The article is reproduced here in its entirety and is republished with permission of Humanities Press Inc.; permission conveyed through Copyright Clearance Center, Inc. Since the publication of the article, more books have appeared on the "Goldhagen affair," but in general, the controversy has died down.

I am indebted to my friend and fellow historian Dr. Valur Ingimundarson for his assistance in preparing this review article.

terest. Before its publication, Goldhagen's Harvard University dissertation had already gained attention and had won a prize for best dissertation in political science. Alfred A. Knopf made the most of the publishing rights, aggressively promoting the book in the media. The work would not only "radically transform our understanding of the Holocaust and of Germany during the Nazi period," claimed the publisher; it also represented a "radical revision of what has until now been written." The *New York Times* and other U.S. publications quickly jumped on the bandwagon with many articles on the book and on the book's reception in Germany.[1] Goldhagen became a celebrity overnight in the United States, appearing on television shows and in other public forums.

Most specialists in German history were less enthusiastic, not only because of the crass commercialism at work here but also because of the self-confident tone of the book. After all, Goldhagen has dismissed most works on the Holocaust as problematic if not outright wrong. More substantially, historians raised three major objections to the book. First, it provided no convincing evidence for its basic premise, namely that "ordinary Germans" willingly took part in the Holocaust; this, because they had developed a unique, specifically German, "eliminationist anti-Semitic mind-set." Second, the book unwarrantedly extrapolated data on the genocidal behavior of one police unit of "ordinary Germans" to German society as a whole. And third, Goldhagen made selective use of both primary and secondary sources and ignored evidence that did not fit into his thesis.

To be sure, Goldhagen has his defenders both among scholars and publicists, including Elie Wiesel, Andrei S. Markovits, and Dan Diner, all who have praised the work.[2] But the majority of historians and political scientists—such as Raul Hilberg, Yehuda Bauer, Omer Bartov, Fritz Stern, Hans-Ulrich Wehler, Dieter Pohl, Christopher Browning, Eberhard Jäckel, Hans Mommsen, Robert Wistrich, David Schoenbaum, Henry Friedlander, Kristen R. Monroe, Ruth Bettina Birn, and Norbert Frei—have been sharply critical of the book in reviews or in public forums.[3] Other historians and publicists such as Gordon Craig, Volker Berghahn, Paul Johnson, and Josef Joffe have been less passionate and more generous in their treatment of the work, even if they have dismissed some of its more extreme positions and extrapolations.[4]

Some historians undoubtedly went overboard in their criticisms by resorting to ad hominem attacks and by belittling Goldhagen in public. Goldhagen's spirited and articulate defense aroused widespread sympathy among lay audiences, for example, during a symposium at the United States Holocaust Memorial Museum in Washington in the spring of 1996. Jealousy may have been part of the reason for the violent professional critique. Historical works seldom become bestsellers, and it is even less common for historians to become public figures. As Josef Joffe put it, "one can imagine the resentment of scholars who have worked hard for decades on the history of the Third Reich without getting anything like the attention given to Goldhagen."[5]

With some exceptions,[6] German publicists and historians were also quick to condemn the book before the publication of the German edition in September of 1996. The publisher of *Der Spiegel*, Rudolf Augstein, termed the value of the book "practically zero," and historian Eberhard Jäckel found it "simply bad."[7] At first, what has aptly been described as a defensive reaction to *Hitler's Willing Executioners*, swept the German intellectual establishment. German scholars implied that the book was so bad as not to be worth reading,[8] and they interpreted Goldhagen's assertion that no distinct line could be drawn between the Nazis and "ordinary Germans" in the slaughter of Jews as signifying the revival of the collective guilt thesis. Again, the German people as a whole were being blamed for the Holocaust.

During the summer of 1996, however, a gradual change took place in the terms of the public discussion in Germany. Intellectuals set out to integrate the message of *Hitler's Willing Executioners* into the broader debate over the country's handling of its tortured past, its *Vergangenheitsbewältigung*. The reinterpretation began with the publication of numerous critical articles in the weekly *Die Zeit*, which stressed the moral value of the book and downplayed its methodological deficiencies. What Goldhagen had accomplished, according to this view, was to portray the Holocaust in a new way. Instead of relying on sanitized academic techniques, Goldhagen may have come closer to the truth about the Holocaust by writing with passion, and in excruciating detail, about the atrocities of the Germans.

In a rare move *Die Zeit* gave over almost its entire book review section for Goldhagen to reply to his attackers, which he did under the title "The Failure of the Critics."[9] Intent on giving no ground, Goldhagen claimed that the critics had misunderstood him or distorted his views and that he stood by all his arguments. When Goldhagen went on a ten-day German tour to promote the book in the fall of 1996, the stage was set for a major confrontation. But then something curious happened: Goldhagen's journey, which took him to all the major cities—Hamburg, Berlin, Frankfurt, and Munich—turned into a triumph. Thousands of people scrambled for tickets to see the articulate and handsome Harvard assistant professor take on his critics. Yet, in stark contrast to the angry tone of his book and of his *Die Zeit* article, Goldhagen was courteous and deferential in public. In panel discussions the German critics quickly mellowed and, in the face of potential public hostility, opted for an exit strategy; they simply agreed to disagree with Goldhagen. Instead of a shouting match, there was much "civilized discussion" about the book. This echoed what the Germans value so much, namely *Streitkultur,* a euphemism for non-confrontation. Needless to say, little of substance came of the pubic discussions; both sides held to their respective positions without really engaging each other. But the audience always sided with Goldhagen, whose stamina under intense pressure and media scrutiny was justly praised.

To cap it all, publicists began to attack the German historians for their supposed willingness to suppress the horrors of the Holocaust. That these historians had spent most of their long careers trying to analyze it was conveniently forgotten. As some German publicists and journalists, such as Evelyn Roll of the *Süddeutsche Zeitung* noted, generational conflicts may have played a role here: the desire of the third generation to pose the question of guilt with more force than the children of the perpetrators were capable of.

Goldhagen concedes only once, and then only in an endnote, that eliminationist anti-Semitism is not part of the German national character: "By no means should this be understood to imply that a *timeless* German character exists. The character structure and the common cognitive models of Germans have developed and evolved historically and, especially since the loss of the Second World War, have changed dramatically."[10] It is hard to see how such a miraculous transformation could have taken place in a relatively short time following upon many centuries of alleged irrationality and murderous Jew hatred. When in Germany, however, both Goldhagen and his admirers put a much greater emphasis on this sudden post-World War II transformation, thereby offering spiritual solace to the postwar generation of Germans.

The Goldhagen phenomenon is still very much alive in Germany. *Hitler's Willing Executioners* has sold over 160,000 copies. Shortly after his promotional tour, a book appeared in German on the Goldhagen controversy.[11] Goldhagen has become a celebrity and is being widely praised for increasing public awareness of the German people's complicity in the Holocaust. Goldhagen even received the prestigious Democracy Prize of the political science journal, *Blätter für deutsche und internationale Politik* in a ceremony in Bonn attended by no fewer than two thousand people. In this sense Goldhagen accomplished what he set out to do: to draw attention to the German (as opposed to Nazi) complicity in the Holocaust.[12] In other respects, however, his book is far less successful. Its line of reasoning is one-dimensional and its argument is marred by unwarranted extrapolations and exaggerations. The book reads like a sermon with all its trappings: a sense of self-righteousness, disdain for differing opinions, and constant repetitions. Its angry and passionate tone, while very popular, contradicts the detached style systematically cultivated by the foremost Holocaust historians ever since the appearance, in 1961, of Raul Hilberg's now classic *The Destruction of the European Jews*. The idea has always been to let the facts speak for themselves.

Hitler's Willing Executioners is divided into three parts: the first deals broadly with the role of anti-Semitism in German history. The second part contains, in turn, three case studies: the story of a police battalion involved in the Final Solution; Jewish slave labor camps; and Jewish "death marches" following the breakup of the extermination and concentration camp system. The third part of the book is a long conclusion that summarizes the argument.

As the German historian Hans-Ulrich Wehler and others have pointed out, Goldhagen deals with problems that have been inadequately explored.[13] Numerous studies have been devoted to the Nazi murder machine, such as the "task forces" (*Einsatzgruppen*), "special commandos" (*Sonderkommandos*), and SS as well as Wehrmacht units. But only one other major study, Christopher Browning's *Ordinary Men: Reserve Police Battalion 101 and the Final Solution in Poland*, has been published on the police battalions that actively participated in the killing operations.[14] Browning offered a multicausal explanation of the motives of the perpetrators: peer pressure, careerism, wartime acclimatization, and obedience. Goldhagen, in contrast, brushes all such nuances aside. He insists that the brutality of the police reservists toward the Jews can only be explained in terms of an "eliminationist anti-Semitism," a viral strain of anti-Semitism that "resided ultimately in the heart of the German political culture, in German society itself."[15] "Ordinary Germans" took part in the executions because they wanted to kill Jews.

Goldhagen can certainly be criticized for advocating such reductionism. But since he came to a radically different conclusion than Browning, one could justify his approach. His decision to explore Jewish slave labor camps in Poland and the "death marches," which are described in vivid and horrifying detail in the book, is also valid, since few studies have been published on the two topics. Nor is there anything wrong with shifting the focus from the role of such faceless bureaucrats as Adolf Eichmann to the brutality of the individual perpetrators.

The problem with Goldhagen's treatment of these issues is that it is devoid of any sense of contingency, acclimatization, political and historical context, and comparisons. How can one claim that German anti-Semitism was sui generis before the Nazi seizure of power without contrasting it to other forms of anti-Semitism? What should we make of the Dreyfus affair in France, the pogroms in Russia, and the prevalence of anti-Semitism in Eastern Europe, if "a demonological anti-Semitism, of the virulent racial variety, was the common structure of the perpetrators' cognition and of German society in general"?[16] How is it possible to argue that Jews were treated differently from other victims, such as Slavs and Gypsies, without systematically comparing their fates? The Nazis pursued brutal programs of eugenics, euthanasia, sterilization, and ethnic cleansing. Even when emphasizing the centrality of the Holocaust one should not ignore the other Nazi mass murders: that of the Poles, the Gypsies, the homosexuals, the over three million Soviet prisoners of war, and German "Aryans" with hereditary or mental illnesses.

Goldhagen is far too quick to rationalize other genocides, including the genocide of the Armenians in Turkey in 1915, while treating the Holocaust as the result of total German irrationality. What is the basis for the contention that only the Germans were capable of certain acts of brutality without an attempt to compare German behavior to that of other nationalities? Goldhagen compares the Germans only with the Danes and the Italians, the two nations out of three in Europe that were the least inclined to participate in the genocide.[17] (The Bulgarians were perhaps even more remarkable in this respect.) But what about the brutality of the Luxembourgers, who were members of the Police Battalion 101 and who took part in the killing operations? Certainly, the inhabitants of Luxembourg did not share in the same genocidal national cultural tradition as the inhabitants of Germany. Austrians, of whom Goldhagen says nearly nothing, were overwhelmingly represented among the SS and in the concentration camp personnel. Yet the Austrian tradition under the Habsburgs was not only that of lower-middle class Viennese anti-Semitism but also, and even more so, of multinationalism and the Emperor's categorical rejection of nationalism and racism.

Hundreds of thousands of Estonians, Lithuanians, Latvians, Ukrainians, Romanians, Russians, and members of other nationalities enthusiastically participated in the mass murder of Jews. It is perfectly true that the Holocaust would not have happened without German orders that must be placed within the context of the policies of the Hitler regime and Nazi ideology. Goldhagen rejects the notion of "collective guilt," but it is implied throughout the book. He states that the conclusions drawn from the acts of ordinary Germans in the police units "can, indeed must be, generalized to the *German people in general.* What these *ordinary* Germans did also could have been expected of other *ordinary* Germans."[18] This raises serious questions about the validity of Goldhagen's methodology.

The early reviews of *Hitler's Willing Executioners* centered critically on its most basic premise, namely that the Germans had developed a special brand of anti-Jewish sentiment. The critics pointed out that this premise was based on a superficial discussion of German anti-Semitism before Hitler's rise to power and on selective reading of such secondary (mostly American) sources, which fit into Goldhagen's theory. Critics also pointed to such errors in the book as that the majority of Germans were "conservatives and Volkish nationalists" in the nineteenth century and that Hitler came to power "through electoral means."[19] In reality at the last truly free parliamentary elections, in November 1932, 67 percent of Germans cast their vote for other than the National Socialist Party. Goldhagen portrays German political culture unconvincingly, especially when he reduces German history to a struggle of Germans against the Jews and when he sees an unbroken historical continuity all the way from the anti-Judaism of the Christian churches in the Middle Ages to the racial anti-Semitism of the nineteenth and twentieth centuries.

To argue that the Germans embraced "eliminationist" anti-Semitism since the early nineteenth century ignores several facts. First, that while there were laws against Catholics, Socialists, and Poles in the Second Reich, the Jews were gaining more rights. There was no shortage of anti-Semitic Germans at that time, some of them in important positions, but there were just as many if not more Germans, again some of them in important positions, who for one reason or another felt that the Jews should be made legally equal to the other Germans. Jews rose to much greater prominence in Germany than, for instance, in the United States. Second, if "racial anti-Semitism," "pregnant with murder," was as wide-spread in Germany as Goldhagen argues,[20] then why did hundreds of thousands of Jews flee from Russia and Eastern Europe to Germany, and why were they allowed to settle there and even to thrive? Or how is one to explain the friendly reception and assistance the Jewish population offered to the German armies in Eastern Europe during World War I, not to speak of the pronouncedly pro-German attitude of the Jewish elite in New York City before America's entry in that war? Third, as noted above, anti-Semitism was more pronounced in pre–World War I France than in Germany. Tensions between Protestants and Catholics were actually more palpable in the Germany of Bismarck than the "Jewish question." Fourth, in his attempt to portray the German people as collectively anti-Semitic, Goldhagen explains away material that contradicts his assertions. A case in point is his rendering of an observation offered by an elderly woman in the wake of the *Kristallnacht*, who said that "We Germans will pay dearly for what was done to the Jews last night." What appears to be an act of opposition is interpreted by Goldhagen as "anxiety at the prospect of the Jews revenging themselves upon Germany." Goldhagen fails to mention that the woman in question is reported—in the very

The Goldhagen Controversy

source he cites—as having hidden Jews and having aided them in various other illegal ways both before and during the war.[21]

There is practically nothing in Goldhagen's account on historical contingencies, the social tensions of the First World War, the political conflicts of the Weimar era, the economic hardships of the Great Depression, the rise of the Nazi Party, the tyrannical nature of the Nazi regime, and World War II. Goldhagen does not deny that all these things mattered, but since they had been treated elsewhere, he argues, he did not need to dwell on them.[22] Yet if "the road to Auschwitz was not twisted,"[23] as he claims, then he should have included the discussion of these historical developments in his analysis. They could, after all, pose a serious challenge to his theory. This would not necessarily have made the book too long; omitting only some of the many repetitions would have freed space for such a serious analysis.

Since few critics had access to the archival material that Goldhagen used in his study, they tended to be less critical of the book's central part: the three case studies. To be sure, some historians faulted Goldhagen for dealing mostly with Police Battalion 101, which differed from others because its almost exclusive function was the mass murder of Jews. Historians also objected to Goldhagen's extrapolating Battalion 101's experience on German society as a whole. It would have been fruitful to examine other units as well, such as Police Battalion 306, which engaged in the mass murder of Soviet prisoners of war before the Holocaust. Others were skeptical of Goldhagen's almost exclusive reliance on testimonies of accused war criminals in postwar trials.

In his rebuttals Goldhagen has admitted that his chapter on anti-Semitism may be open to debate. But he claims that the central part of the study about the implementation of the Holocaust can stand on its own. What he has shown is "that not a small number of Germans, but a bare minimum of 100,000 Germans and probably many more, were perpetrators; and that these ordinary Germans were, by and large, willing, even eager executioners of the Jewish people, including Jewish children."[24]

Recently two book reviews have been published that focus on Goldhagen's three case studies. Both are critical of what they consider Goldhagen's selective use of the documents. In an article in the *Vierteljahrshefte für Zeitgeschichte*, the German historian Dieter Pohl, who recently published a book on the mass murder of Jews in East Galicia, deals with the historiography of the Holocaust within the context of the Goldhagen controversy.[25] His article is measured in tone and by no means dismissive of Goldhagen's book as a whole. Pohl agrees with Goldhagen that, with some exceptions, historical literature has neglected the role of the perpetrators.[26] To Pohl, anti-Semitism was, indeed, a central motive for the mass murder of the Jews, although in contrast to Goldhagen, he believes that other institutional and social factors played an important role as well. On the other hand, Pohl argues that Goldhagen does not offer any proof for his contention that "ordinary Germans," who had no links to the institutional apparatus established by the Nazis to implement the Final Solution, wanted to kill Jews. Together with many other critics, Pohl raises serious questions about Goldhagen's thesis that the Holocaust was carried out during the war on the basis of an anti-Semitic contract between the German people and Hitler. That anti-Semitism was widespread in Germany during the 1930s does not mean that "ordinary Germans" welcomed the extermination of the Jews.[27]

Moreover, Pohl concludes that Goldhagen's three case studies offer no evidence for his thesis regarding the complicity of "ordinary Germans." First, by ignoring the institutional development of the police battalion in question, Goldhagen underestimates the degree of Nazification it went through. From 1941, there were direct institutional links between the police units and the SS. Second, since the Jewish labor camps were a distinct part of Himmler's extermination apparatus, the brutality of the guards cannot be equated with the behavior of "ordinary Germans." Besides, Goldhagen overlooks the similarities of these camps to other camps like Dora-Mittelbau, where non-Jewish prisoners were worked to death.[28] Third, contrary to what Goldhagen says, the "death marches" were not a central element of the Holocaust since other nationalities were involved. The death marches also have to be viewed within the framework of the chaos during the last phase of the war. Finally, Pohl argues that Goldhagen leaves out evidence that contradicts his thesis—for example, evidence about German guards, especially the older ones, who did not abuse the "marchers."[29]

As we all know, documents lend themselves to widely divergent interpretations. In his recent review of Goldhagen's book, the Hungarian Holocaust historian László Karsai takes up the experiences of such Hungarian Jews who, although deported to Auschwitz in the spring and summer of 1944, survived the Holocaust. Their road had led from Auschwitz to a German factory or mine, often to a forced march across Germany toward the end of the war, and then to liberation. After the war, detailed interviews were conducted by Jewish organizations in Budapest with 4,600 such survivors. About 3,700 of these protocols are available today, an important documentary source for researchers. Among them, Karsai found 102 such protocols in which the interviewees praise the behavior of the German factory management, the workers, and the factory guards, and even 63 such protocols in which the survivors express their appreciation of the humane treatment they received from members of the SS, SA, and other camp supervisory personnel. Several former deportees, who complain of the cruelty of Polish fellow workers or of that of the Ukrainian guards, emphasize that they were saved by the intervention of Germans, even of SS personnel. What does all this prove, Karsai asks. Simply, that "one should not draw general conclusions regarding the German people and German culture from the behavior of such Germans who participated in mass murder. After all, it would be equally wrong to assert that such Germans who saved Jewish lives were representatives of the 'true' Germany."[30]

Ruth Bettina Birn, chief historian of the war crimes and crimes against humanity section of the Canadian department of justice, is more critical of the book than Dieter Pohl or even Karsai, accusing Goldhagen of slender and unreliable research. She claims that Goldhagen's case rests on a sample of "fewer than 200 excerpts" from statements made by perpetrators in postwar trials. Like other historians, Birn, who has published an important book on the SS, criticizes Goldhagen for his extrapolations—his "leap from a limited quantity to a collective quality, by which real events are grossly relativized."[31] She maintains that Goldhagen should have paid more attention to other police battalions, which were also active in the Holocaust and were not composed of reservists, but of career police officers or volunteers. Birn also gives specific examples of what she terms Goldhagen's questionable use of evidence; for instance, that he either rejects expressions of shame and disapproval in the perpetrators' testimonies for methodological reasons or ritually discredits them as insincere.[32] Birn goes even further when she writes that by "using Goldhagen's method of handling evidence, one could easily find enough citations from the Ludwigsburg material to prove the exact opposite of what Goldhagen maintains."[33]

Like many other historians, Birn stresses the lack of comparative perspective in Goldhagen's analysis of the perpetrators. She claims that Goldhagen highlights the brutalization of Jewish victims but ignores that of non-Jews, even if examples of both are to be found in the same statement. She finds fault with Goldhagen's assertion that the Germans dealt with everybody but Jews in a manner that was dictated by economic rationality. Millions of Soviet POWs were systematically starved to death before it dawned on the Nazis that they had a problem with labor shortage. Like Pohl, Birn contradicts Goldhagen's contention that the death marches were exclusively directed against the Jews. Non-Jewish inmates were often treated just as harshly.[34] In other words, there is evidence to suggest that the perpetrators slaughtered other minorities with equal enthusiasm and that other motives than anti-Semitism were important here.

There is no need to agree with all aspects of Martin Broszat's or Hans Mommsen's structural explanations of the Holocaust as some kind of "cumulative radicalization" or to subscribe uncritically to "intentionalist" notions of Hitler's genocidal anti-Semitism. But to treat the Holocaust and German anti-Semitism as something outside the realm of human possibility for peoples other than the Germans is unhistorical. Indeed, Birn makes the valid point that Goldhagen uses the word "Germans" excessively throughout the book. It is certainly consistent with his stress on the peculiarity of the German nationality, but it is wrong to eliminate social function as a source of study of the perpetrator.

It has been argued that, to his credit, Goldhagen has broken three taboos: named the perpetrators again (the Germans), described their brutal deeds in detail (thus providing the countertext to Hannah Arendt), and stressed the role of anti-Semitism as the driving force behind the Holocaust. There is, indeed, a tendency within the scholarly literature to overuse the term "Nazi" at the expense of "German." Unfortunately, Goldhagen goes too far in the other direction by overemphasizing nationality and unduly minimizing status. Goldhagen should be criticized neither for his choice of topic nor for his vivid descriptions of mass murder. And although the thesis that anti-Semitism was an important factor in the Holocaust is hardly new, it should be emphasized. But the end should not justify the means. What stands out is the book's preconceived notions and unsubstantiated claims; its intended shock value instead of its historical value.

Despite the book's undoubted merits, the publication of Goldhagen's work and its dazzling success are worrisome phenomena. Writing in the *Times* of London, the Holocaust expert Gitta Sereny warns that Goldhagen is skirting danger when he cries: "Stop referring to them as Nazis. They were Germans, Germans, Germans." Gitta Sereny concludes: "[M]urderous bigotry is not ingrained in the character of any one nation but is part of the human condition. It is not only young Germans who, as did happen after 1945, needed to be retaught humanity, but all children, white, black, brown and yellow, need to learn this now and for evermore."[35]

4

THE HOLOCAUST IN OTHER LANDS

A GHETTO
IN LITHUANIA

Kovno, Kaunas, Kowno, Kauen: all denote a single city in Lithuania that, in typical East European fashion, has gone by many names. "Kovno" is Russian and Jewish, bringing to mind the long periods of Russian domination and the ancient but now nearly defunct Jewish presence there. "Kaunas" is Lithuanian and draws attention to that small nation, which in recent history lost, regained, lost again, and may soon recover its independence. "Kowno" is Polish, evoking the many centuries of Polish-Lithuanian joint rule but also Polish expansion into the region. Finally, "Kauen" is German, recalling the Germans who had a part in building the city and were merchants there, but also recalling Nazi occupation. The city is said to derive its name from a Prince Koinas who allegedly founded it in 1030.

Avraham Tory partly wrote, partly dictated his ghetto diary, which begins on June 22, 1941, the day Germany attacked the Soviet Union, and ends on January 9, 1944, a short time before he escaped from the ghetto and before the Jewish community of Kovno ceased to exist.[1] Prior to his escape he hid the diary in five crates, along with the original copies of German orders and decrees, badges, insignia, photographs, and drawings by ghetto artists. Following the Red Army's occupation of Kovno in the summer of 1944, Tory returned to the city and recovered much of this material from the ruins. He keeps the diary's Yiddish original in Tel Aviv, where he now lives. A Hebrew language edition appeared in Israel in 1988, but this is the first publication in any other lan-

---

It was on November 8, 1990, that the *New York Review of Books* printed my review of Avraham Tory, *Surviving the Holocaust: The Kovno Ghetto Diary* (translated by Jerzy Michalowicz; Cambridge MA: Harvard University Press, 1990). The article is reproduced here in its entirety.

guage. Superbly complemented by Martin Gilbert's introduction and Dina Porat's notes, the diary is a historical document of major importance. It helps us to understand the relations among Germans, Lithuanians, and Jews; the complex hierarchy within the Jewish slave society created by the Nazis; the role of Jews and Christians in saving Jews; and the phenomenal achievements of Jewish Council members, teachers, artists, and medical workers.

Avraham Golub was born in 1909. (He adopted the name Tory only after moving to Israel.) He attended the Hebrew Gymnasium at Marijampolé in Lithuania, then studied law at the Universities of Kovno and Pittsburgh (he spent one year there), and then became an assistant to a Jewish professor of law at the University of Kovno. A good athlete and a dedicated Zionist, he took part as a gymnast in the first Maccabiah Games in Tel Aviv in 1932. When the Soviet Army set up bases in Lithuania in October 1939, Tory worked for the local Soviet military construction administration but was dismissed after five months because of his Zionist past. After being interrogated repeatedly by the Soviet NKVD, he went into hiding to avoid deportation to Siberia and emerged just in time to see the German troops enter Lithuania on June 23, 1941. A month later, after the Nazis had decreed that a ghetto must be created, he became deputy secretary of the local Council of Elders until his escape two and a half years later. He went into hiding with Lithuanian peasants, reappeared when the Red Army reentered Kovno in 1944, and after the war made his way to Palestine. He still practices law in Tel Aviv. Tory emerges from the diary as a deeply religious, sober, and modest man who rarely shows great passion and who preserved admirable self-control when confronted with indescribable horrors.

Great and Small Lithuania

People with a remarkable number of languages and confessions lived together for centuries in what is today Lithuania; it was a workable arrangement as long as human beings were distinguished not by ethnicity but by tribal law or by their status within the feudal system. With the arrival of national ideologies early in the nineteenth century, the situation grew increasingly difficult, culminating in the vast hecatomb that has been the price of modern nationalism. At least today's Lithuania prides itself on being a true nation state. Yet it is not quite that. Although this north European country comes closer to being the home of one national ethnic group than neighboring Latvia and Estonia (there are very few Jews and Germans left in the country and not many Poles and Byelorussians), new immigrants have come from deep in the Soviet Union. The most important recent change, however, is that whereas Jews, Germans, and Poles used to make up a large part of the educated classes, today's elite consists primarily of ethnic Lithuanians. The Soviet immigrants are mostly manual workers. That the native elements are at the top of the social scale in Lithuania, and in the rest of Eastern Europe, is indeed one of the most important social developments in the region's recent history.

The origin of the Lithuanian people is no less mysterious than that of other East European nations. All we know is that tribes speaking Lithuanian have lived in the region from ancient times and that they and the related Latvians speak an ancient Indo-European tongue bearing some striking resemblances to Sanskrit. Neither Lithuanian nor Latvian is a Slavic language. Nor, for that matter, is Estonian, which resembles Finnish and belongs to the Finno-Ugric language group, of which Hungarian is another well-known member. Estonian is thus wholly unrelated to Latvian and Lithuanian, which are as foreign to Polish and Russian as English.

In the Middle Ages Lithuanians had great leaders such as Mindaugas, Gediminas, Algirdas, Kestutis, and Vytautas,[2] who transformed Lithuania into a vast and powerful state. Lithuanians remained pagans longer than any other European nation, but at last, Mindaugas accepted baptism in 1251 and was crowned king at the order of the Pope, only to recant and sacrifice prisoners to his ancient gods. Gediminas called himself a grand duke, a title that would be borne by Lithuania's rulers for centuries. He is said to have founded Vilnius (in Polish "Wilno," to Russians and Jews "Vilna") in 1323. Under the brothers Algirdas and Kestutis, Lithuanian power extended to the shores of the Black Sea and came close to Moscow, and under Algirdas's son, Jogaila, the crowns of Poland and Lithuania were united in 1386. Jogaila, better known as the Polish King Wladyslaw II Jagiello, also restored the University of Kraków, which bears his name. On the powerful equestrian statue in New York City's Central Park, the crossed swords raised above Jagiello's head symbolize the union of Lithuania and Poland.

The Lithuanians did not easily accept union with Poland. Soon Kestutis's son, Vytautas (Polish "Witold"), reasserted his country's independence, at least for a short time. Vytautas, too, performed great deeds, among them at Grunwald in 1410, when his Lithuanians—and allied Poles, Russians, Tartars, and Czechs—defeated the German Teutonic Knights. (Poles, of course, hold that the battle was won by Jagiello's Polish army and that the others were allies.) During the next 150 years the Polish-Lithuanian alliance was confirmed repeatedly but the balance gradually tipped in favor of Poland.

By joining with Poland, the British historian Norman Davies writes, "the Lithuanians opened the door to many changes. Their pagan religion was abolished, the sacred oak groves ritually felled, and the people baptized in legions. Their closed world was thrown open to Western influences, and their *boyars* began to demand the same rights and privileges as the Polish nobility. In due course, all but the lowest levels of society were thoroughly Polonized—both in language and in outlook. The 'Polish connection' in Lithuania came to have the same connotation as the 'British' connection in Scotland. The 'Lithuanian connection' in Poland brought still further enrichment of its rich multinational heritage."[3] At the end of the sixteenth century, the lands of the Polish crown aggrandized to a far greater extent than those of Lithuania, and Polish laws and customs were adopted in Lithuania.

By the eighteenth century, Polish-Lithuanian political life had become a farce; the king had lost most of his power to the nobility represented in the country's parliament, but the nobles became so insistent on making decisions democratically that they could neither legislate nor govern. Beginning in 1772, the dual state gradually succumbed to its absolutist neighbors, Prussia, Austria, and Russia, and in 1795, most of what is today's Lithuania was acquired by the tsar. Granted autonomy at first, Lithuania was later subjected to intense Russification. After the Polish revolt of 1830 the tsarist regime prohibited the use of the Polish language in the region (a prohibition from which the Lithuanian national movement profited indirectly), and the very name of the province was abolished. Following a great Polish revolt in 1863, Roman Catholic schools, the mainstay of both education and of the spirit of national revival, were closed. Nobles and intellectuals from what is today Lithuania participated in all the nineteenth-century Polish uprisings against Russia.

The Lithuania eulogized in the works of the great Polish Romantic poet Adam Mickiewicz during the 1850s was, despite its regional peculiarities, a part of Polish culture; however, during the last half of the nineteenth century, a new movement, inspired partly by journalists and other intellectuals and partly by embattled Catholic clergy, claimed that Lithuania's language and ethnic identity defined it as a separate nation. Lithuanian nationalists participated in the 1905 Russian revolution, but even the Russian progressives who contemplated autonomy for Poland did not contemplate it for Lithuania.

Toward the end of the German occupation of the Baltic region during World War I, Lithuanian, Latvian, and Estonian nationalists, Russian and local Bolsheviks, counterrevolutionary White Russians, Poles, and a German Free Corps battled each other in a confused war of all against all. Meanwhile, however, prominent Lithuanian leaders such as Antanas Smetona and Augustinas Voldemaras proclaimed their country's independence; the Russian Bolsheviks recognized it in July 1920, and the newly independent Polish government on

October 7. Two days later, however, the soldiers of the Polish Free Corps invaded Vilnius/Vilna, and in 1922 the city was officially incorporated into the Polish republic. Having lost its capital, Lithuania persisted in a state of war with Poland for sixteen years, although without further bloodshed. Kaunas/Kovno became the country's temporary capital.

Not to be outdone by their fellow East Europeans, Lithuanians organized their own Free Corps in 1923, invading the port city of Klaipeda (in German, "Memel") and taking it over from the Weimar Republic. Lithuania was now seen as an enemy by both Germany and Poland. Nor was there much hope that the Soviets would not soon reassert Russia's traditional interest in the Baltic states.

Lithuania between the wars was poor, although not desperately so. Its economy was mainly agricultural, and it exported butter, beef, live pigs, eggs, flax, and the pride of the country, fattened goose liver and white down, to Great Britain and Germany. A major land reform, which expropriated the lands of the Polish and Russian gentry, achieved the dual purpose of satisfying the peasants and ridding the country of some rich foreigners. Meanwhile, newly independent Latvia and Estonia had achieved the same result by expropriating the lands of the famous German Baltic barons. Illiteracy was much higher in Lithuania, which was largely rural and Catholic, than in the mostly Lutheran and somewhat more industrialized countries of Latvia and Estonia. Lithuanian commerce and industry were largely in the hands of Jews and Germans, who together made up 11 percent of the country's population of nearly three million.

After a promising democratic start, virtually everything went wrong with Lithuanian political life in the early 1920s. The contesting parties refused to allow stable governments to be formed and, as in most of the other East European states, a strong man took over. Simultaneously with the 1926 coup d'état of Marshal Pilsudski in Poland, Antanas Smetona seized power in Lithuania. He and his young officers and intellectuals abolished the opposition parties, curtailed civil liberties, executed a few Communists, and imprisoned a number of socialists, social democrats, and even Christian Democrats. Like most other East European strongmen, Smetona proved more of a conservative than a radical. In 1934 he imprisoned his former nationalist colleague Augustinas Voldemaras, whose fascist organization, the "Iron Wolf," had long threatened the regime. All in all, under Smetona, nonpolitical citizens, Jews included, could live in peace.

Smetona's position was greatly weakened in 1938 when he was forced by an ultimatum to renew diplomatic relations with the Polish government dominated by the foreign minister, Colonel Beck. This was true again in March 1939 when Nazi Germany seized the harbor city Klaipeda/Memel. Since Latvia and Estonia were weak and uncooperative, Lithuania at the beginning of World War II hadn't a single friend or protector. It was at the mercy of Nazi Germany and the Soviet Union: both countries now proceeded to divide Eastern Europe between them.

There followed a curious interlude of semi-independence, when, as the secret agreement between Stalin and Hitler provided, the Soviets returned Vilnius/Vilna to Lithuania but also forced Smetona to accept Red Army garrisons in his country—the garrisons for whom Avraham Tory worked. In July 1940 the Soviets put an end to this awkward situation by invading and annexing the three Baltic states and then imposing a reign of terror in which hundreds of Lithuanians were killed; according to one source, at least forty thousand were deported to Siberia. Large parts of the economy were nationalized.[4] The Lithuanians responded with anti-Soviet revolutionary conspiracies, directed in part from Berlin, the only place where the Lithuanian leaders could find refuge and assistance. Smetona himself went into exile, never to return; his place was taken by extreme nationalists. Assured by the Germans that a war with the Soviet Union was impending, Lithuanians prepared for an anti-Soviet uprising, working with a desperate sense of urgency in order to present the German invaders with the *fait accompli* of an existing Lithuanian government. In fact, a national uprising preceded the arrival of the Nazis in 1941 by a few hours; when the German motorized units entered Kovno, the hunt for demoralized Red Army soldiers, local Communists, and Jews had already been in full swing. During one night, Lithuanian "freedom fighters," called partisans, butchered at least a thousand Jews and robbed, tortured, or imprisoned even more.

The Jewish Presence

How are these savage attacks to be explained? Jews had lived in the region since the fourteenth century, although some sources say that the first Jewish arrivals were prisoners of war captured by Grand Duke Vytautas at the Battle of Grunwald in 1410. More came later, thanks to the hospitality of Polish-Lithuanian rulers and noble landowners. Some Jews may have been of southern European Khazar descent, that is, racially not Semitic; others were refugees from West European persecution. In 1755, 750,000 of Europe's 1.25 million Jews lived in Poland-Lithuania. Jews were intermittently excluded from Kovno and other cities but never from Slobodka (Lithuanian "Vilijampolé"), now a part of Kovno, the ancient Jewish settlement that the Nazis would soon convert into the Kovno ghetto. Many more Jews lived in Vilnius/Vilna, and thousands of others lived in such places as Siauliai and Marijampolé.

Of these places, the most extraordinary was undoubtedly Vilna: capital of the Grand Duchy of Lithuania, center of Polish Catholic culture, and seat of Jewish piety and learning. Nineteenth-century Lithuanian patriots revered Vilnius as the center of renewed Lithuanian greatness. For Poles, Wilno was a legendary city celebrated in Adam Mickiewicz's *Pan Tadeusz,* the Polish national epic. Roman Catholics embraced it as the home of the wonder-working image of the Virgin of Ostra Brama, a great cathedral, and some twenty-five other churches and chapels. The tsarist authorities chose Vilna as a center for their Russification drive. Finally, for Jews, it was a place that had led Napoleon to exclaim before its chief synagogue that Vilna was indeed "the Jerusalem of Lithuania."

The most famous Jew to reside there was Elijah ben Solomon Zalmen (1720–1797), better known as Elijah Gaon or simply the Vilna Gaon, who in the words of Lucy S. Dawidowicz, "gave Vilna its reputation as the fortress of rabbinic Judaism, the bastion for the study of Torah and especially *halakha,* the Jewish law. Even in his own day, he became a legendary figure, the embodiment of intellect, rationality, and scholarship."[5] A rentless enemy of hasidism, which he accused of dividing the Jewish people and undermining the rabbinic foundations of Judaism, the Vilna Gaon succeeded in limiting the influence of that movement in the city. Other local masters of Jewish scholarship and writing included Abraham Mapu, the creator of the modern Hebrew novel; the Hebrew poet and critic Judah Loeb Gordon; and Isaac Meir Dick, the first popular Yiddish novelist. But Vilna was also the cradle of the Jewish labor movement and the Jewish Labor Bund.

For the Lithuanian Jews, tsarist rule during the nineteenth century alternated between outright oppression of and grants of civil rights. In 1858, for instance, Jews were allowed to settle freely in Kovno, but in the early 1880s two pogroms organized by Russians resulted in hundreds of Jews either being killed or driven out of their homes. By World War I Kovno had a Jewish population of perhaps thirty thousand. As the German army approached, the Russian government sent most of them into the interior of Russia, but many returned a short time later. The Russian regime did not want Jews living under German rule since the Jews on the whole sympathized with Germany, and scores of them were helpful to the occupation authorities—understandably in view of traditional tsarist anti-Semitism and the more liberal practices of Germany and Austria-Hungary.

Following the establishment of a free Lithuania after World War I, the new democratic regime granted special rights to all ethnic minorities and thus also to the Jews. A ministry of Jewish affairs was set up in Kovno as well as a Jewish national council. Jews served in the Lithuanian administration, in parliament (where they were free to address their audience in Yiddish), and as officers in the army. Street signs in Hebrew characters were permitted in Kovno. In 1919 both the minister of Jewish affairs and the deputy foreign minister were well-known Zionists.

There were good reasons for such behavior on the part of President Smetona, the then still moderate Prime Minister Voldemaras, and their colleagues. There was relatively little traditional anti-Semitism among the Baltic peoples; for them, the Russians and the Poles were the problem, not the Jews. The Lithuanian leaders felt that their young but old nation, made up almost exclusively of peasants and intelligentsia, needed the skills of Jewish traders and artisans. They also mistakenly believed that the Jews, through their international connections, would be able to guarantee the country's independence and help fend off Polish and Russian aggression. Lithuanian Jewish leaders, in turn, saw the coming of a Golden Age, in a kind of East European Switzerland in which they would enjoy complete cultural and educational autonomy.

All this was not to last, of course. First, by far not all the Jews of the former Lithuanian grand duchy were included in the new state; most found themselves in Soviet Russia and Poland. The question they faced was what would happen to them if the Jews of Lithuania chose to become Lithuanian patriots. Second, the Jews were deeply divided among a nonpolitical Orthodox majority and militant minorities made up of Bundists, other socialists, several varieties of Zionists, and Folkists, with each group having a different idea of precisely what attitude to take toward the new Lithuanian state. Third, the first census showed that independent Lithuania was much less of a multiethnic state than had been originally assumed; there was no need to think of creating a commonwealth of nations. Finally, no sooner had the new state been created than the rural population began to move into the cities, beginning a process of "Lithuanization" that put in doubt the need for Jewish skills. According to Ezra Mendelsohn, "In 1897 only 11.5 percent of the urban population of Kovno (Kaunas) Province, then under Russian rule, was Lithuanian, but already in the mid-1920s the city was more than 50 percent Lithuanian."[6] Within a few years autonomous ethnic institutions were abolished under the slogan of "Lithuania for the Lithuanians." By the mid-1930s, as the result of vigorous assistance from the government, there were more Lithuanian than Jewish shopkeepers in Kovno.

This campaign, too, paralleled similar pressures for ethnic nationalism in other East European countries; in each case a new native middle class was demanding the positions and the wealth held by people they claimed were foreigners.

Still, Jewish life in Lithuania was less troubled than it was, for instance, in Poland, and as late as 1940, five Yiddish dailies were published in Kovno. The Jews who made up more than a quarter of Kovno's 150,000 inhabitants were largely Yiddish speakers, and most were not assimilated into Lithuanian national and cultural life. Only a minority identified with the Lithuanian nation and another small segment was drawn to the Communist movement. Altogether, more than 150,000 Jews lived in Lithuania between the wars; they amounted to 7 percent of the total population. That proportion was greatly increased by the German-Soviet agreement of October 1939 to return Vilnius/Vilna to Lithuania and by the arrival of large numbers of Jewish refugees from both German-occupied and Soviet-occupied Poland.

No doubt there was a disproportionate number of Jews in the Lithuanian Communist movement (some sources say that they made up one-half of its members, which would have meant one thousand Jewish Communists). They were recruited mainly from among younger members of the intelligentsia.[7] Between 1940 and 1941, a few thousand Lithuanian Jews, such as the NKBD director Todes, served in the Soviet administration, the Red Army, and the political police, and they incurred the hostility of Lithuanians for doing so. Other Jews, usually the well-to-do and the politically independent, were harassed by the Soviets, and when the largest deportation to Siberia took place, between June 14 and 18, 1941, that, too, included a disproportionate number of Jews. The Soviet decision suddenly to jam forty thousand people into cattle cars and send them to Siberia (most of them never to return) drove the Lithuanian people to fury. Thousands escaped to the woods to avoid arrest, only to return a few days later when the Lithuanian national uprising began, which was soon followed by the German invasion. The Red Army fled immediately and the Lithuanians managed to kill only a few stragglers. Local Communists were not easily recognizable, but Jews were; in any case, extreme rightist propaganda had made the Jews responsible for the tragedy of Lithuania.

The Early Months of Terror

If the Lithuanians thought that they would now regain their freedom, they were soon to be disappointed. The Germans would not hear of a free Lithuanian state within what soon became the Reichskommissariat Ostland, a vast region annexed by the great German Reich. The Germans allowed the Lithuanians to set up all sorts of councils and head local administrations, but none of these institutions had any influence on the SS, SD, SA, Einsatzgruppen, Gestapo, Kripo, Sipo, NSDAP, and Volksdeutsche offices, or on the Feldgendarmerie, the various German civilian administrations, the Wehrmacht, the Todt organization, and the rest of the bewildering assemblage of competing institutions in charge of the Nazi occupation.

As Avraham Tory recalls, the German authorities announced in July 1941 that a ghetto would be created and within a month about thirty thousand people were locked up there. This figure no longer corresponded to the original number of Jews in Kovno and its surroundings because Einsatzgruppe A, the SS police battalion specially assigned to the Baltic nations, had meanwhile begun its killing.[8] Lithuanian partisans working with Einsatzgruppe units murdered thousands of Jews in the nearby Seventh Fort and Ninth Fort, huge military fortresses built by the Russians during World War I. It is important to note that Einsatzgruppe A, consisting of about one thousand men, was assigned to the rear guard of the entire German Army Group North; this meant that no more than a few Einsatzgruppe soldiers, as well as some SS men from other units, could be spared for the specific actions at Kovno. Even with the Jews who were completely bewildered and obedient, the liquidations could not have succeeded without extensive local assistance. As every document demonstrates, hundreds of Lithuanian auxiliaries accompanied every major convoy of Jews, shooting some on the way and killing the rest at the forts.

Early in August there were still 30,000 people in the ghetto, but on August 18, SA Captain Fritz Jordan and Mikas Kaminskas, the Lithuanian head of the Kovno municipality, requested that 500 intellectuals volunteer for scientific work in the city archives. As Tory reports, a total of 534 did so; they were taken to the Ninth Fort and killed. Other *Aktionen* followed in quick succession.

Survivors in the ghetto immediately began working for the German military and other enterprises, and some were given special identity cards, generally referred to as "Jordan certificates" or "lifesavers." Doctors and nurses and other health workers also thought their lives would be spared, but on October 2, the ghetto hospital for contagious diseases was boarded up on the orders of Jordan and Kaminskas; two days later it was burned down, along with all its patients, doctors, nurses, and technical personnel. Children, including babies in swaddling cloths, were taken from the children's home to the Ninth Fort and there shot dead.

In late October a *Grosse Aktion,* as the Germans called it, began when SS Captain Heinrich Schmitz and Master Sergeant Helmut Rauca of the Gestapo requested that ten thousand people be selected for "transfer" during a general assembly of the entire ghetto population. As Tory writes, the Council of Elders wanted the people of the ghetto to resist the order, but on the advice of Chief Rabbi Abraham Kahana-Shapiro, who spent a horrible night consulting Talmudic and rabbinical sources, the SS order was finally obeyed. In the morning of October 28 twenty-seven thousand people appeared on Demokratu Square so that Rauca could make his selection. He directed the members of the Council of Elders, the ghetto police, and holders of Jordan certificates and their families to go to the left side of the square, which later turned out to be "good" side. There, too, went a special brigade employed by the Gestapo, whose members bore a conspicuous "Gestapo" next to their Stars of David. People characterized by Rauca as "trash," including single women, nonexempt families with children, the old, and the sick, were sent to the right. Selection went far into the night, and the next morning the ten thousand selected were taken by the militia to the Ninth Fort in full view of the other ghetto inhabitants and Lithuanian spectators. Once there, the victims were stripped naked, pushed into the pits, and machine-gunned. (Sergeant Rauca emigrated to Canada after the war and became a Canadian citizen. He was tried in Toronto in 1984, with Tory testifying as a witness, and was deported to the German Federal Republic; he died in a prison hospital.)

The selections for execution ended soon thereafter, and on February 8, 1942, SS Colonel Karl Jäger reported to Berlin, in a triumphant statistical analysis, that thus far 138,272 *Exekutionen* had taken place in Lithuania. The figure included 136,241 Jews, 1,064 Communists, 56 partisans, 633 insane persons, 44 Poles, 28 Russian POWs, 5 Gypsies, and 1 Armenian. Of the total number, Jäger reported, 55,556 were women and 34,464 children.

Precarious Survival

Following the orgy of killing in 1941, the next two years were relatively calm, disproving, if further proof is needed, the historian Arno Mayer's strange contention that there was a close relationship between the Final Solution and setbacks suffered by the German army on the Eastern front.[9] According to Mayer the Germans' primary motive was anti-Communism and only secondarily anti-Semitism; they liquidated the Jews mainly because they had been unable to liquidate the Bolsheviks. In reality, in the Baltic countries at least, mass executions took place well before any German military setback; thereafter, most of the survivors were kept alive to help support the German war effort. In Vilna there was to be a second great wave of extermination in the spring of 1943, but in Kovno those who died in 1942 and 1943 did so mostly because of malnutrition and diseases such as typhoid. In the spring of 1944 another large group of Jews was killed at Kovno, and in July the last survivors were sent to Germany, where again many perished from sickness and hunger. At the end, only 17 percent of the Lithuanian Jews survived, a horrifyingly low figure matched only by the rates of Poland and Greece.[10]

For those of us who have read of mass killings to the point of nausea, the most welcome portion of Avraham Tory's diary describes the relatively peaceful months of 1942 and 1943, when the ghetto was organized under the wise leadership of Dr. Elchanan Elkes. Thousands marched off every morning to work on construction sties or in German households. They returned in the evening, some of them smuggling in the food they needed to stave off starvation. Small factories producing mainly clothing and shoes for the German army thrived within the ghetto. And in the spring of 1942 the Germans slightly increased the supply of food, which allowed the Council of Elders to set up a soup kitchen. There was an excellent symphony orchestra; secret schools carried on classes; some women gave birth, even though this had been strictly forbidden by a Gestapo order issued on July 24, 1942. There were political parties and several underground organizations; the council created an impeccably clean secret bakery and a pharmacy as well; in the fairly well-equipped hospital typhoid patients were carefully hidden. Tory himself visited Kovno city almost daily to negotiate with the Germans or to be given orders.

Some Germans, especially civilians and even members of the SA, proved to be fairly decent in their relations with Jews; a few, such as SA Lieutenant Gustav Hermann, who headed the German labor office in the ghetto, were solicitous and helpful. Others persisted in being bullies. The Germans were proud of "their" ghetto and liked to show it off to visiting Reich dignitaries. A well-functioning ghetto, after all, could save their lives as well; the alternative was service at the front. Most Germans were willing to accept bribes, as were the Lithuanian guards; this fact alone assured temporary survival. But no one ever doubted that if the order for liquidation came from Berlin it would be obeyed.

Unlike some other Jewish councils, the council at Kovno succeeded in reducing compliance with German orders to an absolute minimum, and again, unlike some other places, for instance Vilna, the Jewish ghetto police were anything but zealous in assisting the Gestapo. Its members kept in close contact with the underground organizations, and they helped to build hiding places, an activity for which many Jewish police officers were later to pay with their lives. Thousands of illegal refugees from other Jewish communities and Jews who had to come out of hiding found shelter in the ghetto. A few inhabitants accumulated small fortunes through trading and smuggling; the rest barely survived. Contacts were maintained with sympathetic Lithuanians, even with the Kovno Bishop Vincentas Brizgys, who in the early days of the German occupation had sent a telegram of thanks to Hitler and even later forbade his clergy to assist the Jews. By 1943, however, Brizgys, like many other Lithuanians, had second thoughts and declared himself ready to help Jewish children. The mood had changed significantly. Now Lithuanians were being persecuted as well, and thousands evaded conscription into the German army by escaping to the forests. The anti-Nazi partisan movement grew swiftly.

There came a time when some Germans showed more sympathy for Jews than for Lithuanians; food confiscated from the local population was occasionally donated to the ghetto, and the Jewish police were used to help evict Lithuanian families from houses the Germans needed. A few Jewish policemen used the occasion to vent their hatred on the Lithuanians—for which, Tory writes, they were severely reprimanded by the Council of Elders. Lithuanians in turn called the ghetto police "Jewish Gestapo" and "Jewish SS." Nevertheless, thousands of Lithuanian families were living in former Jewish flats, using Jewish furniture, and wearing Jewish clothes.

A few amazingly brave Poles and Lithuanians, such as Irena Adamowicz (of whom Tory writes) and Sofija Binkiene, regularly visited the ghetto, bringing news from other ghettos and helping some to escape. The Kovno priests V. Vaickus and Bronius Paukstys, both friends of Tory, were no less heroic; the latter, incidentally, later spent ten years in solitary confinement in a Soviet prison.

Summaries of a few of Tory's diary entries show how periods of near normalcy alternated with periods of horror:

> January 14, 1942: The Germans ordered all Jewish cats and dogs to be delivered to the small synagogue, where they were shot.
>
> June 23: Master Sergeant Rauca came to the ghetto to order a statue of a naked woman from the sculptress Gehrscheim. The Jew Joseph Caspi gave a party at his house in the city that was attended by Rauca and other Gestapo officials. [Caspi, a journalist who had volunteered his services to the Germans because of his hatred for the Soviets, worked as a Nazi agent. He alternately helped and harassed the Council of Elders. He and his family were later shot by the Germans, as was Benjamin Lipzer, the head of the Jewish Gestapo brigade, who also had had excellent connections with the Germans.]
>
> July 7: Bathing in the Vilija river was permitted to Jews. [The book shows a photograph of an attractive woman wearing a bathing costume on the river shore.]
>
> December 13: The German ghetto commandant attended a concert given by the Jewish police orchestra.

February 15, 1943: Jewish workers in the city attempted to give food to some starving Russian POWs.

April 7: News of the massacre of 5,000 Vilna Jews at Ponar has reached the ghetto. [A total of 70,000 to 100,000 people were murdered at Ponar during the war.]

July 14: The ghetto police were authorized by the German authorities to deal with civil and criminal matters according to the laws of the defunct Lithuanian republic. [No information on these trials was released to the Gestapo.]

The inhabitants of the ghetto never felt secure. There was no end to rumors of impending disaster or to the horrible news from Warsaw and elsewhere. The Germans had so often and so brazenly lied to the Council of Elders that no one believed them even when they gave orders for what later turned out to be a normal labor assignment. The Jewish police had to hunt down those selected for jobs.

The End of the Ghetto

In November 1943 the ghetto was officially renamed a concentration camp; by then a part of its population had been transferred to work in the other Baltic countries. In January 1944, with the Red Army approaching, an extensive cleanup of the Seventh and Ninth Forts began: forty-five thousand corpses were burned in the Ninth Fort alone. On March 23, Tory escaped from the ghetto; a few days later twelve hundred people, mostly children, were killed, but meanwhile, well over a hundred members of the underground had escaped to the forest. During the following month the Council of Elders was abolished and in July, after further killings, the remaining eight thousand Jews were shipped to Germany. Dr. Elkes died in Dachau. The ghetto was burned to the ground.

By July much of Lithuania was on the move. Lithuanian peasants hid in the woods, and German peasants from the Klaipeda/Memel region attempted to flee the country; if caught by partisans or the Red Army, they, too, were butchered. The new Soviet administration deported thousands of Lithuanians to the interior of the Soviet Union and murdered others.

Some Lithuanians pretend that the Jewish massacres in 1941 were the work of criminal elements who had infiltrated the ranks of the freedom fighters. Some Jews claim that most Lithuanians were fascists. Both are wrong, but it is probably useless to argue with them. That many Lithuanians participated in the early spontaneous killings and that many volunteered for militia service under the Germans does not make the Lithuanian situation any different in these respects from that prevailing in the Ukraine, Byelorussia, Hungary, Romania, Croatia, Slovakia, Austria, or France. Most of the countries that were occupied by the Nazis or were allied with them produced roughly the same proportions of butchers, of the indifferent, of sympathizers, and of active rescuers. However, it was not the same thing to offer to help the Jews in the East and in the West. In Lithuania and Poland gentiles who tried to rescue Jews were routinely executed and in many instances so were their families. How many Americans could conceive of risking and even sacrificing their lives and those of their families for the sake of a stranger? Some Lithuanians and many Poles took that risk and made that sacrifice.

What did the East Europeans who assisted the Nazis gain? Not much, I would argue, for even though World War II enabled them to speed up the process of "nationalization" and even though the native elite are now firmly in power, the ethnic Germans and the Jews would have been very likely either to assimilate or to leave in any case. Having found refuge in Eastern Europe over the centuries, the Jews began their reverse migration westward well before World War II. There is every reason to believe that, because neither side needed the other any longer, emigration of Jews and Germans from the region would have continued at a quicker pace. The mutually beneficial symbiosis of Jews and East Europeans was coming to an end.

Threatened by fascism and acutely aware of Nazi anti-Semitism, a number of East European Jews embraced the outdated concept of international workers' solidarity, which, in the case of the Communists among them, ultimately meant serving Soviet imperialism. This was exploited by the Germans and by the East Europeans who became their allies in their determination to "settle the Jewish question." The Lithuanians were outraged by the terrors of Soviet occupation in which some Jews took part; and some, although far from all, ethnic Lithuanians lent their services to the Germans in the Final Solution. Others turned against the Jews or at least washed their hands of them. Avraham Tory quotes what Matulionis, a moderate Lithuanian politician, told a Jewish visitor early in July 1941: "I am a practicing Roman Catholic; I—and other believers like me—believe that man cannot take the life of a human being like himself. Only God can do this. I have never been against anybody, but during the period of Soviet rule I and my friends realized that we did not have a common path with the Jews and never will. In our view, the Lithuanians and the Jews must be separated from each other and the sooner the better. For that purpose, the Ghetto is essential. There you will be separated and no longer able to harm us. This is a Christian position." The guilt of the Lithuanians pales next to that of the Germans; still, some committed grave crimes, while other Lithuanians, to repeat, showed their humanity under the most adverse conditions.

Vilnius, Kaunas, and Klaipeda were once marvelously colorful, cosmopolitan cities, enriched by the learning and the skills of their multinational populations. The color and the excitement are now gone, as they are from most other places in Eastern Europe.

ROMANIA

KILLING FIELDS

AND REFUGE

1

If the art of survival is—as it probably must be—central to the politics of small nations then the Romanians may be counted among the greatest practitioners of that art. At the cost of much suffering and a good deal of social corruption, they have, over several centuries, managed to preserve both their national pride and their rich culture in a difficult and often hostile environment.

Surrounded by Slavic and Hungarian speakers, Romanians have persisted in preserving their Romance language, which is akin to Latin, French, and Italian. Invaded by Tatars, Poles, Hungarians, Ottoman Turks, Austrians, Russians, Germans, and finally, the Soviet Red Army, they have succeeded in absorbing or at least pacifying every occupier.

From the fifteenth century until, at least formally, 1878, the two original Romanian principalities, Moldavia and Wallachia, were subjected to Ottoman rule. Required to pay tribute to the Ottoman emperor's Sublime Porte, they were also forced to suffer the presence of viceroys who, especially in the eighteenth century, were often no better than bandits. Yet despite Ottoman domination the Romanians gave up neither their Eastern Christian religion nor their social and cultural institutions. During the first half of the nineteenth century (and again between 1944 and 1958) Russian soldiers occupied the country, yet in few places have the departing Russians left behind less of a tangible legacy than in Romania.

With the title "Survivors," this essay first appeared in the March 5, 1992, issue of the *New York Review of Books*. Reproduced here are only such sections that discuss Romanian history to the end of World War II and not the numerous sections on communist Romania and the December 1989 revolution. The original essay also appeared in German and Czech journals.

By their own efforts as well as by those of Napoleon III the two Romanian principalities were united in 1859, yet because they sensed the growing importance of Bismarck's Germany in the region, the Romanian political leaders invited a Prussian prince, Karl (or Carol I, as he came to be known) to be their ruler. The new prince, who became king in 1881, concluded a secret alliance with Germany and Austria-Hungary, but when World War I came, the Romanians reneged on his commitment. Two years later, having squeezed a maximum of concessions and promises from the Entente Powers, they declared war on their former allies.

Romania was quickly defeated and largely occupied by the German and Austro-Hungarian armies; after Bolshevik Russia left the war in the spring of 1918 it, too, was forced to sign a humiliating peace treaty with the Central Powers. Still, nearly two weeks after the collapse of Austria-Hungary and just one day before Germany's surrender, Romania managed officially to reenter the war and thereby secure a place for itself on the side of the victors.

Territorial gains at the Paris peace conferences were proportionally greater for Romania than for those of any other power. By acquiring Bukovina from Austria, Bessarabia from Soviet Russia, southern Dobrudja from Bulgaria, and Transylvania as well as other provinces from Hungary, the country more than doubled in size. Indeed, the territory it seized from Hungary was greater than all that remained of the latter state after the peace treaty.

It is difficult, however, to see in just what way the Romanian people profited from these territorial gains, unless one counts an inflated national pride that was to contribute to subsequent national tragedies. Flanked by embittered neighbors between the two wars, this greater Romania had a hard time dealing with its newly acquired ethnic minorities and even with its new ethnic Romanian citizens, millions of whom had lived for centuries under vastly different regimes.

After World War I, Romania's minorities—consisting, in descending order of magnitude, of Hungarians, Germans, Jews, Ruthenians and Ukrainians, Russians, Bulgarians, Gypsies, Muslim Turks and Tatars, Gagauz (Christianized Turks), Czechs and Slovaks, Poles, Greeks, Albanians, and Armenians—made up approximately 28 percent of the total population. As for ethnic Romanians, those in Transylvania tended to gather in one political camp and those in the old country, or "Regat," in another.

Until 1938 Romania had a parliament and a multiparty system, but gradually its leaders, like so many others in the region, adjusted to the spirit of the times by resorting to coercion and political assassination. The Romanians in the Regat had inherited from the Ottoman Empire a long tradition of bureaucratic laxness and corruption that reached record levels in those years. Its practitioners ranged all the way from King Carol II and his mistress Magda Lupescu to the humblest railway ticket collector. Undoubtedly, the system of payoffs grossly favored the rich and the well-connected, but some of the people who used it were also practicing the art of survival in a society dominated by a vast and underpaid bureaucracy. Among other things, bribery of officials helped to save thousand of Jewish lives during World War II.

By 1940 Romania had become a one-party state with all the fascist trappings under the dictatorial rule of Carol II. But the king's neutral foreign policy did not satisfy the Führer, who now allowed his allies to seize Romanian territory. On June 27, following Stalin's ultimatum, Romania ceded Bessarabia and northern Bukovina to the Soviet Union; on August 30 Germany and Italy ordered the transfer of northern Transylvania to Hungary, and a week later Romania had to return southern Dobrudja to Bulgaria. On September 5 General (later, Marshal) Ion Antonescu formed a government, and on the following day Carol II fled the country, leaving his nineteen-year-old son, Michael I, as king.

Because both France and Great Britain had utterly failed as Romania's protectors, it is small wonder that Antonescu joined in the international race for the favor of Hitler. For a while he governed in alliance with the Iron Guard, the leading Romanian Nazi movement, but because the Führer wanted order in Romania and because the conservative Antonescu was more to his taste than the radical Iron Guard, he soon gave permission to the Romanian dictator to wipe out the Romanian Nazis.

Like other East European governments in the interwar years, the Romanian government, too, was suspicious of, if not outright hostile to, the national minorities and often adopted harsh measures against them. Yet the minorities, especially the Germans and the Hungarians, generally lived better than the Romanian natives. The sense of racial, social, and cultural superiority claimed by both the Germans and the Hungarians has contributed enormously to the unending trouble between them and the Romanian people. Many Romanians feel and often act like second class citizens in their own country.

Romania has a long tradition of official anti-Semitism. Even in the relatively liberal pre–World War I period the Bucharest government tried to ignore its international obligation, solemnly undertaken at the 1878 Congress of Berlin, to grant equal rights to Jews. Romania was the only European country where, until 1923, native-born Jews were systematically denied citizenship. Yet perhaps nowhere else did well-to-do Jews control a greater proportion of the landed wealth through the system of lease-holds or have a greater influence on trade and finance.

During World War II, Romania was one of only two German satellites (the other was fascist Croatia) to attempt to organize its own Final Solution, murdering between two and three hundred thousand Romanian and non-Romanian Jews. It did so on its own initiative and in parts of the country under its exclusive control. Yet in 1943, after the war had turned against the Germans, the same Romanian regime successfully protected the country's remaining Jews, some three hundred thousand of them, against the German Nazis. Aside from Finland with its very small Jewish minority, Romania, alone in Nazi-controlled Europe, refused to send its Jews to the German death camps. (In Denmark most of the Jews were saved, but a few hundred Danish Jews ended up in a German concentration camp. Bulgaria, too, protected all of its own Jews but delivered to the Nazis nearly all the Jews from the Greek and Yugoslav territories under Bulgarian military occupation.) About one-half of Romanian Jews survived the war.[1]

In 1941 and 1942, Romania contributed the largest of all satellite military contingents to Hitler's anti-Bolshevik campaign. Romanian troops committed many atrocities in the Soviet Union and suffered horrendous losses at Stalingrad and other sectors of the Eastern front. Yet after the Red Army had occupied the northeastern part of the country King Michael, the government, the army, and the people made a unique volte-face. On August 23, 1944, Germany's most devoted satellite became one of Germany's most dedicated enemies, and Romania soon was able to send into action the fourth largest Allied military contingent (after those of the USSR, the United States, and Great Britain) for the final drive against Nazi Germany. Again, the Romanian army suffered enormous casualties, but once more Romania emerged from the war in a remarkably advantageous political position. True, it did not regain Bessarabia and northern Bukovina, territories it had lost to Stalin in 1940, but at the 1946 Paris peace conference it regained all the territories it had lost to Hungary in that same year.

During the war Hungary and Romania were official allies; their armies fought shoulder to shoulder against the Red Army. But the Hungarian and Romanian leaders' hatred of Bolshevism paled in comparison to their hatred of each other. In 1940 Hungary regained northern Transylvania with the help of Hitler and Stalin. In these reannexed lands the Hungarian authorities often mistreated the Romanian minority population.[2] In June 1941 Hungary and Romania, both currying favor with the Nazi government, joined Germany in the war against the Soviet Union. In late 1944 the Romanian militia entering northern Transylvania behind the Red Army took triumphant revenge for the atrocities committed by the Hungarians a few years earlier. This pattern of mutually ruinous rivalry and unrelenting hatred, hidden behind the mask of ideological and political affinity, has marked Hungarian-Romanian relations to this day. As if in unison the two countries have moved during the last century and a half from feudalism to liberal politics to conservative authoritarianism to fascism to communism and finally to post-Communist experiments with democracy, all the while eyeing each other with the utmost suspicion.

2

Romania's chief fascist movement was Corneliu Codreanu's "Legion of the Archangel Michael," also called the Iron Guard. The Legion flourished in the interwar years, preaching Christian Orthodoxy, xenophobia, antiparliamentarism, anti-Semitism, a mystical attachment to nebulous historical glories, and above all, a worship of the peasantry. In pursuit of its sacred goals the Legion practiced astonishing brutality. Between 1933 and 1940, its members murdered four active or former prime ministers and scores of other high functionaries. In one famous incident that took place in 1936, ten Legionaries entered the hospital bedroom of the traitor Mihail Stelescu, an Iron Guard leader who had gone over to another anti-Semitic organization. According to an official account, the intruders fired 120 shots into him, then "chopped up the body with an axe, danced around the pieces of flesh, prayed, kissed each other and cried with joy."[3]

The story of fascist Romania, dominated by the Iron Guard and the dictator Marshal Ion Antonescu, is well illustrated but not completely told in Siegfried Jagendorf, *Jagendorf's Foundry: Memoir of the Romanian Holocaust, 1941–1944*, which is introduced and commented upon by Aron Hirt-Manheimer (New York: HarperCollins, 1991). It is in part an eyewitness account, in part a historical narrative of the Romanian massacre of Jews in World War II. In general, much more needs to be written about the years between 1938 and 1944. Now that the Bucharest government no longer pretends that the Romanian Holocaust never took place or that Romania's participation in World War II began with that country's going to war on August 23, 1944, against Nazi Germany, new writing on the subject is perhaps possible.

Jagendorf's Foundry consists of the memoirs of a Jewish engineer from Bukovina, Siegfried Jagendorf, who persuaded the Romanian gendarmes and military, in the midst of the worst massacres of Jews in 1941, to let him set up a foundry run by Jewish workers and engineers. Even if only half of what Jagendorf tells in his memoirs (written in the United States) is true, there can be no doubt that he brilliantly exploited the snobbishness, stupidity, greed, and—occasionally—the goodness of Romanian commanders, thus saving hundreds, perhaps even thousands, of lives.

The Romanian Holocaust began after the abdication, in September 1940, of King Carol II and the proclamation of a National Legionary State under the joint command of the conservative nationalist Marshal Antonescu and Horia Sima, the head of the Iron Guard. In January 1941 the Iron Guard attempted, or was at least later accused of attempting, to seize complete control in Bucharest. During these events the Legionaries butchered hundreds of Jews. Antonescu had many members of the Iron Guard killed but then proceeded on his own to fulfill the Iron Guard program of "purifying Romania" of Jews. In the Moldavian capital of Iasi alone, between six thousand and ten thousand people were killed.

In his useful explanatory comments on Jagendorf's memoirs, Aron Hirt-Manheimer quotes from the eyewitness account, *Kaputt,* of the Italian war correspondent Curzio Malaparte: "Hordes of Jews pursued by soldiers and maddened civilians armed with knives and crowbars fled along the streets. . . . Squads of soldiers hurled hand grenades . . . into the cellars where many people had vainly sought safety. . . . Where the slaughter had been heaviest, the feet slipped in blood."

Jews who escaped the initial onslaught were packed into sealed trains that rolled through the countryside with no purpose other than to exterminate its human freight. Malaparte describes what happened when the trains stopped from time to time: "The soldiers climbed into the car and began throwing out the corpses one by one. . . . A crowd of peasants and gypsies who had gathered from all over were stripping the corpses . . . men and women dripping with perspiration, screaming and cursing, were doggedly trying to raise stubborn arms, bend stiff elbows and knees, in order to draw off the jackets, trousers and underclothing."

Curiously, Antonescu never succeeded in carrying out his extermination program in the principal Romanian provinces. After the initial killings the Jews in Moldavia, Wallachia, and southern Transylvania were spared. This was not so in Bukovina, which also formed a part of post-1918 Romania but from which thousands were deported eastward into Bessarabia (until recently, Soviet Moldavia), following Romania's entry into the war in the summer of 1941.

The Romanian authorities justified their actions by referring to the alleged communist sentiments and pro-Soviet collaborationist attitudes of the Jews in territories occupied by the Red Army between 1940 and 1941. But the overwhelming majority of the Jews, generally pious and Orthodox in that region, did not and would not have collaborated with the godless Communists. Moreover, southern Bukovina and the northernmost part of Moldavia had never been occupied by the Soviet army, yet Jews were now being deported from those regions as well. These deportees, together with the two hundred thousand Romanian Jews native to Bessarabia, were then either killed or driven east into Transnistria, now a part of Ukraine but at that time freshly incorporated into greater Romania.

Not even in Transnistria were the Jews given any rest. Joined by more than two hundred thousand Jews native to that province, the refugees were forced to move back and forth across the land, often ending up at the demarcation line between the German and Romanian occupation forces. The Germans were outraged at the sight of such disorder and pushed the deportees back into Romanian territory until, at last, most died of hunger and exposure. Others were finished off by Romanian and German soldiers. In Odessa alone twenty-five thousand were killed on Antonescu's orders.

While all this was going on, the Jewish engineer Jagendorf, who was himself deported to the Ukrainian city of Moghilev-Podolski, made an agreement with the Romanian gendarmerie to set up his foundry there. He established his family in a comfortable house, occupied an office shielded by secretaries and a padded door, wore kid gloves and polished boots, and smoked cigarettes in an eight-inch holder. Later, he was even allowed to drive a car. Maybe it was his German engineering diploma that impressed the Romanians or maybe it was the fact that he had once served as an officer in the army of Francis Joseph. In any case, his scheme worked. While thousands wasted away in the camps around the city or in the streets of Moghilev-Podolski itself, Jagendorf's employees were paid decent wages and had enough to eat. Among the most important commissions of his Jewish foundry was a monumental crucifix erected in memory of the fallen Romanian and German soldiers.

By the winter of 1943–1944 the leaders of the Antonescu regime were making plans to survive in the face of the coming Allied victory. The main beneficiaries of this tentative move toward the Allies were the Jewish survivors of the Romanian Holocaust. There was to be one more tragedy, however, this time in Hungarian-occupied northern Transylvania from which nearly all the Jews, perhaps 150,000 in all, were sent to Auschwitz in the early summer of 1944. Few of them survived the war. The Hungarian authorities not only lent Eichmann a helping hand in this operation but actually initiated it, thereby demonstrating a self-destructive madness not displayed by the Romanians. No group in

Transylvania, aside from the non-Jewish ethnic Hungarians themselves, had been more patriotically Hungarian and more proud to speak Hungarian under Romanian rule than the Jews of that province.

Romania's post-1944 trials of Nazi collaborators were considerably milder than in other countries. Only a few were executed, and, interestingly, those tried for collaboration included a number of Jews. There was even an unsuccessful move to charge Jagendorf.

3

The Romanians are an old people, but their independence is of recent vintage. To make up for that lateness, Romanian politicians and intellectuals have created a series of national myths: of Romania having always been the last bastion of Christianity against the infidel; of Romanian bravery and virtues having been ignored by an ungrateful West; of Romania being the subject of much slander; and of the Romanians being alone in the world. One only has to listen to Croatian or Serbian politicians today to realize that such emotions are not unique. Nor have they ever been unique in East Central Europe where all peoples tend to feel unrecognized, unrewarded, and unloved. Yet it does little good to remind the Romanians that their grievances are shared by others. As a former Hungarian, I would like to add that the grumblings of the East Central Europeans about a callous, uncaring, and ungrateful West are, in fact, not wholly unwarranted.

THE EUROPEANS
AND THE HOLOCAUST

1

Jews have been in Italy since Roman times. At the end of the fifteenth century they were expelled from southern Italy, then a Spanish possession, at the same time as the Jews from Portugal and Spain. Consequently, many southern Italians were hardly aware of Italian Jews even during the Fascist period. Jews were never expelled from Rome or other papal possessions in central Italy, in part because the Church needed them as living reminders of the sufferings of Christ. Yet life was not easy for Jews in Rome, at least not after the sixteenth century, when a ghetto was set up there. They were then forced to attend church to hear weekly sermons exhorting them to convert and to be exposed to the taunts of the populace.

Jews fared best in the north. Enlightened princes brought in many of them to promote commerce and Jewish emancipation began early in the nineteenth century. The Royal House of Savoy, which united Italy between 1860 and 1870, was especially philo-Semitic. In return, as Alexander Stille points out in his excellent *Benevolence and Betrayal: Five Italian Jewish Families Under Fascism* (New York: Summit Books, 1991), the assimilated and prosperous Jews of Turin, Genoa, and other northern cities were fierce royalists. Italian Jews became bankers, doctors, lawyers, judges, cabinet members, police chiefs, and army officers in numbers and proportions exceeding those in all other countries, except perhaps the Austro-Hungarian monarchy. During World War I fifty Jewish generals served in the Italian army, a bewildering figure, for it means that

---

The more extensive original of this article appeared in the November 5, 1992, edition of the *New York Review of Books*, under the title "Holocaust Heroes."

more than one out of every thousand Italian Jews was a general. This may have exceeded the proportion of generals within the Prussian Junker class.

After World War I such educated and assimilated Jews who did not happen to be Socialists, and not many were, enthusiastically embraced fascism, which presented itself as a necessary defense against Bolshevism and anarchy. Two hundred and thirty Jewish Fascists marched on Rome with Mussolini in October 1922; Jews sat in the Duce's cabinet and in the Fascist Grand Council. As late as 1938, at the time the first anti-Jewish measures were adopted in Italy, more than ten thousand Jews, or about one out of every three Jewish adults, were members of the Fascist Party; this constituted a much higher proportion of party membership than among the gentile population. Even Jews who were not party members took part in holiday parades wearing Fascist uniforms of one kind or another, as, of course, did much of the rest of the Italian population.[1] Within the party a few Fascist leaders had been anti-Semitic from the start, while others were philo-Semitic, but for most Fascists "the Jewish question" simply did not exist. Nor did it concern the general public, among whom the forty-seven thousand Jews (one-tenth of 1 percent of the total population) were distinguished neither by physical characteristics nor by language and only a little by customs and habits.

Mussolini does not seem to have had strong feelings about the Jewish issue, except when it suited the interests of this most accomplished of all opportunists. He carried on a long affair with Margherita Sarfatti, a Jewish journalist whom he first met in his socialist days and cast aside in the 1930s. During the first fifteen years of his rule, he welcomed Jews into the Fascist ranks, in part because he felt, quite naively, that they had influence in the Western democracies. Even after he had broken with Great Britain over the Ethiopian war in 1935 and 1936, the Duce would alternately support the Fascist Jews and incite them against other Western European Jews and against Zionism, or he would shunt aside the Jewish Fascists and flirt with Zionists, saying that he and the Zionist movement would together conquer the Middle East.

All this changed under the influence of Mussolini's growing friendship with Hitler, which led to the adoption of Italy's first racist laws in 1938. What happened next to the Italian Jews is the subject of three fine new books. One is the abovementioned *Benevolence and Betrayal*, a quietly written yet exciting and heartbreaking account by Alexander Stille, an American writer whose paternal grandparents were Jews who emigrated to Italy from Russia after World War I. The second, *The Italian Refuge: Rescue of the Jews During the Holocaust* (Washington DC: Catholic University of America Press, 1989), which is edited by Ivo Herzer, is a collection of twelve essays mostly by Italian, American, and Israeli writers. The third is Jonathan Steinberg's *All or Nothing: The Axis and the Holocaust, 1941–1943* (New York: Routledge, 1990), which deals with German Nazi influence on Mussolini's policy toward the Jews.

Of the 44,500 Italian citizens who were defined by the law of 1940 as Jews, 7,682 perished during the Second World War, most of them in Nazi concentration camps. Very few among them would have died without some form of Italian collaboration in the Final Solution, yet this still meant a survival ratio of 83 percent, surpassed only in Denmark, Finland, and Bulgaria.

The generally benevolent behavior of the Italians toward the persecuted Jews has been discussed by, among others, Susan Zuccotti in her valuable *The Italians and the Holocaust: Persecution, Rescue and Survival* (New York: Basic Books, 1988). However, the three new books provide much more detail and attempt to give new explanations as to why Italian Fascist society, so destructive in many ways, proved to be racially more tolerant than many non-Fascist societies in Europe.

In *Benevolence and Betrayal* Alexander Stille describes the lives of five Jewish families, in some cases large clans. They lived in four different Italian cities: the Di Verolis in Rome, the Teglios in Genoa, the Schönheits in Ferrara, the Foas in Turin, and the most controversial and fascinating of all, the Ovazzas in Turin. Some of these families lived in modest circumstances, others were very rich; some produced a number of militant anti-Fascists, others many ardent Fascists, but even the poorest among them, the Di Verolis in Rome's ancient Jewish ghetto, were Italian patriots. They all believed that "it could not happen here," a belief that doomed many of them, for they refused to seek shelter even after their non-Jewish friends and neighbors offered to help them to flee abroad or to hide.

As in the rest of Europe the anti-Jewish measures hit poor people the hardest: whereas the better-off Jews were at first often able to circumvent the law, the Di Verolis suffered acutely from being forbidden to peddle goods in the Roman streets. This was one of the absurdities of organized anti-Semitism, which, according to its own theory, ought to have directed its attacks not at poor Jews but at those who had risen above such traditionally permissible occupations as peddling.

The worst effect of the early anti-Jewish measures was psychological, and none suffered more in this respect than the Ovazzas of Turin, who were among the most enthusiastic Italian patriots. Three Ovazza brothers and their father had all served with distinction during World War I; one brother later became a career cavalry officer and another, Ettore, a banker, writer, and ardent Fascist, edited a Jewish Fascist paper, *La Nostra Bandiera* (Our flag), which praised

Mussolini's "corporative" state and his attempts to revive national pride. In 1929 Ettore finally was given an audience with Mussolini, which he later described as follows: "His Excellency Mussolini remembers having read a book of mine, *Diary of My Son,* and asks me: 'And your son?' I answer: 'He is six years old, Excellency!' . . . But when he learns that Il Duce asked me about him! Marvelous faculty of a Man so absorbed by the important affairs of State, to remember so clearly and follow the needs of his faithful! . . . On hearing my affirmation of the unshakable loyalty of Italian Jews to the Fatherland, His Excellency Mussolini looks me straight in the eye and says with a voice that penetrates straight down to my heart: 'I have never doubted it.'"

When the party turned against Ettore Ovazza and his family, he accused not the Duce or the party's anti-Semites but the Zionists and foreign Jews who had, he said, caused anti-Semitism in the first place. Having criticized the Zionists in his newspaper for many years, Ettore, during the fall of 1938, led a squad of patriotic Jews to the offices of a Zionist paper in Florence and burned it down. In October 1943 he and the immediate members of his family were caught by the German SS while trying to flee to Switzerland; they were executed the next day.

The political climate became particularly dangerous for the Jews as a result of Italy's prematurely announced surrender in September 1943, after which the Germans, in effect, captured the Italian army and set up a radical neo-Fascist puppet government in northern Italy. Some of those whose lives are discussed in *Benevolence and Betrayal* became the victims of these neo-Fascists; many more were captured, deported, or killed by the Germans. Yet the difference between Italian and German behavior was striking. Whether they were ordinary working people, nuns, priests, or policemen (the Germans considered the Italian police, unlike their counterparts in France and most other countries, to be hopelessly unreliable) the Italians very often helped Jews. Compared with people in other countries, fewer Italians were indifferent to the persecution of Jews and, often, even the anti-Semites among them could be bribed. This was not so of the Germans, who were supremely methodical. They invested enormous amounts of time and energy in hunting down a few Jewish women and children hiding in a convent; they transported a dying woman, at least ninety years old, all the way from the Fossoli camp in Italy to Auschwitz, though they knew that she would die a few minutes after being thrown into the cattle car.

The Bulgarian authorities, it has often been observed, refused to surrender a single Bulgarian citizen to the Nazis, and therefore not a single Bulgarian Jew was killed. But it is perhaps less well known that the same officials handed over all the Jews in the territories occupied by the Bulgarian army in Greece and Yugoslavia. By contrast, the Italian diplomatic service and army high command fiercely protected all Jews in the territories occupied by Italian forces in Greece, Albania, Yugoslavia, and France. Thus, in contrast to the situation in the rest of Hitler's Europe, the Italian authorities as well as ordinary Italian gendarmes, policemen, and soldiers went out of their way to save the lives of Jews who were not even their fellow citizens. In Budapest, for instance, persons as assimilated and educated as the fictional Italian Jewish family in Giorgio Bassani's *The Garden of the Finzi-Continis* as well as Vittorio De Sica's celebrated film of the novel would have generally survived the war in relative safety and comfort, but poor refugee Jews from abroad generally did not survive in Hungary. The Italians, however, saved about the same proportion—80 percent—of the forty thousand–odd non-Italian Jews who were living under Italian protection as they did of Jews who were Italian citizens.

Ivo Herzer, the editor of *The Italian Refuge,* survived German and Croatian Fascist persecution thanks to the Italian army. As he writes in the introduction, he was born and lived in Zagreb until the Croatian Fascist Ustasha state was created in 1941. He and his family then attempted to flee: "Our train was blocked from continuing the journey at one point and we were stranded in *Ustaša* territory, where the Italian Second Army maintained garrisons. We asked for help from the first Italian soldiers we saw, and their sergeant took upon himself to escort us and several other fleeing Jews to the railroad station. We then boarded an Italian military train with the sergeant at our side; he managed to bring us across the demarcation line into the Italian zone. Ours was quite a typical story of how the lower ranks of the Italian army spontaneously saved Jews during the *Ustaša* terror of the summer of 1941."

Both *The Italian Refuge* and Jonathan Steinberg's *All or Nothing* explains that it was not only the lower ranks for whom such behavior was typical. General Mario Roatta, General Mario Robotti, and General Giuseppe Pièche of the *carabinieri* (gendarmes), and other commanders, defied the Germans, Croats, and the Duce by granting asylum to the Jews. In Italian-occupied southeastern France, General Vittorio Ambrosio and his staff, with the help of the Italian foreign ministry, successfully resisted repeated French and German attempts to deport the many thousand Jewish refugees huddled in the small Italian zone.

Italian junior officers besieged their government with letters protesting the inhumanity of Nazi persecution, and the generals and diplomats, who knew perfectly well that Jews were being gassed, put pressure on Mussolini not to go along with the Final Solution. Caught between the pressures of such Nazi diplomats as Martin Luther, Prince Otto von Bismarck (grandson of the Iron

Chancellor), and Hans-Georg von Mackensen, who demanded deportation, and Italian Fascist Party leaders, foreign service officials, and military men who called for just the opposite, Mussolini hesitated, issued contradictory orders, and tolerated the sabotage of his anti-Semitic decrees, in which he himself did not really believe.

Both Steinberg and the authors of *The Italian Refuge* advance interesting explanations as to why all this happened. They refer to the liberal tradition of the nineteenth-century Italian *Risorgimento,* the small number of Italian Jews and their successful assimilation into Italian life, the fact that the Italian army had always included many high-ranking Jewish officers, and the importance of Jews in the early Fascist movement. No doubt, too, some Italian generals were jealous of German successes and enjoyed irritating their fanatical allies when it came to the treatment of the Jews. The authors refer, moreover, to the beneficial effects of the anarchic tendencies of Italian life and of the conservative mentality of the army officers. When a German general demanded that Jews be deported, General Paride Negri said heatedly, "Oh, no, that is totally impossible, because the deportation of Jews goes against the honor of the Italian army."

The concept of honor must indeed have been important to these brave officers, yet conservative officers in Germany, Hungary, Romania, and elsewhere, equally proud of their honor, often condoned or took part in the murder of Jews. There is something to be said for Hannah Arendt's view that what happened in Italy was "the outcome of the almost automatic general humanity of an old and civilized people." Yet it is also well to remember that the Fascist regime was capable of much brutality, that it was the Italian air force that first perfected terror bombing in Ethiopia, that Italian generals won the war there largely through the heavy use of mustard gas, and that during World War II the Italian military concentration camps in Yugoslavia could be hellish places for their south Slav inmates.[2]

Norway's Response to the Holocaust, by Samuel Abrahamsen (New York: Holocaust Library, 1991), is a book sponsored by the "Thanks to Scandinavia" Foundation (Victor Borge, national chairman), but having read this eminently objective account, I wonder why Jews should be particularly thankful, at least in the case of Norway. Nearly half of that country's minuscule Jewish population of 1,600 (0.05 percent of the total population) was killed during the war and as Abrahamsen, a professor emeritus at Brooklyn College in New York, points out, none would have died without Norwegian collaboration. Norway had only a few convinced Nazis but enough anti-Semites and law-abiding policemen and bureaucrats to make the Final Solution a near-success. To begin with, the small number of Jews in Norway was the result of a long and, at least to me, astonishing tradition of anti-Semitism combined with an extremely restrictive interwar immigration law that kept out nearly all refugees fleeing Nazi terror. During the war many Norwegians who would otherwise not have helped the Germans took part in registering, arresting, and handing over Jews to the German authorities. As for the powerful Norwegian resistance movement, it resembled all the other European resistance movements in caring little about what happened to the Jews. Just as elsewhere, however, there were thousands of decent Norwegians who helped hundreds of Jews escape, for the most part across the Swedish border.

2

As Poland has been the home of more European Jews than any other country, many studies are understandably devoted to the controversial subject of Polish-Jewish relations. One of them, Richard C. Lukas, ed., *Out of the Inferno: Poles Remember the Holocaust* (Lexington: University Press of Kentucky, 1989), is a collection of brief reminiscences by mostly simple people who did what they could to help Jews, most of whom they had never met before. As the book reminds us, the difficulties were almost insurmountable, and it was far easier for a Pole to be a part of the underground resistance than to help a Jew. The story of Barbara Makuch, a young member of Zegota, the Polish underground organization dedicated to helping Jews, can serve as an example.[3]

Makuch became active in saving people in 1942 when her family took in Malka, a Jewish girl they had not known previously, and to whom they gave the Polish-sounding name Marysia. Soon Makuch had to flee from Sandomierz with Malka to Lwow, where she placed her protégée in a convent and at that time joined Zegota, as two of her relations had done before her. Sometime later she was arrested by the Gestapo while carrying huge packages full of forged documents and money. In prison Makuch was whipped and beaten mercilessly and lost all her teeth. She was taken to the Ravensbrück concentration camp in 1943 from which she was liberated at the end of the war by the Americans. Malka and her mother also survived the war; Barbara Makuch was honored by Yad Vashem for saving Malka's life.[4]

"My Brother's Keeper?": Recent Polish Debates on the Holocaust, edited by Antony Polonsky (New York: Routledge, 1990), contains fascinating polemics by a number of Polish and Polish-Jewish intellectuals on Polish anti-Semitism, on what Poles neglected to do during the Holocaust, and on whether or not they, and humanity in general, had an obligation to help. Antony Polonsky, who is a professor of Judaic and Social Studies at Brandeis University in Massachusetts,

taught history at the London School of Economics when this book was published.

The debate in Poland on past and present Polish anti-Semitism was given new force by the showing of Claude Lanzmann's film *Shoah* in that country; the film is often mentioned in the essays and exchanges contained in Polonsky's collection. The book also discusses the wave of anti-Semitism that swept through Poland immediately after the war, leading to the murder of at least forty Jews in the July 1946 pogrom in Kielce. This and similar pogroms were provoked, as Polonsky points out in his introduction, partly by fears that the returning Jews would try to regain their property and partly by the feeling that the presence of many Jews in the Communist regime tended to confirm prewar fears of Judeo-communism (*Zydo-Komuna*).

Much of the discussion in *"My Brother's Keeper?"* centers on an article, reprinted in the book, by the prominent literary historian Jan Blonski. The article originally appeared as "The Poor Poles Look at the Ghetto" in the dissident liberal Catholic weekly *Tygodnik Powszechny* in 1987. The article takes as its point of departure Czeslaw Milosz's poem "A Poor Christian Looks at the Ghetto," written shortly after the destruction of the Warsaw ghetto, and demands that Poles accept their share of responsibility for the death of the Jews. Polish guilt, Blonski argues, did not consist of mass murder but of withholding help that might have been given. This, in turn, was caused by a tradition of anti-Semitism: "Yes, we are guilty. We did take the Jews into our home, but we made them live in the cellar. When they wanted to come in the drawing-room, our response was—Yes, but only after you cease to be Jews, when you become 'civilized.'"

Blonski's article provoked a flood of protests, some of which are reproduced in this volume. His critics, especially those among them who were themselves prisoners in Auschwitz or other camps, feel that Blonski went too far in his accusations. The journalist Witold Rymanowski, whose 1987 article is reprinted in *"My Brother's Keeper?,"* demanded that Blonski be prosecuted under articles 178 and 270 of the Polish criminal code for "slandering the Polish nation." Others are more moderate, and while the former underground fighter Wladyslaw Sila-Nowicki feels that Polish society did all it could during the war, the Catholic dissident Kazimierz Dziewanowski, now Poland's ambassador to the United States, and others are much less certain. As in Germany, the Netherlands, Hungary, and France, national responsibility for the murder of the Jews is now being debated in Poland with candor, vehemence, and the participation of leading thinkers—a contrast with the muted treatment of the subject until fairly recently.

Finally, Józef Garlinski, whose 1975 book about the Warsaw uprising, *Fighting Warsaw,* became an international best seller, has published a much more personal story, *The Survival of Love: Memoirs of a Resistance Officer* (Cambridge MA: Blackwell, 1991). Garlinski, then a young Polish officer, was wounded during the German attack in 1939. He later rejoined his British-born wife in Warsaw, and together they were in the resistance movement, he as the leader of a counterintelligence unit. Betrayed by a former schoolmate in April 1943, Garlinski was arrested by the Germans and taken to Auschwitz where, as he freely acknowledges, life for him as a member of a penal unit was often more bearable, because he was a Pole, than that of a Jew in a nonpenal unit. His wife survived also, and the two were reunited, in Glasgow, after the war. The photographs in the book are harrowing, and the author's prose is simple and convincing—even the most suspicious reader will acknowledge that it is the work of a brave and humane person.

3

"The state of Croatia... no longer exists. It was a short-lived German satellite, set up by the Germans and the Italians after the collapse of Yugoslavia in April 1941." So begins Menachem Shelah's essay on genocide in World War II Croatia in Michael Berenbaum, ed., *A Mosaic of Victims: Non-Jews Persecuted and Murdered by the Nazis* (New York: New York University Press, 1990).[5] Clearly Croatia has shown much greater vitality than anyone would have imagined when the book was published in 1990.

To what degree is the new Croatia a spiritual heir of the World War II state, whose political leaders and Fascist militia, the Ustashas, committed unspeakable crimes? To what extent has Croatia and the rest of the region changed since World War II? One looks in vain for a reasonable answer in the political literature coming out of the former Yugoslavia today,[6] which should have been all the more reason to welcome a new work on the subject of Croatia during World War II by the late Vladimir Dedijer, an internationally known scholar who spent the last decades of his life mostly outside Yugoslavia. His *The Yugoslav Auschwitz and the Vatican: The Croatian Massacre of the Serbs during World War II* (translated by Harvey L. Kendall; Buffalo NY: Prometheus Books/Ahriman-Verlag, 1990) provides some insight into the horrors of the period, but unfortunately, it hardly helps us to understand the civil war during the 1940s or the crisis there now.

The crimes of Ante Pavelić's Ustasha dictatorship are often mentioned today, especially in Serbian protests against those who now condemn their own barbaric program of "ethnic cleansing"; however, it is still worth recalling that during World War II Croatian campaigns of extermination were waged against Serbs, Jews, and Gypsies, and that many Eastern Orthodox Serbs whose lives had been spared were forced to convert to Roman Catholicism. Characteristically, Croatian Fascist propaganda asserted that most Eastern Orthodox "are as a matter of fact Croats who were forced by foreign invaders to accept the infidel faith," but the same regime then proceeded to the wholesale slaughter of these allegedly redeemable "ex-Croats." Croatian clergymen, especially Franciscan monks, gave strong and enthusiastic support to the anti-Serb measures, directed as they were against "infidel" fellow Christians.

Dedijer, who died in 1990, had been Tito's companion in the Partisan war; he wrote, among other books, a well-known biography of Tito and held many state posts. When he fell out with Tito and the regime, he taught history at various U.S. and British universities. One might have hoped that he was capable of writing a clarifying study of the horrible civil war among his countrymen, a conflict whose antagonists seemed to outsiders nearly indistinguishable from one another in appearance, language, and customs. What we get instead is over four hundred pages of anti-Croatian polemics, with wild conspiratorial theories about an eternally conniving, imperialistic, and bloodthirsty Catholic Church. Dedijer seems to divide the Croatian people into "Yugoslavs," that is, the people of whom he approves, and the "Croats," who are murderers and fascists (although in fact a considerable number of Croats joined the Partisan forces with Tito). Dedijer gives neither a general historical view of the subject or even a summary of his book, which consists simply of hundreds of examples of Croatian and Vatican treachery and brutality.

Dedijer writes that "over 200,000 people, mostly Orthodox Serbs, met their death" at the Jasenovac camp, the Croatian "Auschwitz." In a "Preliminary Note" to the same book, Mihailo Marković, the former dissident philosopher who is now closely associated with President Milošević's regime, assures us that "750,000 Serbs were exterminated [at Jasenovac], together with Jews and Gypsies." The claim that 750,000 Serbs were killed in a single Croatian camp is often made in Serbian propaganda publications, yet even the much more reasonable total of 200,000 is meaningless unless some evidence and careful estimates are produced to corroborate it. Marković refers to unnamed "German sources" to support his statement, yet we know that the Germans tended to exaggerate murder statistics, whether as part of an effort to shift responsibility onto their allies and local auxiliaries or as a reflection of the internal power struggles so characteristic of the Nazi system. Fascist Croatia was a protegé of Ribbentrop's foreign ministry, and so the German SS, often at odds with the foreign ministry, tended to take up the cause of the Orthodox Serbs against the

Catholic Croats. In doing so the SS wildly overestimated the number of Serbs killed by the Ustashas.

The irresponsible estimates of Serb propagandists allow Croatian apologists to minimize the number of victims at the Jasenovac camp and elsewhere. Nobody knows how many were killed at Jasenovac, but a rational guess would be somewhere between sixty thousand and eighty thousand, still a horrendous figure, especially when we consider that the camp's executioners lacked the sophisticated murder weapons available to the Germans. As Dedijer shows, the Ustashas used revolvers, a few old machine guns, hand grenades, knives, axes, hatchets, mallets, and any other instrument they could lay their hands on. In 1942, at the time of the worst massacres, they were led by a Franciscan monk, Miroslav Filipović-Majstorović.[7] The viciousness and cruelty of the Croatian Ustashas, to whom thousands of Croats fell victim as well, were extraordinary even in our vicious and cruel age. The Croatian government and society have barely begun to acknowledge this terrible record, much less atone for it.[8]

Characteristically, Dedijer does not have a word to say either about counteratrocities by the Serbian Chetniks or about the massacre by Communist Partisans at the end of the war of many thousands of Chetniks, Croats, Slovenes, ethnic Hungarians, and Germans, whether they were fascist, nonfascist, or antifascist. Dedijer fell out with the Communist regime in later years, but unlike his former comrade Milovan Djilas, he never forthrightly confronted the Communists' massacres of their internal enemies before and after they took power. That Dedijer, a Communist internationalist and a cosmopolitan intellectual, produced at the end of his life so prejudiced and so nationalistic a book suggests how dim are the prospects for ethnic and religious reconciliation in the former Yugoslav republics.

A HUNGARIAN
ADMIRAL ON HORSEBACK

In 1920 Miklós Horthy, a former officer in the Austro-Hungarian navy, was elected regent of Hungary by the Hungarian parliament. He remained in that post until 1944—a very long stretch by contemporary Central European standards. During Horthy's tenure, Hungary was still officially a kingdom, but it had no king—the last king, who was the last Habsburg emperor as well, went into exile in 1919. Although Horthy always wore his Habsburg admiral's uniform, Hungary no longer had a navy, since it had been cut off from the Adriatic Sea by the post–World War I peace treaties. This regent without a king and admiral without a fleet often attended public events on a white stallion—hence the title of Thomas Sakmyster's informative and often wryly humorous book, *Hungary's Admiral on Horseback* (East European Monographs; New York: Columbia University Press, 1994). A University of Cincinnati historian, Sakmyster has conceived the most important work on the admiral to date.

As with most discussions of Horthy, Sakmyster makes much of the paradoxes and ambiguities of his life and political career. Like the other "strong men" who governed a good part of Europe in the first half of the twentieth century—Franco, Salazar, Pétain, Antonescu, and others—Horthy was neither very cultivated nor bright, but he was cunning enough to make himself popular and to maintain control of Hungary in the most trying times. He was a patriot who fought to preserve his country's independence, but because he was also staunchly anti-Bolshevik and antiliberal he alternately courted and defied Hitler. Horthy has been described, in various places, as an archreactionary, a liberal conservative, a constitutional head of state, a dictator, a proto- or semi-

---

This essay appeared in the April 8, 1999, issue of the *New York Review of Books* under the title "Survivor in a Sea of Barbarism."

fascist, and simply a fascist. An "ideological hybrid, a blend of elements of nineteenth-century conservatism and twentieth-century right-wing radicalism," as Sakmyster calls him, Horthy changed his views and methods often, depending on the prevailing political situation and on who, at one time or another, had the greatest influence over him.

A cosmopolitan coterie of land-owning nobles, bureaucrats, and army officers (many of whom were commoners) governed the Habsburg monarchy (or Austria-Hungary) when Miklós Horthy was born there in 1868. The country was populated by Germans, Hungarians, Italians, Slovenes, Serbs, Croats, Bosnian Muslims, Romanians, Ukrainians, Poles, Slovaks, and Czechs, as well as a sprinkling of Armenians, Bulgarians, and others. Horthy's family came from the Great Plain of central and eastern Hungary, which was dominated by the Calvinist gentry whose sons rarely entered the service of the Catholic Habsburgs. But the Horthys were different from other members of the gentry: like his elder brother, Miklós entered the Austro-Hungarian naval academy in 1882. He had been an indifferent student. That he was admitted to the academy must be attributed, at least in part, to the fact that the armed forces tended to favor Hungarians—the most reluctant members of the turbulent Habsburg family of peoples—in recruiting young men for the officer corps.

An army officer was expected to be familiar with several languages and a navy officer with even more. Horthy soon learned to speak German, Hungarian, French, Italian, and Croatian, as well as some Spanish, Czech, and English. (When his ship was in the Adriatic port of Pola in 1904, he took English lessons from James Joyce.) Because he was charming, polite, handsome, a superb sportsman, an accomplished pianist and singer, as well as an amateur painter, those who met him were generally enchanted.

He rose quickly through the ranks. In 1909 he was made an aide-de-camp to the Austrian emperor and Hungarian king Francis Joseph, with whom he served for five years—an experience that greatly influenced his later life. He wrote in his memoirs that he had always asked himself, when confronted with a great dilemma, what Francis Joseph would have done to achieve a noble and humane solution. His decisions, however, were not always in keeping with those of the old emperor. Francis Joseph had always upheld the law; Horthy encouraged his officers, after World War I, to engage in counterrevolutionary terror. And although the emperor did not tolerate religious or ethnic discrimination, Horthy was responsible for introducing anti-Semitic laws in Hungary. By 1913 Horthy had risen to the position of a naval captain (the equivalent of colonel). He traveled widely on naval tours, met with dignitaries, hunted for big game, and admired British social and naval traditions. Although he subsequently opposed the British in two world wars, he never tired of repeating that the Royal Navy would win those wars.

At the start of World War I Horthy was sent back to sea. In 1917, while most of the Austro-Hungarian fleet was bottled up in Adriatic ports, he won a significant victory over British, French, and Italian ships in the Straits of Otranto. In February 1918 he helped to break a naval mutiny. Later that month, King Charles appointed him commander-in-chief of the Austro-Hungarian fleet, ahead of a number of officers who were senior to him. When the war ended in defeat soon afterward, however, Horthy had the humiliating task of handing over the fleet to the enemy. The monarchy was dissolved, and Horthy emerged from the war hating the socialists and Slavic nationalists whom he blamed for the loss of the war and for the dissolution of the Habsburg monarchy.

In March 1919 radicalized members of the Social Democratic Party joined forces with the Communists to overthrow the weakened and pro-Western government. The Bolshevik leader Béla Kun, a former prisoner of war in Russia, became the unofficial head of the Hungarian Soviet Republic. Kun immediately undertook a drastic program aimed at building a dictatorship of the proletariat. He also launched an "international proletarian war" against the Romanian and Czechoslovak armies that were overrunning northern and eastern Hungary. Kun intended to join forces with the Soviet Red Army and bring Lenin's revolution to the rest of Europe.

By early summer a popular counterrevolution against Kun's regime was rapidly spreading through the country, bringing it close to civil war. In response, the Bolsheviks cracked down on the peasantry, and some five hundred Hungarians were killed by thugs carrying out a "Red Terror." Meanwhile, a group of officers, aristocrats, and bureaucrats had begun to form a counterrevolutionary movement in Szeged, in southern Hungary. Horthy soon joined the counterrevolutionaries and was made minister of defense and commander in chief of the newly christened National Army.

In Szeged, Horthy was greatly influenced by the young, radical right-wing officer corps of his new army; its members assured him that the Communists, Socialists, and Jews were responsible for Hungary's dismemberment and called for a wave of "White Terror" to counteract Kun's policies and rid the country of its Jewish population. (Although most Hungarian Jews had no sympathy for the Bolshevik revolution, almost all of the Bolsheviks who seized power in March 1919 were young Jewish intellectuals, and this set off a wave of intensified anti-Semitism across Hungary.) Since the French, who were then occupying southern Hungary, were somewhat ambivalent about the development of Hungarian nationalist forces, the counterrevolutionaries could neither acquire arms nor attract many dedicated followers. Consequently, the National Army did not fight a single skirmish against the Hungarian Reds; they left that task to the Romanians who had invaded central Hungary.

On August 1, 1919, the Romanian army entered Budapest, and Kun's Communist regime collapsed after only 133 days. Horthy transferred his headquarters to unoccupied western Hungary where his officers' detachments instituted a reign of "White Terror" that surpassed the "Red Terror" of the Bolsheviks in its scope and brutality. Its chief victims were Jews and members of the revolutionary committees. In his biography, Sakmyster presents clear evidence that, characteristically, Horthy both denied having participated in these "excesses" and justified the atrocities by arguing that there was no room for sentimentality in such an extreme situation. The Communists had broken the country apart, he asserted, and in order to rebuild it his army could not be "softhearted."

After the Romanians evacuated the Hungarian capital in November 1919, Horthy made a triumphant entry into what he called "the sinful city," with the support of the Allied forces. A coalition government was formed, and on March 1, 1920, Horthy asked parliament to elect him to the position of regent of the Hungarian kingdom. The possibility that King Charles, Francis Joseph's successor, would return to the throne was left open, but in the meantime Horthy demanded and received nearly all of the prerogatives previously enjoyed by a constitutional Habsburg ruler. The election took place while armed officers—the real ruling power in Hungary at that time—were in the parliament building; as Sakmyster insists, however, it also reflected the will of much of the war-weary public.

Although Horthy was, as Sakmyster points out, an intellectual lightweight, he had enough political shrewdness to create the impression at home and abroad that he had single-handedly saved Hungary from the Reds. (In 1920, in a private message to the French government, Horthy said he had five hundred thousand "courageous, united, and loyal men" ready to join in the struggle against Bolshevism—despite the fact that Hungary, at that time, could barely muster an army of eighty thousand men, few of whom had weapons.) The Entente powers immediately recognized the new regime, which they considered a bulwark against Bolshevism.

Believing that the French would later help to restore the Hungarian kingdom, Horthy authorized his representatives to sign the Peace Treaty of Trianon on June 4, 1920. This confirmed Hungary's loss of two-thirds of its territory and 60 percent of its population—including more than three million ethnic Hungarians—to Romania as well as to Czechoslovakia, Austria, and Yugoslavia, among other nations. The stage was thereby set for a Central European conflict that would continue through World War II. Ironically, Hungary would eventually benefit from this dismemberment: it was now largely free of the ethnic diversity that would eventually lead to the breakup of Yugoslavia and Czechoslovakia, first during World War II and then after 1989.

Hungary's political experiences during the war and postwar years were largely responsible for the essentially negative ideology of the Horthy regime: antiliberalism, antisocialism, and "Christian nationalism," which as Sakmyster points out, was basically anti-Semitism.[1] From the 1840s to the onset of the First World War, the Hungarian gentry and the Jewish social elite had quietly worked together to modernize Hungary. The Jews had taken charge of economic development, and the aristocracy and gentry had governed the country. It was a collaboration that led to remarkable economic progress as well as to the integration of the mostly German- and Yiddish-speaking Jews into the Magyar national elite. By 1920 the Jews—who made up only 6 percent of the population—controlled most of the country's industrial and banking interests and accounted for nearly one-half of the professional class.

After the war the members of the urban, gentile middle class and intelligentsia demanded state assistance in their competition with successful Jewish businessmen and professionals. And in September 1920 Horthy's parliament passed laws stipulating that the enrollment of students of various "races and nationalities" in Hungarian universities would be limited to their percentage in the population. As Sakmyster demonstrates, Horthy's position on the Jews depended on the persuasive power of those around him; he swung from being moderately tolerant of them to allowing policies that were strongly discriminatory.

When King Charles, then living in exile in Switzerland, twice attempted to reclaim his throne in 1921, Horthy rejected him, citing—correctly—the danger of Czechoslovak and Yugoslav military intervention against a restoration of the Habsburgs. Distraught, Charles was deported by the British to Madeira, where he died a year later at the age of thirty-four. Charles was a deeply religious man, a political liberal, and a supporter of the Jews; his failure to return to the throne was a tragedy for Central Europe.

Still, during the next ten years, thanks to a talented new prime minister, Count István Bethlen, Hungary gradually returned to the combined liberal and conservative political practices—if not the ideology—of the prewar years. The White Terrorist groups were disarmed, and Bethlen reached agreements with both the Social Democratic trade unions and the Jewish-owned banks and industries. As a result, Hungary was allowed to join the League of Nations in 1922, and a large foreign loan put an end to the inflation that flared up in 1923. Even the anti-Semitic law passed in 1920 was now largely ignored. The press was almost entirely free, and the judiciary was independent. Politics were almost as they had been before World War I, except that the country was much poorer and there was now a fascist far-right both within and outside Bethlen's government party. (Although the political power of the government party was guaranteed by the election system, other parties, with the exception of the Communist Party, were allowed some representatives in parliament.) In the Bethlen era Horthy reigned more than he ruled, allowing Bethlen the freedom to formulate policy, while he devoted himself to ceremonial functions, tennis, and hunting.

The Great Depression and Hitler's rise to power put an end to this relatively tranquil period. Bethlen, whom the far right called a "Jew-loving aristocrat," resigned in 1931, and a year later Horthy chose Gyula Gömbös, one of his former White Terror officers and the founder of the Party of Race Defenders, to replace him.

Gömbös brought with him a number of young right-wing radicals who encouraged an ever-widening split in the counterrevolutionary ranks. The fascistic radicals—in effect the New Right—and the conservatives with liberal inclinations were now within the governing party. The liberal and left-wing parties, which were diminishing in size with every election, had no choice but to support the conservatives.

More active during these years than he had been in the Bethlen era, Horthy sometimes listened to his informal circle of elders—made up primarily of aristocrats and led by Count Bethlen—which invariably counseled caution in foreign policy, restraint in enforcing anti-Jewish legislation, and extreme moderation in social reform. At other times Horthy was influenced by his radical cronies from 1919, who urged him to appoint himself a dictator, dissolve the large estates, expropriate Jewish property, and prepare for war in alliance with Germany. A succession of prime ministers appointed by Horthy after the death of Gömbös in 1936 started out with cautious programs but ended up by being more radical and more pro-German than Horthy would have liked. This was primarily because these politicians had been charged with an impossible combination of tasks: to fight Bolshevism, to regain the lost parts of Hungary, to rely on Germany to achieve these two ends, to reduce the Jewish presence in the economy and society, yet also to keep the domestic fascists at bay and preserve Hungarian independence from Germany. Between 1932 and 1944 every cabinet included both anti-Nazis and politicians who were loyal to the Nazis. Horthy did not dare to dismiss the Nazi agents for fear of angering the Germans, yet he also refused to dismiss the anti-Nazis, whom he trusted.

In 1938, now in cooperation with Hitler and German policy, Hungary was on the way to recovering parts of its old kingdom. Its economy had passed from deep depression to something approaching prosperity, thanks primarily to the German rearmament program. Riding a white horse intended to evoke the legend of Árpád—the Hungarian chieftain who had conquered the Carpathian Basin late in the ninth century—Horthy entered southern Slovakia, then northern Transylvania, and finally north central Yugoslavia, all of which had once belonged to Hungary. These were his greatest triumphs, and as Sakmyster points out, by 1940 his "prestige and popularity in Hungary were immense."

In June 1941 Hungary entered the war against the Soviet Union. It is not easy to see how this could have been avoided, since its neighbors and bitter rivals—Slovakia, Romania, and Croatia—had also joined with Germany. Horthy's aim, after all, was to preserve and perhaps enlarge territories that Hungary had recovered from its neighbors since 1938. He later claimed that he had been tricked into the war by his prime minister, who had failed to pass on a friendly message from the Soviet foreign minister, Vyacheslav Molotov, but that is not believable. Horthy was naïve enough to expect that Hungary could take part in the destruction of Bolshevism without heavy losses, without becoming a German satellite, and without Great Britain and the United States resenting his alliance with Hitler.

The German alliance and immense domestic pressure were soon accompanied by a series of anti-Jewish measures. Three major laws, adopted between 1938 and 1941, imposed considerable economic hardship on middle-class Jews and also led to the death of thousands of men sent to the front in Jewish labor formations. Still, the persecution of Jews in other parts of Europe was far worse than in Hungary. When his prime minister, Pál Teleki, urged him to make some concessions to the anti-Semitic Arrow Cross movement in 1940, Horthy replied, "I have perhaps been the first loudly to profess anti-Semitism, yet I cannot look with indifference at inhumanity and senseless humiliations when we still need [the Jews]. Moreover, I consider for example the Arrow Cross men to be far more dangerous and worthless for my country than I do the Jew. The latter is tied to this country from self-interest, and is more faithful to his adopted country than the Arrow Cross men, who . . . with their muddled brains want to play the country into the hands of the Germans."

In March 1944, 95 percent of the Hungarian Jews and the thousands of Jewish refugees from abroad were still alive; many Jewish factory owners and bankers in Budapest had made immense profits from manufacturing arms for the German and Hungarian armies. Whenever Hitler pushed Horthy to take drastic measures against the 825,000 Hungarian Jews, Horthy argued that this would bring about the collapse of the Hungarian war industry.

The argument of some present-day Hungarian nationalists that Hungary collaborated with the Germans mainly to save Jewish lives is unconvincing, but so is the belief, held by the Allies during the war and left-wing critics of the Horthy regime ever since, that Hungary could and should have resisted the Germans outright. How could such a resistance have been successful when the necessary arms could not have been manufactured without German support, when most of the army officers were Nazi sympathizers, and when the public feared the Russians more than the Germans? (In a circular dated October 1932 Horthy claimed that the Bolsheviks had sunk the *Titanic*, caused Hungarian trains to crash, and kidnapped European statesmen.) It is easy to say that the army should have been purged and the public should have been given different information, but such a view ignores the consequences of the Trianon Treaty giving Hungarian territory to its hostile neighbors.

Horthy was right in arguing that the Jewish community would have been annihilated had Hungary resisted. Such was the case in Poland and in the Netherlands. It is true that anti-Jewish legislation in Hungary prepared the way for the wholesale robbery of Jewish property as well as for the 1944 deportation by brutal Hungarian gendarmes of nearly half a million Jews before the eyes of an indifferent public. But it is also true that in such countries as France—where there had been no anti-Jewish laws before the German occupation—thousands of Jews were also deported by brutal French gendarmes before the eyes of an indifferent public. Meanwhile, in fascist Italy—where Mussolini had introduced some anti-Jewish measures as early as 1938—the public (and the Italian occupation forces in France and Yugoslavia) sabotaged the efforts of the Germans and their Italian henchmen to deport Jews to Auschwitz.

In January 1943 a Soviet offensive destroyed the Hungarian army at the River Don. In two weeks, more than half of the two-hundred-thousand-man army became casualties—killed, wounded, sick, or captured—along with forty thousand members of the Jewish labor battalions. Horthy managed to withdraw the remaining Hungarian soldiers from the front lines, and thereafter he tried to get Hungary out of the war. In the following months the anti-Nazi Prime Minister Miklós Kállay made repeated attempts to reach a secret agreement with the Western Allies. (Horthy was not briefed on the details of these attempts, so that he would be able to deny knowledge of them if confronted by

Hitler.) The Western Allies were not interested in a separate armistice, however, and in any case they were nowhere near the Hungarian border.

Meanwhile, Hitler was being kept informed of Hungarian moves by pro-Germans in the Hungarian leadership. In April 1943 he personally reproached Horthy, condemning the performance of his supposedly unenthusiastic troops and his refusal to resolve the "Jewish question" in a way that was satisfactory to the Nazis. The seventy-five-year-old Horthy argued that the Jews were necessary to the Hungarian economy and said, naively, "What am I supposed to do with the Jews then, after I have taken from them all possibility of making a living? After all, I can't have them shot." Later that year, Kállay approved a secret agreement with the Allies, which stipulated that Hungary would surrender unconditionally to Anglo-American troops if they reached Hungary.

On March 19, 1944, the German army and SS marched into Hungary. There was no resistance, largely because Horthy had been summoned to Germany earlier and was held there on the night of the invasion. In any case, he and Kállay had previously decided not to resist in case of invasion, if only because Hungary still desperately needed German protection against the Red Army, which was then only a hundred miles away from the border. Kállay and Count Bethlen went into hiding; numerous other conservatives and liberals were arrested by the Gestapo. Under threat of complete takeover by the German Reich, Horthy then appointed an unconditionally pro-German cabinet that proceeded to remobilize the nation for war. With Adolf Eichmann's assistance the Hungarian authorities also began to roundup any Jews living in the countryside for immediate deportation to Auschwitz as the last installment of Hitler's "Final Solution."

In his memoirs Horthy claimed that he was powerless to stop these deportations. He also claimed to have known nothing of the real goal of the transfer of the Jews. He had, in fact, been informed several times of the true nature of the deportations but he was unable, Sakmyster writes, to imagine that, "with the war at such a critical stage, the Germans would simply kill these Jews rather than use them as workers." He chose to dismiss the reports as "the usual gossip of cowardly Jewish sensation-mongers," until June 1944, when his son passed on a firsthand account written by two prisoners who had managed to escape the systematic murder of Jews at Auschwitz.

Soon Horthy began to receive messages from Pope Pius XII, King Gustav of Sweden, Franklin Roosevelt, and other world leaders urging him to act to protect the remaining Jews in Hungary. In July 1944, when it came time to deport the two hundred thousand Jews still living in Budapest, he took military measures to oppose Eichmann and the gendarmes, who he feared were also planning a coup d'état against him. The smoothness and speed of the deportation of the Hungarian Jews from the countryside was unique in the history of the Holocaust; so was Horthy's decision to order armored units to prevent the deportation of the Budapest Jews. Ultimately, over 40 percent of the Hungarian Jews survived.

Horthy was later asked why he did not resign in the spring of 1944 to show his opposition to such atrocities. He said that if he had done so, the Budapest Jews and the many thousand Jewish men who were performing labor service in the Hungarian army would also have been deported, and power would have fallen into the hands of the Arrow Cross, Hungary's radical fascist party. Immediately after the German invasion a delegation of Jewish industrialists pleaded with Horthy to remain in office. One must add, however, that Horthy was mainly concerned about "good" Jews—decorated war veterans and capitalists, some of whom were his personal friends.

Early in September 1944, following Romania's sudden defection to the Allied side, the Red Army invaded Hungary. Horthy had already dismissed his pro-Nazi prime minister, and he now began to negotiate an armistice with the Allied forces and Russia—hoping for an agreement that would allow the German troops to withdraw unmolested—but discussions proceeded slowly. The Germans knew about these plans; they began to prepare for a coup d'état and as a first step, on October 15, they kidnapped Miklós Horthy Jr., the regent's only surviving son, whose older brother had been killed at the front. Horthy announced his intention to surrender to the Red Army that same day, but the army high command, imbued with the fanatical anticommunism that Horthy himself had encouraged, refused to follow his instructions and the surrender attempt failed. German SS and paratroopers arrested Horthy, and in order to secure his son's safety the old man signed a piece of paper that made his archrival, the Arrow Cross leader Ferenc Szálasi, his successor. Horthy and his family were then put on a train to Bavaria.

Six months of horror followed, as Arrow Cross thugs killed thousands of Jews and terrorized an increasingly reluctant populace into fighting a losing battle at the front—now jut a short streetcar ride away from the center of Budapest. The arrival of the undisciplined and rapacious Red Army meant liberation for the Jews and political prisoners, but the Soviet occupation was greatly resented by the rest of the population.

All of this no longer directly affected Horthy, who was being held prisoner by the Germans. Liberated by the Americans in the spring of 1945, he was treated alternately as an illustrious statesman and as a suspected war criminal. Fortunately for Horthy, Stalin showed sympathy for him. The first antifascist government, appointed in December 1944 by the Red Army, included three of Horthy's generals, one of whom was made prime minister. Horthy was spared extradition to Tito's Yugoslavia, where he was wanted in connection with the massacres committed by local commanders of the Hungarian army in northern Yugoslavia.

After he was released by the Americans he settled in Estoril, Portugal. He had always lived fairly modestly, and as Sakmyster shows, he had never accumulated any wealth. In Portugal Horthy and his wife survived thanks to the generosity of Jewish friends. He died a few months after the 1956 revolution in Hungary, without ever having returned to his homeland.

Horthy's regime is now considered a failure: it could not protect the country against German and Soviet imperialism; it was unable to keep the territory it had reacquired; it turned over nearly half a million of its most industrious citizens to the German murder machine; it did not even succeed in protecting the privileged social classes in whose interests the counterrevolution had been made. As Sakmyster argues, however, it is unlikely that any other ruler would have done better.

Miklós Horthy was neither a fascist nor a dictator; he was not an evil man, but he was not a humanitarian either. Although he claimed to have been a lifelong anti-Semite, under his reign more Jews survived the Nazi terror than in any other country in Hitler's Europe except Romania. Horthy was no more shallow and muddle-headed than Pétain or Franco, and he was certainly less brutal than the Romanian dictator Ion Antonescu. In the conclusion to his excellent book, Sakmyster seems fair when he writes: "In the ultimately hopeless task of preserving Hungarian independence while at the same time working toward a revision of the hated Treaty of Trianon, Horthy at times tilted dangerously toward Nazi Germany. But in the end he always shrank from the employment of totalitarian methods in Hungary.... It was largely through his influence that in early 1944 Hungary was such an anomaly: an island in the heart of Hitler's Europe where a semblance of the rule of law and a pluralistic society had been preserved in a sea of barbarism."

THE HOLOCAUST
IN HUNGARY

In few other places have Jewish/non-Jewish relations been as complex and contradictory as in Hungary. While Jews had been living in that country for many centuries, their numbers multiplied and their presence became crucially important only in the second half of the nineteenth century. From that time on, the Jewish condition has varied between what they themselves have often described as close to paradise and, alternatively, as sheer hell. Nor can it be characterized as a simple process of rise and fall but, rather, one of dizzying and sometimes nightmarish changes.

Because of the near-silence imposed by the Communist regime, especially in its early stages, the Hungarian-Jewish tragedy has been seriously explored only in the past two decades. Today, scholars in Hungary, Israel, and elsewhere are doing notable work on the subject. Several among them contributed to this important book, including Randolph Braham of the City University of New York, the doyen of Hungarian Holocaust studies. My only complaint is that some of what they say has already appeared in a slightly different form in other collections.

Genocide and Rescue: The Holocaust in Hungary 1944 has its origins in an international conference held at the Institute of Contemporary History and Wiener Library in London in 1994, and it has been ably edited by David Cesarani, director of the Institute and Library, who has also provided a useful introduction. The contributors to the collection agree on most aspects of Hungarian-Jewish history; their disagreements begin only when they discuss whether, and how, the genocide of 1944 could have been averted.

This is a review of David Cesarani, ed., *Genocide and Rescue: The Holocaust in Hungary 1944* (Oxford: Berg, 1997). The original appeared in the *Times Literary Supplement* in London on July 3, 1998.

What would have helped the Hungarian Jews in the last years of the war? Perhaps it would have been better for them had the Hungarian Government not attempted to secede from the war but instead continued to cooperate with the Germans, except, of course, in the matter of the Final Solution of the Jewish Question. Hungary's attempt, in 1943 and again in October 1944, to conclude an armistice with the Allies brought about two consecutive German takeovers, each leading to massive slaughter of Jews. Yet the goal of surrendering to the Allies was not achieved, and Hungary was stuck with the double blame of having been Hitler's last satellite and of having helped to exterminate one-half of its Jewish citizens. Both Randolph Braham and Yehuda Bauer are quite categorical in arguing that, in the interest of its Jewish citizens, Hungary should have refrained from trying to surrender. As Bauer puts it: "The paradox lies in the fact that had Hungary remained a loyal ally of Germany, on the Romanian model, there may not have been a German occupation and the chances of Jewish survival would have been greatly enhanced." He adds: "It was [the anti-Nazi Prime Minister Miklós] Kállay's policy of extricating Hungary from the war (in 1943) that brought disaster on the Jews."

These are courageous and honest words, standing in absolute contrast to what Jews and non-Jews had been saying until recently but their implications make one shudder. First of all, Romania remained a loyal ally only until August 23, 1944. On that day, at their king's order, Romanian soldiers turned their weapons around and rounded up their former German comrades. Whether the Hungarians would have been able and willing to achieve such a dramatic volte-face is most doubtful. Furthermore, if collaboration was in the interest of Jews, then resisting the Germans was ipso facto harmful to the Jews. This means that, in this particular instance, Jewish interests ran against the interests of the Allies and even of such non-Jewish Hungarians who sought to save Hungary. After all, it was important for the nation to try to jump off the sinking German ship. If the interest of Jewish and non-Jewish Hungarians were mutually exclusive, why then should the non-Jews care what happened to the Jews? Moreover, Bauer's and Braham's thesis flies in the face of the Hungarian-Jewish contention that they were Hungarians of the Mosaic faith and that, despite all the official and popular anti-Semitism, they too cared profoundly for Hungary. The insoluble problem was that, whereas the Jews needed time, at any cost, to save their lives, the non-Jewish Hungarians, or at least the more intelligent among them, were in a hurry to rescue their social system and also their country.

The question of what would have happened to Hungary and its Jews had the country remained a loyal German ally throughout the war must remain forever open. In all likelihood the Germans would still have invaded it after the Red Army had come too near. As the authors of the book correctly point out, the presence of the Jews was not what primarily motivated the Germans on March 19, 1944. Rather, their main motive was to mobilize Hungary's manpower and material resources for a last-ditch stand against the Soviet armed forces. It is entirely possible, however, that a much delayed German invasion would have drastically increased the Jewish chances of survival. After all, Himmler stopped deportations to the Polish camps at the end of August 1944.

All the contributors agree that Hungarian military resistance to the Germans, either in March 1944 or later, was out of the question because of the army's weakness and the anti-Soviet, pro-German predisposition of the officer corps, the administration, and a large part of the public. Only a small minority, including the conservative aristocrats who had the most to lose from a Soviet victory, understood that a Soviet occupation was inevitable and that Hungary's dignity required at least a token stand against Germany. In fact, anti-Nazi resistance in Hungary never amounted to much.

What, then, could have been done to save more lives? All the authors, but especially Tony Kushner, demonstrate that no one in Hungary or abroad had protested against the deportations undertaken in the spring of 1944, despite the fact that the fate of Jews in Auschwitz was clear to all, both in the Allied camp and in Hungary. However, there were strong protests late in June and in July, when it was too late to save the Jews of the countryside.

Braham argues that the leaders of the Jewish community knew about the Final Solution but that they criminally neglected to alert their flock. Other contributors state that any warning would have been useless, since the Jews of the countryside had nowhere to hide and in any case would not have believed they were in such danger. Leaders of the Jewish community were good Hungarian patriots, and they continued to trust the government even after the deportations. (In fact, the Jewish leaders generally survived, which means that, personally at least, they had not been betrayed.)

Asher Cohen and Robert Rozett make it clear that Jewish armed resistance was an illusion. There had been no preparations; the Jews had no arms; the situation never seemed as hopeless as it was, for instance, in Warsaw in 1943; and the Jewish fighters would not have been supported by other Jews. What the small Zionist groups did best was to forge Aryan documents and safe conducts; the latter were endorsed by such genuine or self-appointed representatives of the neutral powers as the Swiss Karl Lutz, the Swede Raoul Wallenberg, the pseudo-Spanish chargé d'affaires Jorge (Giorgio) Perlasca (who was actually a former Italian Fascist), and the Vatican nuncio Angelo Rotta. These foreigners, the Zionist youngsters, individual police officers, some monks, nuns, ministers, and nameless civilians in Budapest were the real heroes of the epoch: together they saved tens of thousands of lives.

Was this the most that could be expected? No, because more could have been done without great risk to anyone. The Catholic and Protestant Church leaders failed miserably in the spring of 1944 by not publicly condemning the deportations in a country whose government professed to be devoutly Christian. But the bishops were interested mainly in protecting converted individuals and, like the rest of the country, were indifferent to what happened to the other Jews. A little less zealous obedience on the part of the national administration and on the part of the Jewish leaders might also have accomplished wonders. As for the population at large, the vast majority of whom committed no greater crime than to grab the flats and silver left behind by the departed Jews, it could certainly have shown more compassion. After all, in the early summer of 1944 it was only a question of a few more months.

POLES AND JEWS

No issue in Holocaust literature is more burdened by misunderstanding, mendacity, and sheer racial prejudice than that of Polish-Jewish relations during World War II. In his *Facing the Extreme: Moral Life in the Concentration Camps* (on this book, see the chapter titled "Memories of Hell" in this volume), Tzvetan Todorov describes the fundamental disagreements between Polish Christians and Polish Jews during the war. Why did the underground Polish Home Army offer so little help to the Warsaw Ghetto Uprising in 1943? The reason, Todorov believes, is less the certainly existing anti-Semitism in the Polish ranks than the two communities' traditional isolation from each other and also the pro-Soviet position of many of the Jewish fighters. The Home Army was just as hostile to Stalin as it was to Hitler, Todorov writes, and the Hashomer organization, which was the nucleus of the Ghetto revolt in 1943, was unconditionally pro-Soviet.

Because of events during and after the war, many Poles will forever associate all Jews with "Jewish communism." For the most part, however, the Polish Jews were not Communists. One hundred and twenty thousand of them served in the Polish army in 1939, and some thirty thousand were killed in battle. There were some eight hundred Jews among the Polish reserve officers murdered at Katyń and other sites on Stalin's orders.[1] Many Jews, for their part, tend to view

---

This is part of an article that appeared in the June 26, 1997, issue of the *New York Review of Books*, under the title "Memories of Hell." Because the essay discussed Polish-Jewish relations, there was an inevitable flurry of letters, mostly accusing Poles of terminal anti-Semitism. In my reply, published in the September 27 issue of the journal, I complained about the mutual prejudices and the irresponsibility of some of the American media in casting hasty judgment on Poles who, next to the British, were the only nation to fight against the Nazis throughout the war and who were nearly wiped out in the process.

the Poles as unredeemable anti-Semites, despite the fact that the ancestors of most Jews in Poland in 1939 were invited there by the Polish nobility and were given extraordinary privileges. There are more trees at Vad Yashem in Jerusalem dedicated to the memory of Polish helpers of Jews than all other such memorial trees combined.[2]

Several documentary collections exist on the sufferings of Jews in Poland under Nazi rule. Two of the best are *The Diary of David Sierakowiak: Five Notebooks from the Lodz Ghetto* (edited by Alan Adelson, translated by Kamil Turowski; New York: Oxford University Press, 1996), and *Am I a Murderer? Testament of a Jewish Ghetto Policeman* (edited and translated by Frank Fox; Boulder CO: Westview Press, 1996). Their authors, both young men, died before the Nazis withdrew. David Sierakowiak, the author of *Five Notebooks,* died of starvation in the Lodz Ghetto in 1943, when he was nineteen. Calel Perechodnik, a member of the Jewish police force in 1943 in the Otwock Ghetto, not far from Warsaw, killed himself at age twenty-seven, during the great 1944 Warsaw Uprising, after contracting typhus and being discharged from the Polish Home Army. His book is not a diary but a memoir written while in hiding after the ghetto was destroyed and most of its inhabitants killed.

Both Sierakowiak and Perechodnik were rich boys, well-educated and familiar with many languages. Although starving, Sierakowiak conscientiously did his homework on Cicero and Ovid for the ghetto school; in fact, he was indignant that the ghetto still lacked a university. A convinced Communist, he studied Lenin's *What Is to Be Done* and other Marxist-Leninist tracts. While he was serious, honest, and mature for his years, Perechodnik was beset by emotional contradictions. Frank Fox, the young policeman's translator and editor, describes him as "by turns mordant and sentimental, accusatory and self-pitying, sardonic and sorrowful." Before the war he had belonged to a Zionist organization but was also an ardent Polish patriot. Like Sierakowiak, he remembers the period of the German attack on Poland in September 1939 as one of great fraternity between Poles and Jews; in fact, he claims that before the war he never encountered any manifestation of Polish anti-Semitism. Unlike many later memoirists, who could only recall their prewar family lives as idyllic, these two young men utterly disliked their fathers and were at odds with the other members of their families.

Sierakowiak hated Chaim Rumkowski, Elder of the Lodz Ghetto, who ruled the ghetto like a king and decided to help the Nazis deport its children and old people in order to save the healthy adult population—a strategy that failed horribly, with Rumkowski himself ending up in Auschwitz. Sierakowiak writes about the enormous class differences within the ghetto and describes how some lived comfortably while he and others were wasting away from hunger. His mother was selected for death by two Czech-Jewish doctors, and he watched her being taken away; he often complains about his father, who refused to work but devoured everything in the meager family larder. Yet the father died before his son, and the rest of the family perished as well. The terrible story of the Lodz Ghetto has been told many times before; what is unforgettable about the diaries is the heartbreaking dedication of a young man to learning and to a practical cause in which he desperately wanted to believe.

The young ghetto scholar particularly despises the Jewish ghetto police who served the Germans, arrested fugitives, and if the fugitive could not be found took hostages from among members of his family. Calel Perechodnik was such a policeman, but he was still not sufficiently privileged to save his own wife and child. Although he loved them, Perechodnik seems to have disliked more or less everybody else. He dislikes most Jews, whom he believes are cowards; he accuses the Poles of having betrayed their Jewish friends; he hates the Ukrainian militia, who often behave worse than the Germans; he curses his own superiors in the police who misled him into believing that his family would be exempted from deportation. Policemen, he writes, "lead their own fathers and mothers to the cattle cars; themselves close the door with the bolt—just as if they were nailing the coffins with their own hands." He himself watches as the Germans cram his wife and child into the train.

Above all, Perechodnik hates himself—small wonder in view of what took place. Still, he goes into hiding and so, separately, do his parents and some other close relations. This costs money but the family has plenty of it. Perechodnik blames the Jewish religion for everything: the conceit of the Jews and their conviction that they were the chosen people. What indeed do Jews have in common? What, he asks, binds the French socialist Léon Blum, the Soviet leader Kaganovich, and himself, Perechodnik, a fierce anti-Communist?

This is not a story in which Tzvetan Todorov will find evidence that virtue and decency survived, even though here, too, one encounters a few noble characters, including some Poles, especially "Magister," Perechodnik's close friend who ends up preserving Perechodnik's memoirs. Perechodnik himself demonstrated neither heroic nor quiet virtues; he was far too busy trying to save his wife, child, and himself. Who can blame him?

5
ONLOOKERS

THE POPE, THE NAZIS, AND THE JEWS

1

Few twentieth-century statesmen have been more enigmatic, contradictory, or controversial than Pius XII, who was Pope from 1939 to 1958 during one of the world's, and the Catholic Church's, most trying periods. Pius was an ascetic; his face pale, his hands nearly translucent. He did not drink, smoke, or have any other obvious vices. His breakfast was a piece of bread and a glass of warm milk; for the rest of the day he ate not much more than that. He saw himself as Christ's most humble servant, yet no other pope in recent times has surrounded himself with more pomp, and none has enforced a more rigid etiquette. He did not doubt that he was God's sole vicar on earth, responsible for the spiritual welfare of all humanity, yet at least according to his critics, he hardly ever spontaneously addressed an ordinary human being: when he took a walk in the Vatican gardens, he expected that workers would vanish into the bushes as he passed.

This is the reprint of an essay by the same name that appeared in the March 23, 2000, issue of the *New York Review of Books*. Because it dealt with the Vatican, with John Cornwell's bestseller book on Pope Pius XII, and with the Holocaust, the article created quite a stir and brought many letters addressed both to the editor and to me privately. I tried to sum up the nature of these letters in the June 15 issue of the journal. Interestingly, it was my statement about Jesus's brothers and sisters, born to the same virgin mother, that brought in the most letters. The mention of Jesus's siblings is in the Gospel of Saint Mark, and I brought it up only to show the importance of unconditional belief for the Catholic faithful. Other readers took me to task on the history of the Church and on what they called my unfair attacks on Cornwell. Again others regretted that I did not condemn Pius XII more sharply for his indifference toward the Nazi persecution of the Jews.

Firmly believing in miracles and in the deepest mysteries of the Catholic faith, Pius solemnly proclaimed the Assumption of Holy Mary in 1950. According to this teaching, the Mother of God ended her terrestrial existence by being assumed, body and soul, into heavenly glory. As John Cornwell states in his fascinating but in some respects flawed book, *Hitler's Pope: The Secret History of Pius XII* (New York: Viking, 1999), this was "the only solemn and irreformable decree made by a pope according to the definition of infallibility at the First Vatican Council in 1870." Today every Catholic must believe not only that Mary was born without the original sin burdening the rest of humanity; not only that she remained a virgin despite conceiving and giving birth to Christ as well as to Christ's four brothers and to his sisters (Mark 6:3); but that, after she died, her body and soul were immediately reunited.

Mystical experiences were not unknown to this pope: he once witnessed the phenomenon of the spinning sun associated with the cult of Our Lady of Fátima in Portugal. Considered a saint in his lifetime, the pontiff was also an accomplished politician whose approach to the great questions of the day, including his response to the Holocaust, was largely one of diplomatic maneuvering. It was not for him to risk martyrdom for the Jews or even for his fellow Catholics.

The Church's supreme leader rejected nearly all recent social and political ideas, yet he was the first pontiff to use the mass media systematically for propaganda purposes; he had a flattering film made about himself during the war. No one questions his piety, yet he has also been accused of cynicism, callousness, and opportunism. He is seen as both a ruthless autocrat and a weakling, a fool who did not understand the nature of totalitarian regimes and a cunning authoritarian himself, and an anti-Semite and a savior of Jews. The writers of the books under review, and many, many others, strive to understand him, yet the enigma remains, as do so many other enigmas surrounding the Holy See. A fine evocation of the papal mystery comes from Sir Francis D'Arcy Osborne, the British minister to the Holy See, who spent World War II in the neutral Vatican, an excellent place from which to observe the doings of the Church hierarchy during a crucial period. Osborne wrote in 1947: "I long ago realized that it is almost impossible for a layman and a non-Catholic, and indeed for most Catholics and ecclesiastics outside the Vatican City, to form a valid judgment or express an authoritative opinion on Papal policy.... The atmosphere of the Vatican [is not only] supranational and universal ... it is also fourth-dimensional and, so to speak, outside of time ... for example, they can regard the Savoy dynasty [Italy's rulers after 1861] as an interlude, and the fascist era as an incident, in the history of Rome and Italy. They reckon in centuries and plan for eternity."[1] Indeed, the royal House of Savoy and Italian fascism have long since disappeared from the scene; the papacy is still with us.

Critics of the Pope ought to be aware of the physical and material weakness of the Papal State. Pius XII was scorned for not having done more for one or another cause during World War II. But the survival of the Vatican state depended entirely on the good will of outsiders, first on the Italian Fascist government, and later on the Nazis, when, after Italy's attempted surrender to the Allies in September 1943, German troops occupied Rome and surrounded the Vatican. It was not merely that the Pope had no military divisions, to use Stalin's derisive expression, but that the Holy See did not have the slightest means of independent existence: its water, electricity, gas, coal, and money all came from the outside. Its sewage and garbage were taken away by municipal services over which it had no control. Had there been a German blockade, the Pope, his cardinals, and his officials would have had nothing to eat. Still, one-hundred-odd Allied diplomats delegated to the Holy See had to be sheltered on its premises, and following the German takeover, hundreds of Jewish refugees were hidden either in the Vatican or in other buildings under Vatican control.

Every criticism of Pius XII, and undoubtedly he deserves many, must take into account that without Italian, or later German, permission, such Vatican newspapers as *L'Osservatore Romano* could not have been published, the Vatican Radio would have fallen silent, and all communications between the Vatican and the rest of the world would have been cut. Those of us who complain about the failure of Pius XII to "speak out" must also consider the question of how and how long he could have done so.

No doubt the suppression of Vatican independence would have caused outrage among Catholics in Fascist Italy and in Nazi Germany, yet it is extremely unlikely that the outrage would have turned into an open revolt. After all, the German and the Italian clergy and Catholic laymen had long lived under regimes that systematically violated Catholic rights. In his periodic outbursts against the Vatican, Hitler threatened to kidnap Pius XII, to "clear out that gang of swine" in the Vatican, and to occupy the place.

Two reasons he did not do any of these things are that Pius XII and the Church proved sufficiently accommodating and that the Führer preferred to be cautious so long as there was a war and so long as the all-important "Final Solution of the Jewish Question" was still being carried out. Even when Pius XII subsequently proved not at all accommodating, as was the case after World War II with regard to communist parties and governments in Eastern Europe, the most powerful weapon he had at his disposal was excommunication. This, as Jonathan Luxmoore and Jolanta Babiuch demonstrate in their excellent book *The Vatican and the Red Flag: The Struggle for the Soul of Eastern Europe* (New York: Geoffrey Chapman, 1999), did not prove powerful enough to help Catholics: the angry Communist regimes still imprisoned large numbers of loyal Catholic clergymen and laymen.

All the recent studies agree that, for much of modern history, the papacy has been on the losing side, assaulted, in an increasingly secularized and nationalistic society, by forces believing that the popes wield immense power. Back in 1077 the penitent Emperor-King Henry IV appeared at Canossa before Pope Gregory VII, begging forgiveness from the real ruler of the Christian world. Yet the East-West schism of the eleventh century and the Reformation of the sixteenth century split Christianity; modern secularism threatened to wipe it out altogether. Popes Pius VI and Pius VII were held in captivity by Napoleon; Pius IX had to flee for his life from revolutionary Rome in 1848; the Papal States, encompassing central Italy, were seized in 1870, and the sole territorial guarantee of papal independence was lost. Thereafter, the pope lived as a prisoner in the capital of a foreign country and was the object of widespread contempt and ridicule.

In the late nineteenth century nearly all European countries, including Catholic France, Italy, and Spain, turned against the Church, abolishing many of its privileges, confiscating much of its property, dissolving monastic orders, banning processions and outdoor services, conscripting priests, legalizing mixed marriages, placing marriage—a Holy Sacrament—under state control, and taking away what the Church perceived to be its absolute right and duty: the education of the young. Even Habsburg Austria-Hungary, the Church's traditional protector, did much to alienate the papacy at that time.

During World War I, Pope Benedict XV failed in his effort to mediate between the warring partners and thus to save Austria-Hungary. In 1918 the Habsburg monarchy fell apart; among the successor states, Czechoslovakia was bitterly hostile to Rome. Yet all this was only a prelude to the Vatican's troubles. In Soviet Russia the far-from-unimportant Catholic Church was virtually eliminated; at the same time, thousands upon thousands of Orthodox Christian bishops, priests, and laymen were shot. Characteristically, the Vatican at first detected signs of hope in the Bolshevik Revolution. Following a firmly established papal tradition, it stood ready to negotiate a concordat (or agreement between the Vatican and a secular government) with Lenin and Trotsky. The goal was to profit from the chaos in Russia with the reconversion of the schismatic Eastern Orthodox to the only true, Roman Catholic, faith. Even Pius XII harbored illusions in this regard and during World War II secretly sent missionaries to the East in the footsteps of the German army. In consequence the Soviets executed scores of missionaries, especially Jesuits.

Between 1926 and 1928 the Mexican government hounded priests, monks, and nuns, and practically forbade the practice of religion. Priests and lay Catholics answered in kind: *Cristero* guerrillas blew up trains and killed soldiers. Beginning in 1936, when Eugenio Pacelli was the Vatican representative in Berlin, anarcho-syndicalists in Spain tortured and murdered priests, monks, and nuns, of whom about eight thousand perished during the Civil War. Official Mexican governmental policy toward the Church eventually mellowed, and in Spain, General Franco's counterrevolution wiped out not only the anarchists but also the Spanish Republic itself, some of whose leaders had also been hostile to the Church. Invoking the name of "Christ the King," Franco's nationalists carried out their own massacres, which in their brutality exceeded those of the anarchists and Communists; however, the killing of priests and nuns remained part of Spanish memory.

The best-known author of the new books on Pacelli's life and career is John Cornwell, whose *Hitler's Pope* has recently been a best seller. A British journalist and author, he has written a clear and informative book in which Pius XII comes very much alive. Cornwell is particularly knowledgeable about Catholic mysticism and religious dogma. The main direction of his argument, with which there is no reason to disagree, is that in his pursuit of Catholic unity, Pius made the Church more centralized, autocratic, and rigid. More controversially, Cornwell also argues that the Pope deliberately abandoned the Catholic political parties in Europe, which he saw as competitors for his absolute power, but which were willing to stand up to fascism and National Socialism.

The trouble with Cornwell's book lies with its sensationalism. Pius XII was not "Hitler's Pope"; the two hated each other, as Cornwell himself admits. In the autumn of 1939, he writes, Pius XII took some risks in supporting a German general's plot to overthrow Hitler. Nor is Cornwell's subtitle, "The Secret History of Pius XII," accurate. The author was able to look into a number of unpublished documents connected to the beatification process of Pius XII, but these documents reveal nothing of great importance. Most of Cornwell's information, including details on the Pope's participation in the plot against Hitler, comes from secondary sources. There is nothing wrong with this in a book of such a wide scope. What is objectionable is Cornwell's claim to have uncovered all sorts of dirty secrets that had caused him to go into "moral shock." Pius's actions are far too well known for that.

What is difficult to swallow is the author's self-assurance. He states, for instance, that in the summer of 1914, when Pacelli was a middle-level official in the Vatican foreign service, he was able to bring about a concordat protecting Serbia's Catholics. This, Cornwell writes, so angered Austria-Hungary, the traditional protector of the not-so-numerous Catholics in Serbia, as to make the war inevitable. In other words, Pacelli was responsible for the outbreak of World War I.

To bolster his claim, Cornwell quotes from the British writer Anthony Rhodes's *The Power of Rome in the Twentieth Century* (Franklin Watts, 1983). Yet he does not mention Rhodes's other statement, that "it is a Papal principle never to refuse a request for a Concordat" and that Pacelli acted in accord with Pope Pius X's instructions. The Austro-Hungarian leaders must have been furious over the Serbian concordat, but the list of their complaints against Serbia was long already. In the major Austrian histories of the period, I have found no mention of the Serbian concordat as having been an issue. It was the assassination of Archduke Francis Ferdinand at Sarajevo that gave the monarchy's leaders their long-awaited excuse to crush Serbia.

It is equally difficult to accept Cornwell's claim of Pacelli's early anti-Semitism. No doubt some of the Vatican publications, such as the Jesuits' *Civiltà Cattolica,* often published diatribes against Judaism, but Pacelli was not one of the contributors and there is little if any evidence of anti-Semitism on his part. Cornwell cites the "palm-frond incident" in 1917, when the Bavarian-Jewish community, wanting to celebrate the Feast of Tabernacles, requested that Pacelli, as papal nuncio, or ambassador, to Munich, obtain palm fronds from Italy, a country with which Germany was at war. Pacelli refused, yet, Cornwell writes, it "might have brought spiritual consolation to many thousands [of Jews]." This, in my view, proves nothing.

Nor do I find convincing Cornwell's second "proof" of Pacelli's anti-Semitism, namely his derogatory views, in the spring of 1919, of the Soviet Republic briefly established by radicals in Munich. In his letters to Rome, Pacelli wrote at length about the "lecherous demeanor and suggestive smiles" of some revolutionary women, who were "Jews like all the rest of them." His description of one of the revolutionary leaders was full of Jewish stereotyping. But then, most leaders of the Bavarian Soviet Republic were in fact Jews, and conservative German Jews found these rather childish and yet often brutal young intellectuals similarly unappealing.

We can be sure that Pacelli did not particularly care for Jews; nor did most other clergymen. Priests saw the Jews as Christ-killers or at least as the Chosen People who had proved deaf and blind to the teachings of Jesus of Nazareth. The clergy tended to feel that Jews were behind the Enlightenment, Freemasonry, rationalism, the French Revolution, liberalism, capitalism, democracy, socialism, communism, anarchism, radicalism, anticlericalism, secularism, materialism, evolutionary theory, and urban immorality: all mortal enemies of the Church and of Catholic teachings. But many priests who disliked the Jews for such reasons also became their brave protectors during the Holocaust; others, like Pius, did help the Jews but too little and too late; and still other priests, for example in Croatia, joined the ranks of the murderers. A few early expressions of anti-Judaic feelings prove little.

Cornwell charges Pacelli with love of luxury when, for instance, as the newly appointed papal nuncio to Munich, he transported sixty cases of embargoed food across neutral Switzerland during World War I. But Cornwell himself writes later that "Pacelli traveled tirelessly in Germany . . . bringing food and clothing to the starving 'of all religions' on behalf of the Holy See." So the sixty cases of groceries may not have been for Pacelli alone.

The scope of Michael Phayer's very valuable *The Catholic Church and the Holocaust, 1930–1965* (Bloomington: Indiana University Press, 2000) is obviously narrower than that of Cornwell's book, which deals with the papacy as whole. But Phayer, who teaches at the Jesuit-run Marquette University in Wisconsin, moves well beyond World War II. Highly critical of Pius XII, he pays much attention to the Vatican's active assistance to escaping war criminals, to Pius's efforts to promote clemency for war criminals, and to his refusal to confront anti-Semitism after the war. Phayer's book is based on a large number of German and American archival sources, printed documents, and memoirs and on a thorough reading of the eleven volumes of documents on the Holy See during World War II that the Vatican published between 1965 and 1967. He has written a fine and judicious book, which can be supplemented by Frank J. Coppa's *Controversial Concordats: The Vatican's Relations with Napoleon, Mussolini, and Hitler* (Washington DC: Catholic University of America Press, 1999). Coppa's work is a valuable compendium of essays on the three dictators' concordats with the Vatican, and it includes the texts of the concordats themselves.

In *The Hidden Encyclicals of Pius XI* (translated from the French by Steven Rendall, with an introduction by Gary Wills; New York: Harcourt Brace, 1997), George Passelecq and Bernard Suchecky discuss a major encyclical that Pius XII's predecessor, Pope Pius XI, planned to issue in 1939. It was to be a strong refutation of Nazi racial theories and the persecution of Jews. Pius XI, the Italian-born Achille Ratti, had issued a papal letter in 1931 arguing that fascism and Catholicism were incompatible; he also had spoken out against nationalism, racism, and totalitarianism. The draft on anti-Semitism was drawn up by three Jesuits—from the United States, Germany, and France. Clearly, the drafters of the document abhorred virtually everything connected with National

Socialism. Yet even they stated that the Jews were responsible for their tragedy because unlike the pagan peoples they were given the light but failed to see it. Pius XI died while the encyclical was in draft form, and Pius XII, on succeeding him, buried the draft in the archives. Garry Wills's introduction to this volume is enlightening; the fact that George Passelecq, a Benedictine monk in Belgium, and Bernard Suchecky, a specialist in contemporary Jewish studies, cooperated in publishing a book so critical of the papacy is a sign of the changes since Pius XII's time.

Finally, in their admirable *The Vatican and the Red Flag,* Jonathan Luxmoore and Jolanta Babiuch discuss the excruciating problems faced by the Vatican in trying to deal with Communist governments in Eastern Europe and particularly with their persecution of Catholic priests and laymen. Luxmoore writes on Church affairs in Eastern Europe for several British, mostly Catholic, journals, and his wife, Jolanta Babiuch, is a lecturer at Warsaw University. They start with what they call "the agonies of Pius XII" in confronting the mortal threat of Stalinism in the post–World War II period, and they carry their story up to the time of Karol Wojtyla, that is, John Paul II. The emphasis of their study, which is written more for specialists than the general public, is on Poland, where the Church dealt most successfully with its Communist enemies.

2

Eugenio Pacelli was born in 1876, in Rome, into a family of church lawyers. One of his brothers was to have an important part in negotiating the concordat with Mussolini in 1929. Eugenio was serious, studious, and intelligent, and he always wanted to be a priest. It would be helpful to know how he dealt with the problem of celibacy, but of this we know nothing. There was some gossip in Rome that the Pope and his housekeeper, a rather overbearing German nun, were lovers, but there is no evidence for this. In 1899 he was ordained a priest and was soon recruited into the elite Vatican diplomatic corps. He earlier participated in the drafting of a new Canon Law that regulated the life of the clergy and enforced even greater conformity and discipline. He never served as a parish priest.

In 1911 Pacelli became one of the more important members of the Vatican foreign service; in 1914 he negotiated the concordat with Serbia; in 1917 he was made an archbishop; and in the same year he was appointed papal nuncio to Bavaria. This was one of the Church's most important foreign posts, more than one-third of Germans being Roman Catholics, with a significant proportion of those in Bavaria. In the 1870s the "Center"—Germany's Catholic political party—the Catholic trade unions, and other Catholic groups had successfully withstood Bismarck's fierce anti-Catholic campaign. By World War I, Catholicism in Germany was thriving as perhaps never before. Pacelli himself learned to speak and write fluent German; he became the Vatican's foremost German expert, and he developed a great fondness for that country.

In 1929, while Pacelli was still in Germany, his superior, Pius XI, concluded a concordat with Mussolini who, even though an inveterate atheist, proved to be more friendly to the Church than had earlier liberal regimes. The Church was accorded a minuscule sovereign state and the right to organize religious life in Italy without much interference from government. Between 1870 and 1929 the popes had resided in buildings that legally belonged to Italy. In exchange for Vatican sovereignty, the Holy See gave up all claims to political activity and abandoned support of the once dynamic Catholic party.

The same spirit marked the concordat with the German Reich in 1933, which was negotiated by Pacelli himself. By then he had left Germany and been Cardinal Secretary of State, that is, the second most important person at the Holy See, for some three years. Most of the writers under review condemn the two concordats as a surrender to dictatorships. Yet defenders of the Vatican point out that the Vatican was weak; even though everyone knew that the agreements would be violated, the concordats were better than nothing in protecting the legitimacy of the Church and the rights of Catholics to worship under regimes that were explicitly hostile.

This defense seems convincing; it was most unlikely that, without the concordat, the German Center Party would have put up resistance to the Nazis. Well before Hitler's assumption of power the Center Party had begun to shift to the right, and Catholic voters threatened to defect to the National Socialists if the Center did not make its peace with Hitler. The few who disagreed with this, such as former chancellor Brüning and some Catholic youth groups, were quickly shunted aside without much, if any, protest by other German Catholics.

The concordat was often violated by Nazi denunciations of the Church, the closing of Catholic schools, the dissolution of Catholic associations, Hitler Jugend attacks on Catholic youth, and the imprisonment of scores of priests charged with sexual crimes or currency speculation. German bishops openly defended Catholic rights and objected to the Nazi proposal to eliminate the deformed and retarded, but with very few exceptions, the bishops did not speak up in defense of the persecuted Jews.

The Italian and German bishops were in a quandary. As Michael Phayer explains, with only a few convinced Fascists and National Socialists among them they were much less anti-Semitic than some of their Eastern European counterparts. But they still preferred the Fascist-Nazi regimes to what they saw as the only other possibilities: soulless Western materialism or Communist atheism, both of which, especially communism, threatened the very existence of the Church. The Fascists and National Socialists advocated the values of the traditional family and opposed divorce and abortion; they had many of the same enemies as the Church, and notwithstanding Pius XI's criticism of fascism, they seemed to want to build the kind of authoritarian, corporate state with a unifying social purpose that many of the bishops found desirable. In addition, there was the call of patriotism. In 1935 the Italian bishops supported Mussolini's war against Abyssinia, even though the Italian army openly boasted of its success in using gas against the local population, many of whom were Coptic Christians. In Germany, too, the bishops at first lined up behind Hitler's national program.

By the mid-1930s, however, the protests of the German bishops against the anti-Catholic propaganda and other practices of the Nazis had enthusiastic support from Pope Pius XI and much milder support from Cardinal Pacelli. In 1937 Pius XI issued the encyclical *Mit brennender Sorge* ("With Burning Concern"), which strongly condemned the deification of race and of the German people as well as the cult of the German state. The Nazi authorities tried to confiscate the encyclical, but it was successfully distributed among the faithful and was openly read from the pulpits. This again showed that, with regard to the Church, the Nazis were quite lenient, at least for the time being; such a development would have been inconceivable in the Soviet Union.

In 1938, as mentioned earlier, Pius XI gave orders for the drafting of his major encyclical against racism and anti-Semitism. It was to be entitled *Humani Generis Unitas*, "The Unity of the Human Race." But this straightforward and resolute man died early in 1939, and his successor, Pius XII, preferred diplomatic methods. In any case, he had long come to the conclusion that Soviet communism was the main enemy of the Church and that Germany ought to be regarded as being in the forefront of that struggle. He tried to prevent the outbreak of World War II, which he perceived as an unreasonable conflict between non-Communist powers. He never protested, not even in secret communications to the Germans, against the devastation of Catholic Poland, the beloved daughter of the Church, by the invading Wehrmacht. He remained silent when the Nazis moved against the Polish intelligentsia, shooting and torturing priests, professionals, politicians, and Catholic professors. As Michael Phayer has shown, the Nazis killed about 20 percent of the Polish clergy. Pius XII's silence in this matter remains more difficult to interpret than his extreme lateness in objecting to the persecution of the Jews.

How much did the Pope know about Nazi atrocities? Experts are divided on the question but it is clear that the Vatican was aware of the extensive killing of Poles and Jews. In Croatia specifically, the Vatican became aware, beginning in 1941, of the genocide of the Serbian Orthodox, Jewish, and Gypsy populations. The fact that Zagreb was close to Italy and that the Croatian Ustasha leaders, at least pretending to be devout Catholics, were received in the Vatican and were visited by Vatican dignitaries both support this assumption. Additionally, the Italian occupation forces that opposed the Croatian fascists and protected the Jews reported regularly on the Ustasha massacres, as did, incidentally, the local SS, which disliked the troubles caused by the Croats with their murderous campaigns.

Some Croatian bishops (though not Archbishop Stepinac of Zagreb) called openly for the forced conversion of the Orthodox. Some Franciscan monks beat, tortured, and machine-gunned their Serbian victims. As Michael Phayer, along with many other authors, demonstrates, the Vatican was well informed about what was happening in Croatia, yet it did nothing. Some have claimed, without documentary evidence, that for the Pope the campaign in Croatia meant the first step toward the reconversion of the Eastern schismatics. If this is true, it would only serve to damn him.

The attitude of the Pope toward the Holocaust remains a controversial issue, but overall, the Pope's behavior in this respect can be deemed less reprehensible than in respect to the Polish Catholics and the Orthodox believers in Croatia. Even though he was very late in reacting, the Pope did do something on behalf of the Jews. All claims to the contrary, he sometimes took the initiative in helping them, and according to statements by a variety of Catholic officials, at many other times he approved the action of the Catholic saviors of Jews.[2]

To be sure, Pius's behavior regarding the Holocaust was often deplorable. In October 1943, for instance, the German SS prepared to deport the Jews of Rome. Jews were at the time already in hiding in private homes, monasteries, and convents. But over a thousand were marched away "under his very windows," to use the title of a book to be published by Susan Zuccotti, a specialist on the Holocaust in Italy.[3] The Pope had been alerted to what was happening, especially by German diplomats to the Holy See who feared that many Italians, driven by indignation at the treatment of the Jews, would revolt. Yet Pius did nothing. He sent no warning messages to the Jewish community, messages that, unlike messages from German diplomats, would surely have been believed; nor did he try to address the SS command. One uncharitable explanation for his behavior is that he did not wish to alienate the Germans, whose presence he desired in Rome as long as possible in order to prevent a Communist-Partisan takeover. A more charitable explanation is that by not protesting the deportation of a thousand or so Roman Jews, he helped to save the six or seven thousand others. He had long since learned, he claimed later, that an open confrontation would only harm the persecuted all the more.

The Pope's defenders often refer to the example of the Netherlands, where both Catholic and Protestant churches were trying to save the lives of at least the Jewish converts. This was promised to them by the German High Commissioner in exchange for their agreement to remain silent about the Jewish persecution generally. The Protestant churches respected the deal and Protestant Jews were spared. However, the Archbishop of Utrecht openly condemned the persecution of the Jews, whereupon the Catholic Jews were deported. Apparently, the Pope believed that forty thousand Catholic Jews were killed as a consequence of the Archbishop's pastoral letter. But there were not forty thousand converts in the Netherlands; rather, it seems that only about one or two hundred Catholic Jews were arrested.[4] It is impossible to tell whether the Pope was in fact moved by what happened in the Netherlands—or what he believed had happened—or whether he used it as an excuse for his silence.

The question is often raised about what exactly the Pope could have done, for instance, in the case of the Roman Jews. Cornwell admits: "Pacelli had only limited scope for action. . . . [His] first priority was to maintain his limited independence." This is certainly true; still, it is hard not to feel that the Pope could have gone to the railroad station where the Jews were waiting, crammed in boxcars. If he had solemnly appeared at the station, in full regalia and with some of his colorful retinue, and if he had indicated that he was against deportation, he might have caused the release of the 1,023 Jews, mostly women and children; this seems possible since some 236 had already been released by the SS for various reasons. At the very least, the news of such an unheard-of gesture would have spread in Europe, and Catholics everywhere might have had second thoughts about what their governments and they themselves were doing. Instead, the 1,023 Jews were sent to Auschwitz. Of those, according to Zuccotti, only fifteen came back after the war.

Zuccotti and other historians have shown that there is no evidence of the Pope's having given any direct instructions to the Italian clergy regarding the defense of the Jews. On the other hand, there is plenty of impressive evidence of the cooperation that took place between Italian-Jewish organizations and local archbishops, bishops, priests, and nuns, all of whom seem to have worked out their own methods of protecting the Jews. The result was the survival of 83 percent of the Italian Jews.

While the Pope was unwilling to intervene with the Nazis on behalf of the Jews, he had no such hesitation with regard to the minor Eastern European governments. He directly appealed to the anti-Semitic Monsignor Tiso, who was the president of Slovakia, and he successfully ordered the intensely anti-Semitic Slovak bishops to adopt measures first to try to save Jewish converts and then all Slovak Jews. Moreover, Pius XII was also the first head of state to protest against the extensive deportation of Hungarian Jews between May and July 1944. It is true that the Pope's cable on behalf of the Jews to Admiral Horthy and the mostly Catholic members of the Hungarian government was written after most Hungarian Jews in the countryside had already been deported and after the Allies had occupied Rome. But other statesmen, such as the King of Sweden and President Roosevelt, were even slower in protesting. Duly impressed both by the protests and by the Allied landing in Normandy, Horthy forbade further deportations. In the end, about 40 percent of the Hungarian Jews survived.

Most of the apostolic nuncios, as well as many priests, under German occupation were active on behalf of the Jews. In Budapest, for example, Monsignor Angelo Rotta again and again addressed protests to the Hungarian government on behalf of the Jews, and he distributed to them forged Vatican passports and letters of protection. Even if he did not have written instructions, Rotta must have acted in a way he thought the Vatican wanted him to act.

Michael Phayer emphasizes the heroism of many nuns and Catholic lay women. Just one example: the Hungarian nun Margit Slachta, who was the mother superior of the Social Mission Society, protested the mistreatment of Hungarian Jews as early as 1941. A year later she traveled to Slovakia from where she described the treatment of Jews as hellish and satanic. She tried to awaken the generally indifferent or anti-Semitic Hungarian bishops to the danger of the Slovak Holocaust spilling over into Hungary, and she personally gave documents to Pius XII on the destruction of Jews in Poland and Slovakia.

In 1944, after the Holocaust had spread to Hungary, she and her order of "Grey Sisters" either hid or gave forged papers to thousands of Jews. Thugs from the fascist Arrow Cross militia shot a member of her order, as well as the Jews the sister had been protecting, and threw their bodies in the Danube. After the war, Margit Slachta led a Catholic women's party that was ridiculed and viciously slandered in the left-wing press. In the 1947 national elections, votes for her party, and for all anti-Communist parties, were falsified at the orders of Minister of Interior László Rajk, a fanatical Communist later executed as an alleged Titoist agent. In 1949 Slachta emigrated to Buffalo, where she died in 1974 at the age of ninety. Today she is largely forgotten even in Hungary.[5]

After World War II and again in 1958, at the time of Pius XII's death, Jewish organizations, political leaders, and ordinary people inundated the Vatican with letters of thanks for Catholic efforts on behalf of Jews. The respected Israeli historian and religious thinker Pinchas E. Lapide went so far as to claim in his *The Last Three Popes and the Jews* (London: Souvenir Press, 1967) that "the Catholic Church, under the Pontificate of Pius XII was instrumental in saving at least 700,000, but probably as many as 860,000, Jews."[6] Since the publication of Lapide's book, his figure of 860,000 has been used by practically every defender of Pius XII, and it has come in handy to Patrick Buchanan in his recent political campaigns. Lapide did not give any factual basis for his estimates, but he is right in accusing other international institutions of even more foot-dragging; he justly condemns the International Red Cross in Geneva for having remained silent about the treatment of Jews in concentration camps.[7]

By November 1944, when the Hungarian Jews suffered a second wave of persecution, Rome had long been under Allied rule. For the papacy this only meant a change of overlords. Before the arrival of the Americans, the Pope's main preoccupations were that the Eternal City not be bombed, that no colored troops enter the city, and that the Communist Partisans not be allowed to take over. In general, he was not to be disappointed.

Now, however, there began one of the most shameful episodes in the history of the Vatican: its systematic assistance to Nazi war criminals enabling them to escape, mostly to Juan and Eva Perón's Argentina. This episode, too, has been the subject of many books, films, and television shows, and a great deal of mythmaking. Phayer and Cornwell show clearly that important prelates at the Vatican were involved in a project that allowed hundreds of mass murderers to escape the gallows, including Dr. Josef Mengele, Adolf Eichmann, the Croat Führer Ante Pavelić, and Franz Stangl, the Austrian commander of the Treblinka death camp. The partial involvement of the U.S. and other Allied secret services in this matter seems undeniable. (Some historians even claim that, indirectly, the Soviets plotted the escapes—for what reason remains unclear.)[8] In any case, the infamous Rat Line, the "underground railroad" of the war criminals, often led through buildings under Vatican protection. Furthermore, money, tickets, and forged documents were provided by prelates at the Holy See.

How much did the Pope know about the Rat Line? The sources are as fuzzy on the subject as they are on the Pope's familiarity with the actions undertaken by his underlings on behalf of the Jews. I would argue that Pius XII approved of both undertakings: saving innocent Jews and saving war criminals. The

Pope and the German bishops also campaigned assiduously for the release of war criminals imprisoned in Germany. All this, Michael Phayer and others argue, was part of the Vatican's attempt to muster all available forces, however tainted, for the battle against communism. The Western Allies rather quickly came to share this papal point of view.

Pius XII must have been the first cold warrior. In contrast to his ambivalence during the Nazi years, he now freely used his chief weapon, excommunication. Anyone joining the Communist Party, or even working with Communists, was automatically under interdict and would, according to the edict, surely land in Hell unless able to show genuine repentance. In Italy the American government and the Vatican coordinated efforts to prevent a Communist victory in the 1948 elections. In Eastern Europe, as Luxmoore and Babiuch show in *The Vatican and the Red Flag,* papal policy was much less successful and the edict was not followed by most of the Eastern European clergy. Under Cardinal Stefan Wyszynski the Polish Church broke with papal policies in order to arrive at a modus vivendi with the Stalinist regime in Poland without, however, surrendering to it. Other Church leaders in Eastern Europe were less skillful or enjoyed less popular support. Hungarian, Czechoslovak, and other clergy went to prison, and some were executed. Wyszynski himself served time in prison. Others surrendered. Some of the worst fellow travelers were the so-called Peace Priests and like-minded Catholic lay intellectuals who followed the regime's orders. As under the Nazis, the Protestant churches proved even more subservient than the Catholic.

Life under communism gradually and fitfully began to change, starting with the East German and Polish disturbances of 1953 and continuing with the Hungarian uprising in 1956, the Prague Spring in 1968, and the Polish unrest of the 1970s. Meanwhile, in the years between 1958 and 1963, Pope John XXIII attempted to reform, modernize, and decentralize the Church. Among many other things, he proclaimed that present-day Jews were innocent of the killing of Jesus, and he became less rigid in papal policy toward the Communist regimes.

The election of the Polish cardinal Karol Wojtyla as Pope John Paul II in 1978 presented a tremendous problem to the Communist leadership. Unable to mobilize the masses themselves, they had to watch helplessly as John Paul spoke to millions of the faithful, who took the occasion of his visit to Poland to demonstrate their opposition to communism. Thus, finally, without a single military division, the Pope did much to defeat the Soviet system.

It is impossible to compare the situation in Poland in the 1970s with that in Rome in, let us say, 1943. In the 1970s there was no war; the Soviets would have run a large risk if they had intervened militarily, and the Eastern European Communists had long since lost any sympathy either for Marxist ideology or for Communist economics. In 1943 the Holy See was surrounded by German soldiers; the Nazi leaders were fanatics and millions of Germans were ready to die for their cause. This explains much of Pius XII's behavior during and immediately after the war, but it does not explain everything.

Pius XII died in 1958 at the age of eighty-two, plagued by many illnesses, of which incessant hiccuping must have been the most excruciating. He was not an evil man. In fact, his behavior must be judged to have been a little better than that of millions upon millions of other Europeans who were even more indifferent toward their Jewish fellow citizens and other victims of the German and Soviet tyrannies. But then Eugenio Pacelli was the Pope, and while little was expected of the others, much was expected of him. Many of his medieval predecessors who had stood up to emperors and kings had thereby helped to preserve a duality of power that was instrumental in the development of Western civilization.

True, that duality had long been eroded by Vatican obscurantism, the rise of nationalism, and the modern state. But could not this Pope have made a single, historic public gesture? If he had, he would likely have saved more Jews, Poles, Serbs, and others than he did through his diplomatic skills. Unfortunately, he proved weak and fallible. He demonstrated no personal courage; he gave no example of the Imitatio Christi, which is what the world expects from the head of a church that traces its authority back to the apostles. Pope John Paul II's current attempt to make Pacelli a saint must be judged a very strange undertaking indeed.

THE BRITISH AND THE AMERICANS

Can it be said that the United States and Great Britain were responsible, at least in part or indirectly, for the Holocaust? Did Allied indifference encourage the Nazis to proceed with their murderous plan? Why did the West not ransom the European Jews? These and related issues have been debated for decades, and the arguments of the critics have been reinforced by newly uncovered documents showing the unconcern, even the anti-Semitism, of certain British and American officials. Still, many critics have been carried too far by their anger. Witness such categorical indictments as those in Arthur Morse's *While Six Million Died: A Chronicle of American Apathy* (New York: Random House, 1968); Monty Penkower's *The Jews Were Expendable: Free World Diplomacy and the Holocaust* (Urbana: University of Illinois Press, 1983); and David S. Wyman's *The Abandonment of the Jews: America and the Holocaust, 1941–1945* (New York: Pantheon, 1985), all of which give away their message in their titles and make the truth seem simple.

These indictments are certainly correct in many respects, but they bespeak a zeal that is sharply critical of nearly every aspect of American and British policy. Driven by righteous indignation, some historians assert that the sinking of the American passenger ship *Lusitania* during World War I was more the fault of Winston Churchill, then First Lord of the Admiralty, than of the German submarine commander who torpedoed the boat or of the German High Command, which joyously celebrated the deed. (Revisionist historians assert that Churchill provoked the sinking of the *Lusitania* in order to drag the United

---

This review of Richard Breitman's *What the Nazis Planned, What the British and Americans Knew* (New York: Hill and Wang, 1998) appeared in the February 15, 1999, issue of the *New Republic*. The editors entitled the article, "Horror and Hindsight."

States into the war.) The aerial bombardment of Germany during World War II, which contributed powerfully to the defeat of the Nazis, has been repeatedly described as a terrible British and American crime, as has the devastation of Japan by conventional and atomic bombs. The U.S. Fifteenth Air Force, which was stationed in southern Italy during the last one and a half years of the war, has been a particular target of criticism: its commanders have been found guilty of refusing to save Jewish lives by not precision bombing the gas chambers in Auschwitz or the railway lines leading to the death camp. As for the cold war, it is often presented as solely the result of American imperialist machinations, with little reference to the Soviet takeover of Eastern Europe.

I disagree with some of the details, and even with one or two of the major contentions, in Richard Breitman's masterful account of British and American behavior during the war. However, his work is neither sensationalist nor dogmatic. Breitman is in the enviable position of having gained first access to some newly uncovered documents, and he has made good use of those sources, presenting a balanced and often novel account. The last sentences in his book regarding Allied responsibility for the horrors of the Final Solution are worded cautiously: "[T]he record generally shows that in 1942 and 1943 the U.S. government . . . did not try to do what might have worked. This makes it very difficult, long, long after the fact, to demonstrate that saving more Jews had been impossible."

What might have worked on behalf of European Jewry, says Breitman, would have been the creation much earlier of the U.S. War Refugee Board, which did not come into existence until January 1944. This organization succeeded, in Breitman's judgment, in preserving a significant number of Jewish lives through such stratagems as sending citizens of neutral countries, who were actually secret representatives of the board, to Eastern Europe. Their assignment was to try to help the local Jews, an endeavor in which at least one agent, the Swede Raoul Wallenberg operating in Hungary, was quite successful.

Breitman takes his time in leading the reader to the fundamental dilemma addressed by his book, namely, what more could the British and the Americans have done? The first section of the book has only a tenuous connection with the Anglo-Americans; instead, it rehearses Germany's road to the Holocaust on the basis of newly opened German and British records. Breitman argues that such relatively unknown Nazis as the Gestapo boss Kurt Daluege, and SS General Erich von dem Bach-Zelewski, the future Nuremberg witness for the prosecution who was, in the eyes of that tribunal, almost simpatico, and SS General Karl Wolff, who early in May 1945 achieved fame for surrendering the German army in Italy to the Allies, played much greater roles in the Holocaust than has been hitherto assumed. Since these men were engaged in 1939 in preparing the destruction of the Polish political elite (a program powerfully assisted by the allied Soviet forces in their won occupation zone), they temporarily soft-pedaled the Jewish question. In 1941, however, it was the turn of the Jews.

As the German tanks rolled toward Moscow, SS *Einsatzgruppen* and battalions of the infamous Order Police, the *Ordnungspolizei,* began the program of systematic annihilation. At this point, Breitman disagrees with Daniel Goldhagen's controversial thesis that the Order Police, made up mainly of middle-aged civilians, were among the most willing of Germany's many millions of willing executioners. In the battalions that he examined, Breitman reports, it was not so easy to say no. Orders had to be followed, though it is true that there is no evidence of anyone having been punished for refusing to kill. In any case, there was no shortage of volunteers, nor was there any lack of approval and active assistance from the regular army.

The official justification for the massacres, as Breitman shows, was that the Jews were looters, and that, in accordance with the usages of war (*nach Kriegsgebrauch*), looters were to be shot. I wonder whether any German policeman believed such nonsense. And anti-Semitism was not, of course, a German monopoly: in the East volunteer murderers from every nationality were easy to find.

As Breitman and others have demonstrated, the planning of the Final Solution began much earlier than the Nazis' notorious Wannsee conference in January 1942. Always ready to translate Hitler's *Mein Kampf* into reality, Heinrich Himmler concocted the idea of the "unmixing" (*Entmischung*) of the Europeans, which stood for the elimination of the Jews and millions of Slavs. Unfortunately, Hitler's most radical statements regarding the "Jewish menace" were missing from *Mein Kampf*'s English editions. This, among many other things, delayed the realization in the West of what Hitler and his companions intended to do.

Yet tendentious translation of *Mein Kampf* was only one of many reasons why the Allies did not protest more vigorously and did not admit more refugees. There was, first, the Western governments' fear of public reaction at home. Both American and British popular anti-Semitism were at their peak in the late 1930s. In Depression-ridden America, moreover, German-Jewish immigrants were resented as unwanted competitors, while East European Jews were perceived, even by many Western Jews, as an unappealing group.

Also, the Allies were reluctant to return to the discredited heavy-handed attacks on German atrocities that had characterized Western propaganda in the First World War. The myth of the barbarous German "Hun" had been vigorously repudiated in the interwar years. (Interestingly, recent findings show that the German soldiers did indeed behave quite barbarously in occupied Belgium and northern France, at least during the first weeks of World War I.) Skepticism about news originating from Polish and Jewish sources helps to explain why reports of the Holocaust met with so much disbelief.

To all these inhibitions, Breitman argues, there must be added the reluctance of the Western leaders to treat the Jews as a separate group for fear of seeming to agree with Nazi racial doctrine. Both Roosevelt and Churchill worried about creating the impression that they were fighting a "Jewish war." There was also concern about German retaliation against Allied prisoners of war. Finally, the British objected strenuously to the immigration of masses of Jewish refugees into Palestine, for fear that it would upset the extremely precarious balance between the British authorities, the Arabs, and the Jewish settlers. As Breitman notes, the Romanian threat to release seventy thousand Jews in 1943 was evaluated in the Foreign Office as a "frightful prospect."

Some of the Allied objections to massive immigration were unreasonable only with the wisdom of historical hindsight. But was anti-Semitism not also at work here? Of course it was. Breitman cites, among other damning documents, the private secretary of Foreign Secretary Anthony Eden, who noted in April 1943 that Eden "loves Arabs and hates Jews." Others in the British Foreign Office and the State Department were no better. And yet the Jew-hatred of officials and bureaucrats cannot explain everything. Even without the presence of these men, Allied policy regarding immigration would not have changed much. This was, after all, a period of worldwide callousness and hostility toward refugees. The United States was actually not the worst culprit. As the writers in FDR and the Holocaust (edited by Verne W. Newton; New York: St Martin's Press, 1996) show, the United States admitted twice as many Jewish refugees (two hundred thousand out of a total of three hundred thousand) as the rest of the world put together. The essays appearing in FDR and the Holocaust attempt to reject, in part emotionally, in part with hard evidence, many of the charges against President Roosevelt. They protest the widespread view that Roosevelt was even more "guilty" than Churchill.

How much did the Anglo-Americans know about the Holocaust? Breitman's answer is quite categorical: they knew quite a lot, and early. But the diffusion of this knowledge was severely limited by the requirements of war. British decoders at Bletchley Park, a justly famous outfit, penetrated the German, Soviet, Japanese, Spanish, Portuguese, and American codes during the war. Having received a duplicate of the German Enigma encoding machine from Polish counterintelligence in 1939, the British developed their celebrated Ultra system, which decrypted some of the most secret German messages, including reports in 1941 of the killing of thousands of Jews in Eastern Europe.

In accordance with the general trend of not seeing the Jews as a special Nazi target, however, while at the same time exalting the Soviet people, Churchill himself interpreted these killings as targeted at "Russian patriots." Soon thereafter he was given more precise figures on the events in the East by Paul Thümmel, a German *Abwehr* (military intelligence) official who worked secretly for the Czechoslovak government-in-exile. Breitman concludes, from what Thümmel told Churchill, that "almost three months before the start of operations in the first extermination camp and more than four months before the Wannsee Conference, British intelligence had a basic grasp of Nazi intentions toward Jews in the Soviet territories."

But intentions are not everything, and in any case British decoding had a great drawback: so as not to give away their secret, Britain's leaders rarely dared to act on their information. Concern for the fate of the Jews in occupied Eastern Europe could not possibly have been a high priority in the Allied camp, especially in 1941 and 1942 when the outcome of the war was still in doubt and when Britain was fighting for survival. Since there was not much that British diplomacy or the military could do at that time, Bletchley Park transmitted fewer and fewer decoded messages about the killings to Churchill. Breitman believes—rightly, in my opinion—that much more publicity about Nazi crimes, especially about crimes committed by the Order Police (which Bletchley Park was able to decode with relative ease), might have persuaded some officials in occupied Europe that the Jews were deported not for labor but for death. Fearing retaliation, these officials might have moderated their zeal to do the Germans' handiwork.

Since they allowed millions of Soviet POWs to die, the German armed forces needed Jewish laborers. In 1943 systematic mass extermination more or less ceased at Treblinka and other death camps, and selection became the rule in such places as Auschwitz. The young and able-bodied were put to work, often only to be killed later; the rest were gassed and burned without anyone bothering to register their names and numbers. British intelligence tracked the changing population in Auschwitz from decoded SS reports, but it was ignorant of the gas chambers.

More information about the factory-type massacres arrived with brave Polish agents such as Tadeusz Chciuk-Celt, who parachuted twice into Poland and in the fall of 1942 sent messages from Budapest about mass executions at Auschwitz. As Breitman shows, both the Polish underground Directorate of Civilian Resistance and the Polish government-in-exile reported regularly on the ovens of Auschwitz. Understandably, the Polish underground also wanted the West to know of the systematic depopulation by the Nazis of such provinces as Bialystok and Lublin. The inhabitants there, mostly peasants, were gassed, deported to Germany, or sold to the new German settlers.

There were other valuable informants as well, such as the German businessman Eduard Schulte, whose reports on the Final Solution reached the Allied authorities via Geneva late in 1942 but were met with disbelief. And there was the Polish underground fighter Jan Karski, later celebrated in the film *Shoah*, who crisscrossed Nazi Europe more than once and late in the autumn of 1942 landed in England with the mission to report on the Nazi attempt to kill all the Jews. Among other things, Karski brought an incriminating microfilm concealed in a key. He met with Churchill, Roosevelt, and other politicians, but he was not believed even by many Jews, including Felix Frankfurter. But again, one must repeat, there was not much that the British and the Americans could have undertaken at the time of their own greatest national emergency.

A joint Allied Declaration, issued in December 1942, denounced the murders and threatened retribution. According to Breitman, the driving force behind the declaration was the Polish exile government. The Declaration was read several times, but not often enough, on BBC Radio. In the opinion of the BBC leaders, this was not what most Europeans wanted to hear, a contention that may have been correct. But Breitman believes that the Declaration nonetheless saved many lives by drawing attention to Nazi crimes. Curiously, one part of public opinion held that publicity about the mass murder would only increase Nazi fury; but I agree with Breitman that, beginning in 1943, many officials in Europe had second thoughts regarding the outcome of the war. Thus even the infrequent warnings issued by the BBC caused some of them to overlook German orders regarding the Jews.

Things began to change following the Allied invasion of southern Italy in September 1943 and the establishment of American air bases there. It is at this point that the criticism of some Holocaust historians becomes quite unreasonable. The critics claim that the bombing of the railway lines and of the gas chambers at Auschwitz could have been undertaken but that it was not undertaken because of the callousness of the military and political leadership of the United States. There were indeed some callous officials, notably Assistant Secretary of War John J. McCloy; I have never understood this argument, not even after reading Breitman's work, which cautiously supports this criticism of American policy.

The obstacles to a bombing attack were overwhelming. Jewish leadership in the United States was profoundly divided over the question of whether the camps should be bombed. No American general would have consented to killing Jews in the camps in order to prevent the killing of other Jews. The Germans may have drawn some propaganda advantage from the affair by claiming that it was the Anglo-Americans who were murdering Jews.

But let us assume that such raids would have been successful and that only a few inmates of the camps would have been killed, even though some barracks were only a few hundred yards away from the gas chambers. And let us assume further that many inmates would have managed to escape. Where would they have gone without any knowledge of the Polish language (by then most Polish Jews were dead), emaciated and dressed in prison garb? In Poland, the penalty for hiding Jews was the execution of the host and his entire family. And even if all the gas chambers and crematoria were destroyed, experience had already demonstrated to the Allies that even greater complexes could become functional again in just a matter of weeks. (In August 1943 the U.S. Army Air Force sacrificed over five hundred airmen and fifty-four bombers in an attempt to smash the vast Romanian oil refineries in Ploesti, which were vital to Germany. Despite horrifying losses, the raids destroyed nearly half of Ploesti's total capacity; within weeks, however, the refineries were producing at a higher rate than before the raid.) Moreover, the Germans would have been able to fall back on their time-honored method of shooting their victims. And if the rail lines had been bombed? The inmates in the cattle cars and those at the departure points would have been allowed to die of thirst, of the heat, or of the cold while the lines were being repaired.

The U.S. air force was fighting a war. Bombing a concentration camp could not have been a high military priority. The Allies had scarce information on the precise location of the gas chambers, even after four Slovak-Jewish inmates escaped from the camp in the spring of 1944, two of whom provided a description of the camp. Their report reached the West in July 1944, three months before the Germans dismantled the gas chambers at Auschwitz. By July, all the major transports had been gassed.

While the British had practiced pinpoint precision bombing, moreover, the Americans had not. The British used their best trained crews, after a long and arduous preparation, to raid such places as the Gestapo headquarters at Amiens in France and at Aarhus and Copenhagen in Denmark. Some of the raids were eminently successful, meaning that Gestapo personnel and papers were destroyed and the political prisoners in the Gestapo headquarters were able to escape. Unfortunately, many among the imprisoned resisters who had not been killed by the bombs were soon recaptured and shot. The aerial attacks on the special targets were prepared in coordination with local resistance and with the agents of the Special Operations Executive who had been parachuted into occupied Europe. The British pilots were provided with accurate maps and a precise description of the target. None of this was available for a raid on Auschwitz.

Moreover, there was "collateral damage" even in the case of precision bombings. In Copenhagen where, on March 21, 1945, waves of British Mosquitos came in, skimming the rooftops, one plane struck a tall light pole and crashed into a Catholic school for children. Pilots in the following waves mistook the burning building for the Gestapo headquarters and leveled it with bombs. Within a few minutes, eighty-six Danish children and seventeen adults were dead. In *FDR and the Holocaust*, James Kitchens reports that an American bomber raid on August 24, 1944, against a V-2 guidance works and an armament factory adjoining Buchenwald concentration camp at Weimar caused the death of 315 prisoners. This, despite precise intelligence.

Kitchens also demonstrates that middle-range bombers could not easily have reached Auschwitz, which was 620 miles away from the bomber base in Foggia. Heavy bombers could have done the job, but at the cost of smashing everybody and everything. As had been proven again and again, bomber crews flying at a very high altitude often dropped their cargo many miles away from the target; sometimes not more than 5 percent of the bombs hit the target area. What would have been achieved, then, by raids on the two major camps in Auschwitz, where, in addition to Jews, there were Poles, Gypsies, Soviet POWs, German political prisoners, German "asocials," and so on, and even British POWs?

Toward the end of this book Breitman discusses the complex and controversial issues surrounding Western efforts to save the Hungarian Jews, the vast majority of whom were still alive in the spring of 1944. He credits Raoul Wallenberg, the Swiss Consul Karl Lutz, and other neutral representatives in Budapest with having saved the lives in the winter of 1944–1945 of more than one hundred thousand Hungarian Jews.

Certainly many Hungarian Jews survived, at least 40 percent of the 825,000 who had qualified as Jews before the German army marched into Hungary on March 19, 1944, precisely in order to solve the "Jewish question" there. But the partial survival of the Jewish forced laborers under Hungarian army command and the partial survival of the Jews in Budapest—as opposed to the Jews of the countryside, who had already been sent to Auschwitz—was owed to more important factors than the extraordinary efforts of foreign diplomats. This is not to belittle the noble achievements of Wallenberg who, after helping the Jews, perished in Soviet captivity; even if the lives he managed to save should be numbered, realistically, at a few thousand, this must still be counted as a significant achievement for the Swedish humanitarian and the U.S. War Refugee Board.

But the historical picture was complicated. Those other fortunate factors included the decision of Regent Miklós Horthy to forbid the deportations early in July 1944, thereby preserving the lives of the Budapest Jews, and the decision of the army high command, hitherto among the most ferocious of anti-Semites, not to surrender its Jewish forced laborers to Eichmann and his colleagues in May–June 1944. Thousands of Jews also found refuge in monasteries, cloisters, and the homes of Christian families. Finally, the Hungarian fascist Arrow Cross regime, which the Germans had put in power in October 1944, set up and operated a ghetto in Budapest. Many of these Jews were killed by Arrow Cross thugs, while others died of starvation, yet the great majority of the ghetto inmates survived: they were freed by the Red Army in January 1945. No doubt the Arrow Cross's nonsensical desire to gain international recognition at this final stage of the war played a role in their decision to spare lives.

Did the Allies know? Yes, a great deal of information was available to them. Still, not all received the facts, not even in the highest political and military circles, and even fewer believed them. Telford Taylor, one of the chief prosecutors at the Nuremberg trials, wrote in his memoirs that he learned about the Holocaust late in 1945, in Nuremberg. Yet Taylor was attached to Bletchley Park during the final years of the war.

It is certainly true that those in the know did not undertake much to help the Jews. This was in large part because there was not much that could be done. Still, it is also certainly true that more active radio and leaflet propaganda, combined with very concrete threats, might have helped. Here, however, the Allies, whether Americans, British, or Soviets, fell prey to their own wartime propaganda, which insisted on characterizing all those deported, arrested, or shot, Jews or not Jews, simply as patriots. It was extremely difficult, consequently, to single out the Jews for special consideration. The Allies also sensed that many people in Nazi-occupied Europe, even some of those ferociously opposed to the German occupation, would not mind if the Jews, or at least the foreign Jews, were to disappear from their midst. In this respect, at least, there was little difference between these Europeans and some Allied officials. The former wanted fewer Jews in their countries, the latter did not want more Jews in their countries. The killings would have gone on in any case; however, it was the moral eclipse of the outside world that completed the tragedy.

NOTES

Who Were the National Socialists?
1. On all this, see especially Sarah Gordon, *Hitler, Germans, and the "Jewish Question"* (Princeton NJ: Princeton University Press, 1984), 119 and 300. All figures regarding German-Jewish survivors are merely rough estimates. On this, see Gerald Reitlinger, *The Final Solution: The Attempt to Exterminate the Jews of Europe, 1939–1945* (New York: Barnes, 1961), 491–92, and Lucy S. Dawidowicz, *The War Against the Jews, 1933–1945* (Toronto: Bantam Books, 1976), 506.

Who Were the Fascists?
1. Hamilton notes, for example, that the vote for Hitler among passengers on five German ocean liners in the July 1932 parliamentary elections was above the national average. But to arrive at this figure he assumes that the ordinary seamen voted for the Social Democrats or Communists. This may be so but then it is hard to understand why the people on the *Tacoma* and the *General Artigas,* freighters with only a few passengers, respectively voted 62.3 percent and 57.1 percent for the Nazis.

Perpetrators
1. The American historian Bruce F. Pauley reminds us in his important work *From Prejudice to Persecution: A History of Austrian Anti-Semitism* (Chapel Hill: University of North Carolina Press, 1992), xviii, that the U.S. laws passed in the 1920s to restrict immigration were aimed to a large extent at the Jews from Eastern Europe. These laws and the many American state laws forbidding racial intermarriage were closely watched and applauded by Austrian anti-Semites. Public opinion polls conducted in the United States between 1938 and 1942 revealed that only one-third of the population would have opposed anti-Semitic legislation if the government had proposed it. Between July 1938 and May 1939, the worst period of open anti-Jewish excesses in Nazi Germany, from 66 to 77 percent of the American public was opposed to raising the immigration quota to help Jewish refugees, even children. Pauley quotes, on the same page, from a work, published in 1935, by a great scholar of anti-Semitism, Count Richard Coudenhove-Calergi:

"[T]he overwhelming majority of non-Jewish Europeans today are more or less anti-Semitically disposed."

2. For National Socialist fanaticism, murderous activities, and postwar self-acquittal of the German regular army from generals down to ordinary soldiers, read Omer Bartov's devastating but scholarly indictment: *Hitler's Army: Soldiers, Nazis, and War in the Third Reich* (New York: Oxford University Press, 1991).

3. Bruce Pauley writes in *From Prejudice to Persecution,* 298, that five thousand Jewish "U-boats" or "submarines" survived in Berlin, but only seven hundred in Vienna, a city that, before the war, had housed considerably more Jews. Even if we take into consideration the unreliability of all statistical data on annihilation and survival and the differing conditions in the two cities, we have no reason to doubt that a Jew in hiding was more likely to find assistance among the notoriously cynical Berliners than among the Viennese.

In Disguise

1. Other works by Nechama Tec, both highly recommended, are *Dry Tears: The Story of a Lost Childhood* (New York: Oxford University Press, 1984) and *When Light Pierced the Darkness: Christian Rescue of Jews in Nazi-Occupied Poland* (New York: Oxford University Press, 1986).

2. There is nothing surprising about Tec's—or was it Oswald Rufeisen's?—mistranslation of Papa Rufeisen's military rank. Many Jews of Central or East Central European origin cherish the memory of an ancestor who served under Francis Joseph, the greatest friend the Jews ever had. It is only natural that the military rank of such a notable forefather inevitably rises with the passage of time. After all, both captains and buck sergeants wore three stars on the collars of their uniform. Who today can tell from faded old photographs the difference between gold stars and white stars?

The Incomprehensible Holocaust

1. Philip Lopate, "Resistance to Holocaust," *Tikkun* 4, no. 3 (May/June 1989): 56.

2. See Pierre Vidal-Naquet, "Theses on Revisionism," in François Furet, *Unanswered Questions: Nazi Germany and the Genocide of the Jews* (New York: Schocken, 1989), 304–19.

3. Translated from the Italian by Stuart Woolf (New York: Macmillan, 1988).

4. Nechama Tec estimates, in *When Light Pierced the Darkness: Christian Rescue of Jews in Nazi-Occupied Poland* (New York: Oxford University Press, 1986), 11, that between fifty thousand and one hundred thousand Jews survived the war in Poland, but it is not clear from her account whether these figures include only Polish citizens or all Jewish survivors in Polish territory. To complicate matters, not all survivors were indebted to Polish Gentiles. Some had been left behind in the concentration camps by the retreating Germans and were liberated by the Red Army; others had been able to "pass" as Gentiles without any Polish assistance, or joined Jewish resistance groups in the forest.

On the other hand, many Jews who had been helped by Polish Gentiles failed to register as Jewish survivors after World War II and are consequently not in the statistics. Consider, too, that the boundaries of Poland—and of the other Eastern European countries—changed radically during and after the war, meaning that statistical data on the dead and the survivors are at best approximations.

5. The SS commander reporting on the Warsaw ghetto revolt was Major General Jürgen Stroop, hanged in Warsaw in 1951. See *The Stroop Report,* translated from the German and annotated by Sybil Milton, introduction by Andrzej Wirth (New York: Pantheon Books, 1979), 29. This report, in fact, contains such statements as: "The Jews and Polish bandits succeeded in repelling the first penetration of the Ghetto by ambushing the participating units, which included tanks and armored cars" (4), and: "The main Jewish fighting unit, which was intermingled with Polish bandits . . ." It is true that Stroop also states: "The Polish population has by and large welcomed the measures implemented against the Jews" (11). As for the admirable behavior of the Italian army in France, Yehuda Bauer writes in *A History of the Holocaust* (New York: Franklin Watts, 1982), 236: "The French police, especially the so-called Garde Mobile who searched intensively for Jews for deportation, were not allowed to function in the Italian zone because the Italians opposed such actions and all other anti-Jewish acts as well."

6. On the nightmare of the Nazi euthanasia program and medical experiments, see especially Robert Jay Lifton, *The Nazi Doctors: Medical Killing and the Psychology of Genocide* (New York: Basic Books, 1986).

7. Zsolt Csalog, *Lajos M., Aged 42* (Budapest: Maecenas, 1989), 18–19. On the troubled reminiscences of a great many survivors, see Anton Gill, *The Journey Back from Hell: An Oral History, Conversations with Concentration Camp Survivors* (Fairfield NJ: Morrow, 1988). Of no less interest and value is Ruth Schwertfeger, *Women of Theresienstadt: Voices from a Concentration Camp* (Oxford: Berg, 1989), which, besides describing life in Theresienstadt, Bohemia (Czech Terezín), contains testimonies in verse and prose as well as contemporary drawings by women inmates. As is well known, Theresienstadt was a "model" concentration camp, designed to mislead foreign visitors and the German public; it had formal autonomy, a welfare system, and schools. Most of its inmates ended up, nevertheless, in the gas chambers. One group comprised highly decorated Austrian Jewish war veterans, who, rather than emigrating, trusted the promises of the Gestapo and paid for it by being deported first to Theresienstadt and then to Auschwitz, where all were killed. Another major publication, David G. Roskies, ed., *The Literature of Destruction: Jewish Responses to Catastrophe* (Philadelphia: The Jewish Publication Society, 1988), contains one hundred articles on the suffering of Jews from the destruction of Solomon's temple in 587 B.C. to Auschwitz.

8. In the same year the young German Communist Jonny Hüttner was arrested in Berlin, the young Austrian Communist Karlo Stajner was arrested in Moscow. Unlike Hüttner, however, who was given three years, then freed, then immediately rearrested and sent to a camp without a new trial, Stajner was given ten years, then retried far away from any court, in a Siberian camp, and sentenced to another ten years. He left the

USSR for Yugoslavia in 1956, after twenty years in Soviet captivity. Perhaps this reveals a difference between the Stalinist and the Nazi concepts of justice. See Karlo Stajner, *Seven Thousand Days in Siberia*, translated by Joel Agree, with an introduction by Danilo Kiš (New York: Farrar, Straus and Giroux, 1988).

9. The film *Lodz Ghetto* which was released in the spring of 1989 and was directed by Kathryn Taverna and Alan Adelson, is based on the documents and photographs in this book. Both the book and the film were inspired in turn by Lucjan Dobroszycki's five-volume work, in Polish, on the Lódz ghetto, which has also been issued in an abridged version as *The Chronicle of the Lódz Ghetto, 1941–1944* (New Haven CT: Yale University Press, 1984).

10. See Gitta Sereny, *Into that Darkness: From Mercy Killing to Mass Murder* (New York: McGraw-Hill, 1974), which analyzes the life of Franz Stangl, an Austrian policeman who became commandant of the Treblinka death camp. See also *Commandant of Auschwitz: The Autobiography of Rudolf Hoess*, with an introduction by Lord Russell of Liverpool, translated by Constantine FitzGibbon (Cleveland: World Publishing Company, 1959); and Peter R. Black, *Ernst Kaltenbrunner: Ideological Soldier of the Third Reich* (Princeton NJ: Princeton University Press, 1984).

11. Nora Levin, *The Holocaust: The Destruction of European Jewry, 1939–1945* (New York: Schocken, 1973), xi–xii.

12. Eberhard Jäckel, "Die elende Praxis der Untersteller," *Die Zeit*, September 12, 1986, as quoted in Charles S. Maier, *The Unmasterable Past: History, Holocaust, and German National Identity* (Cambridge MA: Harvard University Press, 1988), 75–76. On Maier's work, see Gordon Craig's "Facing Up to the Nazis," in the *New York Review of Books* (February 2, 1989).

13. The figure on the number of Jewish victims is that of Raul Hilberg in *Unanswered Questions*, 171; the figure on Stalin's victims is that of Charles Maier in *The Unmasterable Past*, 74. For a detailed analysis of Stalinist terror, see Robert Conquest, *The Harvest of Sorrow: Soviet Collectivization and the Terror-Famine* (New York: Oxford University Press, 1986). The widely used figure of six million Jewish dead was the estimate of Adolf Eichmann.

14. This theme is, incidentally, most thoughtfully explored in Maier, *The Unmasterable Past*, 71–84.

15. On all this, see Ezra Mendelsohn, "Relations Between Jews and Non-Jews in Eastern Europe Between the two World Wars," in *Unanswered Questions*, 71–83.

The Goldhagen Controversy

1. *The New York Times*, March 27 and April 2, 14, 25, 1996.

2. Elie Wiesel, "Little Hitlers," *The Observer*, March 31, 1996; Andrei S. Markovits, "Störfall im Endlager der Geschichte," in *Ein Volk von Mördern?: Die Dokumentation zur Goldhagen Kontroverse um die Rolle der Deutschen in Holocaust*, ed. Julius Schoeps (Hamburg: Hoffmann und Campe, 1996), 228–40. Richard Bernstein and A. M. Rosen-

thal wrote very positive reviews in the *New York Times,* March 27 and, respectively, April 2, 1996.

3. Omer Bartov, "Ordinary Monsters," *The New Republic,* April 29, 1996, 32–38. Fritz Stern, "The Goldhagen Controversy: One Nation, One People, One Theory?" *Foreign Affairs* 75, no. 6 (November/December 1996): 128–38. Hans-Ulrich Wehler, "The Goldhagen Controversy: Agonizing Problems, Scholarly Failure, and the Political Dimension," *German History* 15, no. 1 (1997): 80–91 (this is an expanded version of an article that appeared in *Die Zeit,* May 24, 1996). Dieter Pohl, "Die Holocaust-Forschung und Goldhagens Thesen," *Vierteljahrshefte für Zeitgeschichte* 45, no. 1 (January 1997): 1–48. Christopher Browning, "Dämonisierung erklärt nichts," *Die Zeit,* April 19, 1996. Eberhard Jäckel, "Einfach ein schlechtes Buch," *Die Zeit,* May 17, 1996. David Schoenbaum, "Ordinary People?" *National Review,* July 1, 1996. For Henry Friedlander, see *German Studies Review* 19, no. 3 (October 1996): 578–80. Kristen R. Monroe, *American Political Science Review* 91, no. 1 (1997): 212–13. Ruth Bettina Birn, "Historiographical Review: Revising the Holocaust," *The Historical Journal* 40, no. 1 (1997): 195–215. Norbert Frei, "Ein Volk von 'Endlösern'? Daniel Goldhagen beschreibt die Deutschen als 'Hitlers Willing Vollstrecker,'" *Süddeutsche Zeitung,* April 13, 1996.

4. See Gordon Craig's review in the *New York Review of Books,* April 18, 1996. Volker Berghahn, "The Road to Extermination," *The New York Times,* April 14, 1996. Paul Johnson, "An Epidemic of Hatred," *The Washington Post,* March 24, 1996. Josef Joffe, "Goldhagen in Germany," *The New York Review of Books,* November 28, 1996.

5. Joffe, "Goldhagen in Germany."

6. See, for example, Volker Ulrich, "Ein Buch provoziert einen neuen Historikerstreit: Waren die Deutschen doch alle schuldig?" *Die Zeit,* April 12, 1996.

7. *Der Spiegel,* April 15, 1996. Jäckel, "Einfach ein schlechtes Buch."

8. That was Hans-Ulrich Wehler's characterization. See Josef Joffe, "Goldhagen in Germany."

9. Daniel Goldhagen, "Das Versagen der Kritiker," *Die Zeit,* August 2, 1996.

10. Goldhagen, *Hitler's Willing Executioners: Ordinary Germans and the Holocaust* (New York: Knopf, 1996), 582 n.38.

11. Schoeps, ed., *Ein Volk von Mördern?*

12. See Goldhagen's comments in *The New York Times,* March 27, 1996.

13. Wehler, "The Goldhagen Controversy," 81–83.

14. Christopher R. Browning, *Ordinary Men: Reserve Battalion 101 and the Final Solution in Poland* (New York: HarperCollins, 1992).

15. Goldhagen, *Hitler's Willing Executioners,* 428.

16. Ibid., 392.

17. Ibid., 390.

18. Ibid., 402.

19. Ibid., 56, 85.

20. Ibid., 75.

21. Bern Engelmann, *In Hitler's Germany: Daily Life in the Third Reich*, trans. Krishna Winston (New York: Pantheon, 1986), 138–39, 223ff. The Goldhagen quote is on page 101 of *Hitler's Willing Executioners*.

22. See particularly, Daniel Jonah Goldhagen, "Motives, Causes, Alibis," *The New Republic*, December 23, 1996, 37–45.

23. Goldhagen, *Hitler's Willing Executioners*, 425.

24. Goldhagen, "Motives, Causes, Alibis," 37.

25. Pohl, "Die Holocaust-Forschung und Goldhagen Thesen," 1–48. Pohl's book is *Nationalsozialistische Judenverfolgung in Ostgalizien, 1941–1944: Organisation und Durchführung eines staatlichen Massenverbrechens* (Munich: Oldenbourg, 1996).

26. Pohl, "Die Holocaust-Forschung und Goldhagen Thesen," 15.

27. Ibid., 16–21.

28. See Henry Friedlander's review of *Hitler's Willing Executioners* in *German Studies Review*, 19, no. 3 (October 1996): 580.

29. Pohl, "Die Holocaust-Forschung und Goldhagen Thesen," 16–21.

30. László Karsai, "Történészek, gyilkosok, áldozatok" [Historians, murderers, victims], *Beszélő* (Budapest, June 1997): 34–59. The quotation is on page 53 of the manuscript.

31. Birn, "Historiographical Review: Revising the Holocaust," *The Historical Journal* 40, no. 1 (1997): 197. Birn's book is *Die höheren SS- und Polizeiführer: Hitlers Vertreter im Reich und in den besetzten Gebieten* (Düsseldorf: Droste, 1986).

32. Birn, "Historiographical Review," 198–99.

33. Ibid., 200.

34. Goldhagen, *Hitler's Willing Executioners*, 587.

35. Gitta Sereny, "The Complexities of Complicity," *The Times of London*, March 28, 1996.

A Ghetto in Lithuania

1. I am aware that the place should be called Kaunas, for it is now a large city in Lithuania, but here I will refer to it as Kovno, following the book under review. Place names are, of course, no minor matter for most East Europeans, and I remember well the furious scolding I received as a child from a stranger in a train somewhere in Slovenia when I referred to the country's capital as Laibach, its German and Hungarian name, and not as Ljubljana.

2. As many as half a dozen variations for East European personal names may be in use and this is the case with the Lithuanian heroes mentioned in the text.

3. Norman Davies, *Heart of Europe: A Short History of Poland* (New York: Oxford University Press, 1986), 292.

4. Algirdas Martin Budreckis, *The Lithuanian National Revolt of 1941*. (New York: Lithuanian Encyclopedia Press, 1968), 44.

5. Lucy S. Dawidowicz, *From that Place and Time: A Memoir, 1938–1947* (New York: Norton, 1989), 43. On Dawidowicz's book, see the chapter titled "The Incomprehensible Holocaust" in this volume.

6. Ezra Mendelsohn, *The Jews of East Central Europe between the World Wars* (Bloomington: Indiana University Press, 1983), 255. Much of my information on interwar Lithuanian-Jewish relations was culled from this fine book.

7. On the popularity of communism among young, middle-class Lithuanian Jews, see the memoirs of the Jewish survivor Frieda Frome, *Some Dare to Dream: Frieda Frome's Escape from Lithuania* (Ames: Iowa State University Press, 1988), 7–10. On Frome's book, see the chapter titled "The Incomprehensible Holocaust" in this volume.

8. On the special police battalions in the East, see Yitzhak Arad, Shmuel Krakowski, and Shmuel Spector, eds., *The Einsatzgruppen Reports: Selections from the Dispatches of the Nazi Death Squads' Campaign Against the Jews, July 1941–January 1943* (New York: Holocaust Library, 1989).

9. See Arno Mayer, *Why Did the Heavens not Darken?: The "Final Solution" in History* (New York: Pantheon, 1988). On Mayer's book, see the chapter titled "The Incomprehensible Holocaust" in this volume.

10. The most reliable statistics on this difficult and terrifying subject seem to be in Israel Gutman, ed., *Encyclopedia of the Holocaust*, 4 vols. (New York: Macmillan, 1990), 4:1799.

Romania

1. Because of repeated territorial changes during and immediately after the World War II, all statistical data on the number of Romanian Jews killed are inevitably misleading. Consider that thousands of the Romanians' Jewish victims were Soviet citizens before World War II; yet they were killed in what during the war was officially Romanian territory. Others were Romanian citizens before the war but were annihilated four years after their homeland had been reincorporated into Hungary in 1940. Consequently, thousands of Romanian-Jewish victims figure in the statistics on Soviet and Hungarian Jewish victims or vice versa. In contrast, many survivors remain unaccounted for because, rather than returning to their place of origin after the war, they went to another place or left Europe altogether. Jean Ancel writes in the *Encyclopedia of the Holocaust* (edited by Israel Gutman, four volumes; New York: Macmillan, 1990), 1292–1300, that the Jewish population in Romania numbered 760,000 in 1930, amounting to 4.2 percent of the total population. "Some 420,000 Jews who were living on Romanian soil in 1939 were estimated to have perished in the Holocaust. This figure includes the Jews killed in Bessarabia and Bukovina in July and August 1941; the Jews who died during deportation to Transnistria or after their arrival there; the victims of the pogroms in

Iasi and other places in Romania; and the Jews of northern Transylvania who were deported to Auschwitz and killed there. Not included are the Jews who had been living in the Soviet territory that Romania occupied during the war and who also perished in the Holocaust."

2. Note that, after 1918, Hungary was forced to cede much more than merely the historic principality of Transylvania to Romania. It included a large part of eastern Hungary and the eastern part of the Banat or Vojvodina.

3. Cited in Eugen Weber, "Romania," in Hans Rogger and Eugen Weber, editors, *The European Right: A Historical Profile* (Berkeley: University of California Press, 1965), 548.

The Europeans and the Holocaust

1. A good many Italian Jews were not enthusiastic followers of Il Duce. The early anti-Fascist movement known as Giustizia e Libertà (Justice and Freedom), founded by Carlo and Nello Rosselli, who were from a prominent Tuscan Jewish family, included many Jews, and the manifesto of anti-Fascist intellectuals, edited by Benedetto Croce and published on May 1, 1925, had several Jews among its signers. The arrest of eleven young Jews in Turin in the spring of 1934 for anti-Fascist activities, which led to the first serious manifestations of anti-Semitism in the Italian press, split the Italian Jewish community. "Patriotic" Jews hastened to reassure Mussolini of their loyalty; others became even more hostile to fascism. Following the German occupation of Italy in September 1943 many Jews, including Primo Levi (the author of *Survival in Auschwitz*, among other books) joined the Partisans in the mountains to fight the Germans and the neo-Fascist Republic of Salò.

2. The Italian army in Dalmatia and other parts of occupied Yugoslavia was caught in the local civil war. While joining the Germans in the common fight against the Yugoslav Communist Partisans, the Italian military command tended to support the Serbian Chetniks against both the Titoist Partisans and the Croatian Fascist Ustashas. The Germans meanwhile generally supported the Ustashas against the Serbian Chetniks and the Communists. In the course of this many-sided struggle the Italian army interned not only captured Communist Partisans but local people, particularly Slovenes, suspected of harboring hostile guerrillas. According to Jonathan Steinberg's account, thousands of these captives died of illness and malnutrition. On this, see also Franc Potočnik, *Koncentraciisko taborišce Rab* (Lipa: Koper, 1975), and in Italian translation: *Il Campo di Sterminio Fascista: L'isola di Rab* (Turin: ANPI, 1979).

3. Writing in Israel Gutman, ed., *The Encyclopedia of the Holocaust* (New York: Macmillan, 1990), 1729–31, Teresa Prekerowa explains that Zegota, which was the code name for Rada Pomocy Zydom (Council for Aid to Jews), worked clandestinely in German-occupied Poland from December 1942 to January 1945. The organization was set up at the initiative of the Catholic writer Zofia Kossak-Szczucka, whom the Germans later sent to Auschwitz, and one of its most famous leaders was the writer and historian Wladyslaw Bartoszewski, who was later to be imprisoned in Stalinist Poland. At its most active, Zegota was run by five Polish and two Polish Jewish political movements. The money to

run it came mainly from the Delegatura, the representatives in Poland of the Polish government-in-exile in London, and its main activity was giving financial help to thousands of Jews in hiding as well as providing them, free of charge, with forged "Aryan" documents. All this took place under the threat of torture and execution by the Germans. Prekerowa writes that Zegota was the only organization in Europe "that was run jointly by Jews and non-Jews from a wide range of political movements." In 1963 Zegota was recognized by Yad Vashem in Jerusalem as belonging to the "Righteous among the Nations."

4. Besides Nechama Tec's book *In the Lion's Den,* discussed in the chapter titled "In Disguise" in this volume, another important work on the subject of non-Jewish saviors is Samuel P. Oliner and Pearl M. Oliner, *The Altruistic Personality: Rescuers of Jews in Nazi Europe* (New York: Free Press, 1988).

5. For a discussion of the book *A Mosaic of Victims,* see the chapter by the same title in this volume.

6. Two excellent books, published in the West on twentieth-century Yugoslavia, are Ivo Banac, *The National Question in Yugoslavia: Origins, History, and Politics* (Ithaca NY: Cornell University Press, 1984), and Aleksa Djilas, *The Contested Country: Yugoslav Unity and Communist Revolution, 1919–1953* (Cambridge MA: Harvard University Press, 1991). These books do not deal with contemporary developments, however.

7. Well before the war, Father Filipović had joined the Ustasha movement. Following the German invasion of Yugoslavia and the proclamation of the Croatian state in 1941, he and some of his fellow priests led punitive expeditions against Serbs in Bosnia, where they committed atrocious crimes. For this he was arrested and tried by the German occupation authorities, apparently at the request of the Italian army. He was then suspended from his priestly functions by the Papal Legate in Zagreb. In June 1942 the Ustasha authorities released him from a Croatian jail and sent him to the Jasenovac camp as deputy commander. After several months there, he took up other posts in the Ustasha government. Captured by the British in Austria at the end of the war and handed over to the Tito government, Filipović was tried and executed in Yugoslavia in 1945.

8. On November 21, 1989, *Danas,* a Zagreb weekly, published a brief summary of the still secret findings of an official Yugoslav commission on wartime casualties that had accumulated 2,990 boxes of statistical data in Belgrade in 1964. According to the article in *Danas,* a total of 597,000 people perished as a consequence of the hostilities in Yugoslavia between 1941 and 1945. This is, of course, a far lower figure than the 1,706,000 dead claimed by the Tito government. It is also much less than the number of people killed, according to Marković, in Jasenovac alone, and fewer, for instance, than the 800,000 Hungarians, Jews, and non-Jews combined who are estimated to have died as a consequence of the war. According to the same statistical report of the 597,000 dead Yugoslavs, 346,000 were Serbs, 83,000 Croats, 42,000 Slovenes, 32,000 Muslims, 45,000 Jews, and the rest Macedonians, Montenegrins, Turks, Albanians, Hungarians, Slovaks, and "others."

The statistician Vladimir Zerjavić estimates in his *Opsesije i Megalomanije oko Jasenovca i Bleiburga* (Zagreb: Globus, 1992), 166, that 947,000 people lost their lives in Yugoslavia because of the war. Zerjavic criticizes both those who exaggerate the number of victims at the Ustasha concentration camp at Jasenovac and those who inflate the number of alleged Nazi collaborators and other Yugoslav citizens executed by the Titoist Partisans. Many victims of Titoist revenge had been taken prisoner by the British authorities and were handed over to the Yugoslav Partisans. They were then either immediately executed at the Bleiburg transit camp in Austria or were killed later in Yugoslavia.

On the historical controversy regarding Jasenovac, see also Ljubo Boban, "Jasenovac and the Manipulation of History," *East European Politics and Societies,* vol. 4, no. 3 (fall 1990): 580–92.

A Hungarian Admiral on Horseback

1. In 1922, Horthy enthusiastically greeted the visiting Secretary General of the American YMCA with the words: "I am delighted to meet the head of such an important anti-Semitic organization." Quoted by Sakmyster, 147.

Poles and Jews

1. Simon Schochet, "An Attempt to Identify the Polish-Jewish Officers Who Were Prisoners in Katyń." in *Working Papers in Holocaust Studies II* (Holocaust Studies Program, Yeshiva University, March 1989), as cited in the notes to Calel Perechodnik's *Am I a Murderer?* 228.

2. One of the best treatments of Polish-Jewish relations is Ralph Slovenko's essay "On Polish-Jewish Relations," *The Journal of Psychiatry and Law* (winter 1987): 597–687. (Some advanced undergraduate students who come to my class on East European history at Columbia University are aware of the Warsaw Ghetto Uprising of 1943 but are entirely ignorant of the Warsaw Uprising of the Polish resistance. The event took place between August and October 1944 and claimed some 250,000 lives. Others, often after viewing Claude Lanzmann's film *Shoah,* believe that the Holocaust was the result of a German-Polish conspiracy.)

The Pope, the Nazis, and the Jews

1. Quoted in Mark Aarons and John Loftus, *Unholy Trinity: The Vatican, the Nazis, and the Swiss Banks* (revised edition; New York: St. Martin's, 1998), vii.

2. For a spirited but not unprejudiced defense of Pius XII in connection with the genocide of the Jews, see Jesuit Father Robert A. Graham's writings in *Pius XII and the Holocaust: A Reader* (Milwaukee WI: Catholic League for Religious and Civil Rights, 1988).

3. Susan Zuccotti, *Under His Very Windows: The Vatican and the Holocaust in Italy* (New Haven, CT: Yale University Press, 2000). See also her earlier, fascinating book, *The Italians and the Holocaust: Persecution, Rescue, and Survival,* with an introduction by Furio Colombo (Lincoln: University of Nebraska Press, 1996).

4. Among the Catholic Jewish deportees in August 1942 was the German philosopher Edith Stein, whose religious name was Sister Teresia Benedicta a Cruce. She died in Auschwitz and was canonized by Pope John Paul II in 1998, over the protests of some Jewish organizations that pointed out that Edith Stein had died not as a martyr of the Catholic faith but because she was a Jew.

5. See Mária Schmidt, "Margit Slachta's Activities in Support of Slovakian Jewry, 1942–1943," *Remembering for the Future: Jews and Christians During and After the Holocaust* (New York: Pergamon Press, 1989), 207–11, and Randolph Braham, *The Politics of Genocide: The Holocaust in Hungary*, in two volumes (revised and enlarged edition: New York: Columbia University Press, 1994), 1174 and 1199–2000.

6. Not wanting to appear too favorable to Pius XII, Lapide adds: "It is true that Pope Pius XII was no King of Denmark, who was 'Christian' not only in name. Under his undaunted leadership little Denmark managed to save all but 52 of its 6500 Jews" (213). This is all the more ironic as, all legends to the contrary, King Christian X neither wore nor ever threatened to wear the Jewish star. Nor did he do anything memorable on behalf of the Danish Jews for the simple reason that such a thing was not necessary. No Jew in occupied Denmark was ever obliged to wear the Jewish star. A model satellite, of enormous economic importance to Germany, Denmark was always treated by the Nazis with great consideration. When finally ordered by Berlin to move against the tiny Jewish community, on October 1, 1943, the local German authorities made sure that the Danish people were first able to export most Jews to neutral Sweden. Only about five hundred Jews, mostly old people, were arrested; they were sent to the "model" concentration camp at Theresienstadt where they continued to come under the protection of the Danish government. Those, however, who were forced to give up their places at Theresienstadt for the Danish deportees were sent by Eichmann to Auschwitz where they were gassed. (On all this, see, among others, István Deák, "The Incomprehensible Holocaust," *The New York Review*, September 28, December 21, 1989; February 1, March 29, September 27, 1990; and April 25, 1991.) In fact, under Pius XII's pontificate, many Catholic clergymen and nuns took greater risks and suffered far more on behalf of the Jews than did King Christian of Denmark.

7. For a critical view of the International Red Cross in World War II, see, for instance, the Swiss historian Jean-Claude Favez's *Une Mission impossible? Le CICR, les déportations et les camps de concentration nazis* (Lausanne: Payot, 1988).

8. See, for instance, Aarons and Loftus, *Unholy Trinity: The Vatican, the Nazis, and the Swiss Banks*. Despite the subtitle, the book cover shows clearly that the "unholy trinity" was made up of Pius XII, Hitler, and Stalin. Only an expert in super-murky secret service operations could judge the validity of the authors' arguments and the hundreds of documents cited in the book.

INDEX

Aarons, Mark: *Unholy Trinity,* 205 n.8
The Abandonment of the Jews (Roskies), 185
Abrahamsen, Samuel: *Norway's Response to the Holocaust,* 142
Abusch, Alexander, 36
Abzug, Robert, 70
Adam, Uwe Dietrich, 80
Adamowicz, Irena, 125
Adelson, Alan: (ed.) *The Diary of David Sierakowiak,* 164; (ed.) *Lódz Ghetto,* 79, 198 n.9
Adenauer, Konrad, 36, 38, 41–43
Adorno, Theodor, 19
Agree, Joel, 198 n.8
Algirdas, grand Duke (of Lithuania), 115
Allen, W. S.: *The Nazi Seizure of Power,* 7, 13
All or Nothing (Steinberg), 139, 141–42, 202 n.2
The Altruistic Personality (Oliner), 203 n.4
Ambrosio, Gen. Vittorio, 141
Améry, Jean, 95
Am I a Murderer? (Perechodnik), 164, 165
Amin, Idi, 20
Ancel, Jean, 201 n.1
And I Am Afraid of My Dreams (Póltawska), 75–76
Andreski, Stanislav: "Fascists as Moderates," 21

anti-Semitism: Austrian, 105, 195 n.1; Baltic, 120; British and American, xvii, 25, 185, 187, 188, 195 n.1, 204 n.1; Catholic, 67, 170, 174–76, 177–78; centrality of, in Nazi ideology, 3–4, 30, 69, 81, 83–88, 89–90, 123; Communist position on, 40; debate on the term, 68; fascism and, xiii, 17, 87; French, 81, 104, 106; German, 3, 4, 9–13, 58, 63, 69, 96, 100–110; Hungarian, 149, 150–51, 152, 153, 154–55, 158, 160, 181, 193; Italian, 137–42, 202 n.1; Jewish, 32; Norwegian, 142–43; Polish, 71, 72, 73–74, 91–92, 94, 96, 143–44, 163–65; postwar, xiii, 31–32, 40, 74, 144; Romanian, 131–32, 133; Russian, 81, 104, 106, 119; Slovakian, 181; Ukrainian, 92–93. *See also* Final Solution; Holocaust
Antonescu, Marshal Ion, 20, 131, 133–35, 148, 158
Arad, Yitzhak, 201 n.8
Arendt, Hannah, 19, 81, 110, 142
Armenian genocide, 68, 105
Arrow Cross (Hungarian fascist party), 22, 49, 87, 153–54, 157, 181, 193
Augstein, Rudolf, 102
Auschwitz and After (Delbo), 95, 98
Auschwitz-Birkenau concentration camp (Poland): Carmelite convent at, 74; commandant of, 28–30; killings at, 91,

Auschwitz-Birkenau (*continued*)
94, 96, 197 n.7, 205 n.4 n.6; preventability of killings at, 161, 186, 189–92; social hierarchy at, 67, 97–98, 145; survivor reminiscences of, 70, 76–78, 95, 98, 108–9. *See also* concentration camps

Austria: anti-Semitism in, 105, 195 n.1; concentration camp personnel from, 79–80, 105, 182, 198 n.10; fascism in, 21; Mauthausen concentration camp in, 30–32; murder squad personnel from, 28, 91. *See also* Habsburg monarchy

Austria-Hungary. *See* Habsburg monarchy

Babiuch, Jolanta: *The Vatican and the Red Flag*, 172, 176, 183
Bach-Zelewski, SS Gen. Erich von dem, 186
Baltic states: anti-Semitism in, 120; Holocaust in, 57, 122, 123; participation of, in Final Solution, xvi–xvii, 10; post–World War I fighting in, 29, 116; Soviet invasion of, 118. *See also* names of individual countries
Banac, Ivo: *The National Question in Yugoslavia*, 203 n.6
Bartoszewski, Wladyslaw, 202 n.3
Bartov, Omer, 101; *Hitler's Army*, 196 n.2
Bassani, Giorgio: *The Garden of the Finzi-Continis*, 141
Bauer, Yehuda, 80, 101, 160; *A History of the Holocaust*, 197 n.5
Bauman, Zygmunt: *Modernity and the Holocaust*, 88
Beating the Fascists? (Rosenhaft), 8
Begley, Louis: *Wartime Lies*, 23–24, 49
Belgium, xvi, 98
Belorussia, 49
Benedict XV, 172
Benevolence and Betrayal (Stille), 137, 138, 139

Benz, Wolfgang, 95
Berenbaum, Michael: (ed.) *A Mosaic of Victims*, 89–93, 145
Berghahn, Volker R., 101; *Modern Germany*, 7
Berlin: Congress of, 131; Jews in hiding in, 10, 24, 32–34, 196 n.3; Lithuanian refuge in, 118; Nazi-Communist battles in, 8–9; Nazi supporters in, 4
Bernstein, Richard, 198 n.2
Bessarabia, 130, 131, 132; Holocaust in, 15, 134, 135, 201 n.1
Bethlen, Count István, 152–53, 156
Binkiene, Sofija, 125
Birn, Ruth Bettina, 101, 109–10
Bismarck, Otto von (the Iron Chancellor), 106, 130, 177
Bismarck, Prince Otto von (Nazi diplomat), 141
Black, Peter R., 90, 198 n.10
The Black Corps (Koehl), 13–15
Blätter für deutsche und internationale Politik, 103
Bleiburg transit camp (Austria), 204 n.8
Bletchley Park (England), 188–89, 193
Blonski, Jan: "The Poor Poles Look at the Ghetto," 144
Blum, Léon, 165
Boban, Ljubo: "Jasenovac and the Manipulation of History," 204 n.8
Bohemia (Terezín). *See* Theresienstadt concentration camp
Bolshevism. *See* Communism
Borge, Victor, 142
Borowski, Tadeusz, 95
Bosnia-Herzegovina, 97, 203 n.7
Bracher, Karl D., 19
Braham, Randolph L., 80, 159, 160, 161
Brandt, Willy, 43
Breitman, Richard: *What the Nazis Planned, What the British and Americans Knew*, 185–93
Brizgys, Bishop Vincentas, 125

Index

Broszat, Martin, 80, 83, 110
Browning, Christopher R., 80, 91, 101; *Ordinary Men,* 104
Buber-Neumann, Margarete, 95
Buchanan, Patrick, 182
Buchenwald concentration camp (Germany), 62, 192
Bukovina, 130, 131, 132, 133, 134–35, 201 n.1
Bulgaria, xvi, 86, 88, 130, 131; fascism in, 21; Holocaust in, 29, 69, 105, 132, 139, 140–41; World War II casualties in, xvii
Burnstone, Deborah, 26

Carol I, King (of Romania), 130
Carol II, King (of Romania), 131, 134
Caspi, Joseph, 125
Catholic Church, 169–84; anti-Communist stance of, 171–73, 176, 178, 182, 183–84; assistance of, to Nazi war criminals, 182–83; in Croatia, 15, 16, 21–22, 146, 179, 203 n.7; debate on behavior of, during Holocaust, xiv, 67, 90, 169, 171–82, 205 n.6 n.8; debate on martyrs of, at Auschwitz, 74, 94, 96, 205 n.5; failure of, to condemn Final Solution, 27–28, 75, 162, 175–76, 177–78, 179–80; historical weakness of, 171–73. *See also* Catholicism
The Catholic Church and the Holocaust (Phayer), 175, 177, 178, 179, 181, 182, 183
Catholicism: in Austria, 21, 31; of concentration camp commandants, 29, 79; in Germany, 4, 10, 12, 18, 41, 106; in Lithuania, 116, 119, 127; in Poland, 74. *See also* Catholic Church
Cesarani, David: (ed.) *Genocide and Rescue,* 159–62
Chalmers, Martin, 61
Charles I, Emperor (of Austria) and King (of Hungary), 150, 151, 152
Chciuk-Celt, Tadeusz, 189
Childers, Thomas: *The Nazi Voter,* 3–5, 7
Christian X, King (of Denmark), 205 n.6

The Chronicle of the Lódz Ghetto (Dobroszycki), 198 n.9
Churchill, Sir Winston, 185, 188–89, 190
Civiltà Cattolica, 174
Codreanu, Corneliu, 133. *See also* Iron Guard
Cohen, Asher, 161
collaboration, xi, xiv, 32, 35, 89, 92, 134, 136, 139, 142, 152, 160, 204 n.8; with Gestapo, 79, 123, 124, 125–26; in Ukraine, 10, 74, 89, 98, 109, 165
Colombo, Furio, 204 n.3
Communism: fear of, in Nazi Germany, 11, 83–88, 123; in Hungary, 150–51, 181; papal antipathy to, 171–73, 176, 178, 182, 183–84; popularity of, among Eastern European Jews, 74, 127; popularity of, among German Jews, 38–40, 78; popularity of, among Hungarian Jews, 22, 150; popularity of, among Lithuanian Jews, 121, 201 n.7; popularity of, among Polish Jews, 144, 163–65; popularity of, among Romanian Jews, 134–35; in Weimar Republic, 8–9, 37; in Yugoslavia, 147, 202 n.2. *See also* German Democratic Republic (GDR); Soviet Union
concentration camps: commandants of, 28–30, 79–80; communities adjacent to, 30–32; German, compared with Soviet, 96–97; location of, 9, 92; medical experiments in, 76; "model," 57, 197 n.7, 205 n.6; moral behavior in, 94–99; Red Cross silence about, 182; slave labor in, 29, 90–91, 98–99, 104, 108, 189; social hierarchies in, xv, 67, 76–77, 97–99, 145; survivors of, xiii, 75–79, 108–9; wartime knowledge of, 9, 59, 188–92, 193; in Yugoslavia, 142, 204 n.8. *See also names of individual camps*
"The Concept of Fascism" (Payne), 19–21
Congress of Berlin (1878), 131
Conquest, Robert: *The Harvest of Sorrow,* 198 n.13

The Contested Country (Djilas), 203 n.6
Coppa, Frank J.: *Controversial Concordats*, 175
Cornwell, John: *Hitler's Pope*, 169, 170, 173–75, 180, 182
Coudenhove-Calergi, Count Richard, 195 n.1
Craig, Gordon, 101; "Facing Up to the Nazis," 198 n.12; *The Germans*, 6, 7
Craig, Mary, 75
Croatia, xvi, 25, 136, 154; Catholic Church in, 15, 16, 21–22, 146, 175, 179, 203 n.7; enthusiasm of, for "ethnic cleansing," 132, 141, 145–47; Jasenovac concentration camp in, 146–47, 203 n.8; wartime casualties from, 202 n.2, 203 n.8
Croce, Benedetto, 202 n.1
Crome, Len: *Unbroken*, 78
Curriculum Vitae (Klemperer), 52
Czechoslovakia, xvi, 40, 86, 98, 152; anti-Catholic sentiment in, 172, 183

Dachau concentration camp (Germany), 31, 42, 126
Daluege, Kurt, 186
Danas, 203 n.8
Daniel, Father. *See* Rufeisen, Oswald
Davies, Norman, 115–16
Dawidowicz, Lucy S., 80, 119; *From That Place and Time*, 72; *The War Against the Jews*, 195 n.1
Deák, Gloria: *Picturing New York*, x
Deák, István: "The Incomprehensible Holocaust," x, 23, 67–88, 205 n.6
Death Comes in Yellow (Karay), 99
Death Dealer (ed. Paskuly), 28, 30
Dedijer, Vladimir: *The Yugoslav Auschwitz and the Vatican*, 145–47
Delbo, Charlotte: *Auschwitz and After*, 95, 98
Denmark: Allied bombing of, 191, 192; high Jewish survival rate in, xiv, xvi, 69, 71, 73, 132, 139, 205 n.6
Denner, Arthur, 94

De Sica, Vittorio: *The Garden of the Finzi-Continis*, 141
The Destruction of the European Jews (Hilberg), 104
Deutschkron, Inge: *Outcast*, 34
The Diary of David Sierakowiak (ed. Adelson), 164
Dick, Isaac Meir, 119
Diner, Dan, 101
Di Veroli family (Rome), 139
Divided Memory (Herf), 35–43
Djilas, Aleksa: *The Contested Country*, 203 n.6
Djilas, Milovan, 147
Dobroszycki, Lucjan: *The Chronicle of the Lódz Ghetto*, 198 n.9
Dobrudja, 130, 131
Doctor #117641 (Micheels), 76–77
Dora-Mittelbau concentration camp (Germany), 78, 108
Double Identity (Kubar), 70, 71
Dresden, 51, 57–58, 59, 68
Dressel, Dr. (Dresden physician), 61, 62
Dressen, Willi, 26
Dziewanowski, Kazimierz, 144

Eastern Europe: brutal treatment of prisoners from, 90, 93; Catholic Church in, 176, 181, 183–84; ethnic nationalism in, 25, 83–88, 114–15, 121, 131; fascism in, 17, 21–22, 87; Gentile assistance to Jews in, xiv, 71, 127; Jewish Communists in, 74, 127; Jewish emigration from, 71, 127–28, 187, 195 n.1; place names in, 113, 200 n.1 n.2; role of, in Final Solution, 26, 67, 187. *See also* names of individual countries
East Germany. *See* German Democratic Republic (GDR)
Eden, Anthony, 69, 188
Eichmann, Adolf, 28–29, 79, 104, 182, 198 n.13, 205 n.6; supporting role of, in Hungarian roundups, 135, 156, 193
Einsatzgruppen, 26, 85, 104, 122, 187, 201 n.8

Index 211

The Einsatzgruppen Reports (ed. Arad, Krakowski and Spector), 201 n.8
Elijah ben Solomon (Elijah Gaon), 119
Elkes, Elchanan, 124, 126
The Encyclopedia of the Holocaust (ed. Gutman), 201 n.1, 202 n.3
Estonia, 105, 114; interwar history of, 116, 117, 118; language of, 115
Europa, Europa (Holland), 23–24, 49
Eva's Story (Schloss), 77–78

Facing the Extreme (Todorov), 94–97, 163, 165
"Facing Up to the Nazis" (Craig), 198 n.12
"The Failure of the Critics" (Goldhagen), 102
fascism, 16–22; Austrian, 21; Catholic response to, 173, 175–76, 177–78; Communist response to, 37–40; Croatian, 21–22, 141, 145–47, 179, 202 n.2, 203 n.7, 204 n.8; definition of, xii, xiii, 19–21, 81; demographic basis of support for, 16–19, 21–22, 84–85; Hungarian, 22, 49, 87, 153–54, 157, 181, 193; Italian, 17, 18, 20, 137–42, 155, 202 n.1; Lithuanian, 117; Romanian, 18, 20, 21, 22, 87, 131, 133–36. *See also* National Socialism
"Fascists as Moderates" (Andreski), 21
Faurisson, Robert, 68
Favez, Jean-Claude: *Une Mission impossible?*, 205 n.7
FDR and the Holocaust (ed. Newton), 188
Felice, Renzo de, 19
Field, Noel, 40
Filipović-Majstorović, Father Miroslav, 147, 203 n.7
Final Solution: Allied knowledge of, xvii, 185–93; "death march" program of, 104, 108, 109; euthanasia program of, xiv, 31, 75, 105, 177, 197 n.6; forced labor program of, 10, 15, 29, 30, 56–57, 90–91, 92; German support for, xvii, 9–13, 69, 83–88, 96, 100–110; Gypsy victims of, 27, 30, 91, 93, 105, 179; homosexual victims of, 30, 76, 93, 98, 105; "intentionalist" versus "functionalist" interpretations of, xv, 68–69, 82–83, 94, 110; Jewish assistance in, xiv, 32–34; medical program of, 76; non-German assistance in, xvi–xvii, 27, 69, 74, 105, 122, 126–27; Polish victims of, 75–76, 90, 91–92; Russian victims of, 12–13, 30–31, 56–57, 75, 90, 105, 109; Serbian victims of, 91; Spanish Republican victims of, 30, 98; Ukrainian victims of, 92–93; Wannsee Conference on, 28, 187, 189. *See also* anti-Semitism; concentration camps; Holocaust
The Final Solution (Reitlinger), 195 n.1
Finland, xvi; Holocaust in, 69, 132, 139
FitzGibbon, Constantine, 198 n.10
The Forgotten Holocaust (Lukas), 91
Fox, Frank: (ed.) *Am I a Murderer?*, 164, 165
France, 131, 150–51; anti-Semitism in, 81, 104, 106; participation of, in Final Solution, xvi, 30, 35, 141, 144, 155, 197 n.5; war casualties from, 93. *See also* French Revolution
Francis Ferdinand, Archduke (of Austria), 174
Francis Joseph I, Emperor (of Austria), 86, 135, 149, 196 n.2
Franco, Francisco, xiii, xv, 20, 148, 158, 173
Frank, Anne, 77, 78
Frankfurter, Felix, 190
Frei, Norbert, 101
French Revolution, 25, 84, 174
Friedlander, Henry, 101
Friedländer, Saul, 80, 81, 83
Fritsch, Karl, 79
Frome, Frieda: *Some Dare to Dream*, 70, 71, 201 n.7
Fromm, Erich, 19
From Prejudice to Persecution (Pauley), 195 n.1, 196 n.3
From That Place and Time (Dawidowicz), 72

Furet, François: (ed.) *Unanswered Questions,* 80

Galicia, 47–48
Gaon, Elijah, 119
The Garden of the Finzi-Continis (film by De Sica), 141
The Garden of the Finzi-Continis (novel by Bassani), 141
Garlinski, Józef: *The Survival of Love,* 145; *Surviving Warsaw,* 145
Gebhardt, Karl, 76
Gediminas, grand Duke (of Lithuania), 115
Genocide and Rescue (ed. Cesarani), 159–62
German Democratic Republic (GDR), xvii–xviii, 35–40, 42, 52–53, 60
The Germans (Craig), 6, 7
Germany. *See* German Democratic Republic; Nazi Germany; Weimar Republic; West Germany
Gestapo, 71, 197 n.7; Allied raids on, 51, 191–92; Jewish "catchers" for, 32–34; Jewish collaboration with, 79, 123, 124, 125–26; treatment of Victor Klemperer by, 56, 58, 62, 63
ghettos, xiv, 57, 58, 69, 71, 77, 91, 137, 193. *See also* Kovno (Lithuania): ghetto at; Lódz Ghetto (Poland); Mir Ghetto (Belorussia); Otwock Ghetto (Poland); Warsaw: Ghetto Uprising (1943)
Gilbert, Martin, 80, 114
Gill, Anton: *The Journey Back from Hell,* 197 n.7
Ginzburg, Eugenia, 95
Giustizia e Libertà, 202 n.1
Glazar, Richard: *Trap with a Green Fence,* 95, 98–99
Glemp, Cardinal Josef, 74
Globke, Hans, 42
Globocnik, Odilo, 79
Goldhagen, Daniel: "The Failure of the Critics," 102; *Hitler's Willing Executioners,* xvii, 96–97, 100–110, 187, 198 n.2, 199 n.8
Goldschlag, Stella, 24, 32–34
Gömbös, Gyula, 153
"The Good Old Days," 26–28
Gordon, Judah Loeb, 119
Gordon, Sarah: *Hitler, Germans, and the "Jewish Question,"* 11–13, 195 n.1
Göth, Amon, 79
Graf, Malvina: *The Kraków Ghetto and the Plaszów Camp Remembered,* 70
Graham, Father Robert A., 204 n.2
Great Britain, 67, 73, 131, 149–50, 185–93; anti-Semitism in, xvii, 25, 185, 187, 188; conduct of, in World War I, 185–86; war casualties from, 93; wartime knowledge of Holocaust in, xvii, 188–92, 193
Greece, xvi; Holocaust in, 124, 132, 140–41
Gregory VII, 172
Grill, Johnpeter Horst: *The Nazi Movement in Baden, 1920–1945,* 10–11
Gross, Jan T., 91
Grotewohl, Otto, 36
Gusenbauer, Eleanore, 31
Gustav V, King (of Sweden), 156
Gutman, Israel, 92; (ed.) *The Encyclopedia of the Holocaust,* 201 n.1, 202 n.3
Gypsies, 27, 30, 91, 105, 146; status of, in concentration camps, 76, 98; Vatican's response to killings of, 75, 179

Habermas, Jürgen, 82
Habsburg monarchy (Austria-Hungary), 48, 174; collapse of, 130, 148–50, 151–52, 172; Jewish advancement under, 86–88, 105, 137
Hamilton, Richard: *Who Voted for Hitler?,* 4, 5, 17–18, 195 n.1
The Harvest of Sorrow (Conquest), 198 n.13
Hashomer organization, 163
Hegel, Georg Wilhelm Friedrich, 41
Heimwehr (Austrian fascist movement), 21

Index

Hein, *Polizeimeister* (Belorussian M. Sgt.), 49–50
Henry IV (King of Germany and Holy Roman Emperor), 172
Herder, Johann Gottfried von, 41
Herf, Jeffrey: *Divided Memory*, 35–43
Herling, Gustaw, 96–97
Hermann, SA Lt. Gustav, 124
Herzer, Ivo: (ed.) *The Italian Refuge*, 138, 141–42
Herzl, Theodor, 54
Heuss, Theodor, 36, 38, 42
Heydrich, SS Gen. Reinhard, 83
The Hidden Encyclicals of Pius XI (Passelecq and Suchecky), 175–76
Hilberg, Raul, 67, 80, 101, 198 n.13; *The Destruction of the European Jews*, 104; *Perpetrators, Victims, Bystanders*, 90, 91
Hillgruber, Andreas, 81–82
Himmler, Heinrich, 14, 15, 29, 69, 108, 161, 187
Hirt-Manheimer, Aron, 133, 134
A History of the Holocaust (Bauer), 197 n.5
Hitler, Adolf: cultural preferences of, 6; Great Blood Purge of, 20; *Mein Kampf*, 83, 187; Mussolini's friendship with, 138; parliamentary support for, 38; predilection of, for violence and war, xiii, 85; racist ideology of, 12–13, 81, 187; relationship of, with Admiral Horthy, 148, 155–56; relationship of, with Vatican, 171, 173, 175, 205 n.8; responsibility of, for Holocaust, 9, 68–69, 82–83, 85, 105, 110; secret agreement of, with Stalin, 81, 118; similarities of, to Stalin, xv–xvi, 20–21. *See also* National Socialism; Nazi Germany
Hitler, Germans, and the "Jewish Question" (Gordon), 11–13, 195 n.1
Hitler's Army (Bartov), 196 n.2
Hitler's Pope (Cornwell), 169, 170, 173–75, 180, 182
Hitler's Willing Executioners (Goldhagen), xvii, 96–97, 100–110, 187, 198 n.2, 199 n.8
Holland, Agnieszka: *Europa, Europa*, 23–24, 49
Holocaust: bystanders, 30–32; Catholic Church and, xiv, 27–28, 67, 74–75, 90, 162, 169–84, 204 n.2, 205 n.6 n.8; debate on the term, 67–68; denial, xii, 68; incomprehensibility of, xiv, 63, 69–70, 80, 88; Jews in disguise during, xiv, 23–24, 47–50; literature on, xii–xiii, 23, 67, 82, 100; moral behavior during, 94–99; perpetrators of, 13–15, 26–30, 79–80, 104, 107–10; postwar memory of, 35–43; postwar punishments for, xvii–xviii, 36, 39, 41–42, 182–83, 196 n.2; Slavic victims of, 13, 15, 25, 105, 187; survivor testimonies on, xii, 34, 51–63, 70–79, 108–9, 197 n.7; underlying causes of, 83–88, 89–90; uniqueness of, 23, 68, 81–82. *See also* anti-Semitism; concentration camps; Final Solution; resistance movements; *and names of individual countries*
The Holocaust in History (Marrus), 80
homosexuals, 30, 93, 105; in concentration camps, 76, 98
Homze, Edward, 90
Horthy, Adm. Miklós, 21, 148–58, 181, 193, 204 n.1
Horwitz, Gordon J.: *In the Shadow of Death*, 30–32
Höss, Rudolph, 28–30, 198 n.10
Humani Generis Unitas (Pius XI), 175–76, 178
Hunczak, Taras, 93
Hungary, 25, 148–58, 203 n.8; alliance of, with Nazi Germany, xvi, 21, 153–56; anti-Semitism in, 149, 150–51, 152, 153, 154–55, 158, 160, 181, 193; Communist revolution in, 150–51; counterrevolutionary government of, 150–53; fascist Arrow Cross in, 22, 49, 87, 153–54,

Hungary (*continued*)
157, 181, 193; German invasion of, 156, 160–61; Holocaust in, 69, 135–36, 141, 144, 155–57, 159–62, 181–82, 192–93, 201 n.1; Holocaust survivors from, 78, 108–9; language of, 115; postwar, 40, 42, 183; Soviet invasion of, 157–58; territories of, ceded to Romania, 130, 131, 132–33, 202 n.2. *See also* Habsburg monarchy
Hungary's Admiral on Horseback (Sakmyster), 148–58, 204 n.1
Hüttner, Jonny, 78, 197 n.8

"The Incomprehensible Holocaust" (Deák), x, 23, 67–88, 205 n.6
Ingimundarson, Valur, 100
International Red Cross, 182, 205 n.7
In the Lion's Den (Tec), 24, 47–50, 203 n.4
In the Shadow of Death (Horwitz), 30–32
Into that Darkness (Sereny), 198 n.10
Iron Guard (Romanian fascist group), 22, 87, 131, 133, 134
Israel, 35–36, 37, 38, 40, 43, 47, 50, 188
Italian army: conduct of, in Abyssinian war, 178; conduct of, in occupied Yugoslavia, 202 n.2, 203 n.7; Jewish generals in, 137–38; resistance of, to Final Solution, 73, 141–42, 155, 197 n.5
The Italian Refuge (ed. Herzer), 138, 141–42
The Italians and the Holocaust (Zuccotti), 139, 204 n.3
Italy: fascism in, 17, 18, 20, 137–42; Holocaust in, xvi, 137–42, 180; Holocaust resistance in, 69, 105, 139–42, 155, 179; Jewish anti-Fascists in, 202 n.1; Jewish Fascists in, 138; Jewish settlement in, 137. *See also* Catholic Church; Italian army
I Will Bear Witness (Klemperer), xvii, 51–63

Jäckel, Eberhard, 81, 101, 102

Jagendorf, Siegfried: *Jagendorf's Foundry*, 133–36
Jäger, SS Col. Karl, 123
Japan, 48, 90
"Jasenovac and the Manipulation of History" (Boban), 204 n.8
Jasenovac concentration camp (Croatia), 146–47, 203 n.8
Jehovah's Witnesses, 30, 98
Jelinek, Yeshayahu, 22
Jewish Councils, xiv, 32, 91, 114, 120, 122–26
Jewish Labor Bund, 48, 72, 119, 120
The Jews and the Poles in World War II (Korbonski), 73
The Jews of East Central Europe between the World Wars (Mendelsohn), 201 n.6
The Jews Were Expendable (Penkower), 185
Joffe, Josef, 101, 102
Jogaila (Wladyslaw II Jagiello, King of Poland), 115
John Paul II, 176, 183, 184, 205 n.4
Johnson, Paul, 101
John XXIII, 183
Jordan, SA Capt. Fritz, 122
The Journey Back from Hell (Gill), 197 n.7
Joyce, James, 149

Kádár, János, 21
Kaganovich, Lazar Moiseyevich, 165
Kahana-Shapiro, Chief Rabbi Abraham, 123
Kállay, Miklós, 155–56, 160
Kaltenbrunner, Ernst, 79, 198 n.10
Kaminskas, Mikas, 122
Kaputt (Malaparte), 134
Karay, Felicja: *Death Comes in Yellow,* 99
Karsai, László, 108–9
Karski, Jan, 190
Kater, Michael H., 80; *The Nazi Party,* 3, 5, 7
Kendall, Harvey L., 145
Kent, Evelyn Julia, 77

Index

Kershaw, Ian: *Popular Opinion and Political Dissent in the Third Reich*, 9–10, 11, 12, 13
Kestutis, grand Duke (of Lithuania), 115
Kim, Il Sung, 20
Kirchner, Hadwig, 61
Kitai, Sara, 99
Kitchens, James, 192
Klaipeda (Memel, Lithuania), 117, 118, 126, 128
Klee, Ernst, 26
Klemperer, Eva, 54, 56, 57, 59, 61, 62
Klemperer, George, 53
Klemperer, Victor: *Curriculum Vitae*, 52; *I Will Bear Witness*, xvii, 51–63; *LTI(Lingua Tertii Imperii)*, 52
Knopf, Alfred A., 100, 101
Koehl, Lewis: *The Black Corps*, 13–15
Köhler, Annemarie, 53, 61–63
Kolbe, Father Maximilian, 94, 96
Kolyma camp (Soviet Union), 95
Koncentraciisko taborisce Rab (Potocnik), 202 n.2
Korbonski, Stefan: *The Jews and the Poles in World War II*, 73
Kosovo, 88
Kossak-Szczucka, Zofia, 202 n.3
Kovarikova, Ruzena, 72
Kovno (Lithuania): ghetto at, 71, 113–28; name of, 113, 200 n.1
Kraków, Cardinal Archbishop of, 74
The Kraków Ghetto and the Plaszów Camp Remembered (Graf), 70
Krakowski, Shmuel, 201 n.8
Kren, George M., 70
Kristallnacht, 11, 106
Kubar, Zofia S.: *Double Identity*, 70, 71
Kühnl, Reinhard, 19
Kun, Béla, 150–51
Kushner, Tony, 161

Lamont, Rosette C., 98
Landau, Felix, 28
Langer, Lawrence L., 98

Lanzmann, Claude, 79; *Shoah*, 73, 144, 190, 204 n.2
Lapide, Pinchas E.: *The Last Three Popes and the Jews*, 182, 205 n.6
Lapides, Robert: (ed.) *Lódz Ghetto*, 79
Laqueur, Walter, 80
Larsen, Stein Ugelvikz: (ed.) *Who Were the Fascists*, 16–17, 18–22
The Last Three Popes and the Jews (Lapide), 182, 205 n.6
Latvia, 29, 114, 115, 116, 117, 118; assistance of, in Final Solution, 27, 74, 105
Lenin, Vladimir Ilich, 150, 172; *What Is to Be Done*, 164
Levi, Primo: *Survival in Auschwitz*, 70, 95, 98, 202 n.1
Levin, Nora, 80
Life with a Star (Weil), 71–72
Lifton, Robert Jay, 80; *The Nazi Doctors*, 197 n.6
Linz, Juan J., 19, 20
Lipset, S. M., 21
Lipzer, Benjamin, 125
The Literature of Destruction (ed. Roskies), 197 n.7
Lithuania, 113–28; assistance of, in Final Solution, 27, 74, 105; ethnic nationalism in, 71, 114–15, 116–17, 120–21; German occupation of, 121–22; Holocaust in, 70, 71, 77, 118, 121–28, 201 n.10; interwar dictatorship of, 117–18; Jewish settlement in, 118–21; language of, 115, 200 n.2; Soviet occupation of, 48, 118, 121; union of, with Poland, 115–16; union of, with Russia, 116, 119–20
Lódz Ghetto (ed. Adelson and Lapides), 79
Lodz Ghetto (film by Taverna and Adelson), 198 n.9
Lódz Ghetto (Poland), 79, 164–65, 198 n.9
Loftus, John: *Unholy Trinity*, 205 n.8
Lopate, Philip, 68
LTI (Lingua Tertii Imperii) (Klemperer), 52

Lukas, Richard C.: *The Forgotten Holocaust*, 91; (ed.) *Out of the Inferno*, 92, 143
Luther, Martin (Nazi diplomat), 141
Lutz, Karl, 161, 192
Luxembourg, 105
Luxmoore, Jonathan: *The Vatican and the Red Flag*, 172, 176, 183
Lyon, Cardinal of, 74

Mackensen, Hans-Georg von, 142
Maier, Charles S., 80; *The Unmasterable Past*, 198 n.12 n.13 n.14
Majdanek concentration camp (Poland), 80
Makuch, Barbara, 143
Malaparte, Curzio: *Kaputt*, 134
Mao Tse-tung, 9, 20, 68
Mapu, Abraham, 119
Marković, Mihailo, 146, 203 n.8
Markovits, Andrei S., 101
Marrus, Michael: *The Holocaust in History*, 80
Matulionis (Lithuanian politician), 127
Mauthausen concentration camp (Austria), 30–32
May, Karl, 6
Mayer, Arno: *Why Did the Heavens Not Darken?*, 67–68, 69–70, 83–88, 123
McCloy, John J., 190
medical experiments, Nazi, 14, 76, 197 n.6
Meinecke, Friedrich, 19
Mein Kampf (Hitler), 83, 187
Mendelsohn, Ezra, 120; *The Jews of East Central Europe between the World Wars*, 201 n.6
Mengele, Josef, 182
Merker, Paul, 36, 39–40, 41
Merkl, Peter H., 22
Micheels, Louis J.: *Doctor #117641*, 76–77
Mickiewicz, Adam, 116; *Pan Tadeusz*, 119
Milošević, Slobodan, 146
Milosz, Czeslaw: "A Poor Christian Looks at the Ghetto," 144

Milton, Sybil, 93, 197 n.5
Mindaugas (Lithuanian ruler), 115
Mir Ghetto (Belorussia), 49–50
Une Mission impossible? (Favez), 205 n.7
Mit brennender Sorge (Pius XI), 178
Modern Germany (Berghahn), 7
Modernity and the Holocaust (Bauman), 88
Moldavia, 129, 134–35
Molotov, Vyacheslav, 154
Mommsen, Hans, 83, 101, 110
Monroe, Kristen R., 101
Morse, Arthur: *While Six Million Died*, 185
A Mosaic of Victims (ed. Berenbaum), 89–93, 145
Mosse, George L., 80
Müller-Claudius, Michael, 11
Mussolini, Benito: compared with Hitler, xv, 20; concordat of, with Catholic Church, 176, 177, 178; Jewish policy of, 138–42, 155, 202 n.1
"My Brother's Keeper?" (ed. Polonsky), 143–44
The Myth of The Twentieth Century (Rosenberg), 56

Nasjonal Samling (Norwegian Nazi Party), 19
The National Question in Yugoslavia (Banac), 203 n.6
National Socialism, 3–15; anti-Semitism and, 3, 4, 9–13, 63; Catholic support for, 4, 18, 177–78; Communism and, xv–xvi; fascism and, xiii, 22; parliamentary support for, 38; popular support for, 3–9, 17–18, 106, 195 n.1; postwar advancement of, 42; Protestant support for, 4, 6, 7, 17–18, 75; SS membership and, 14, 26, 28, 30. See also Nazi Germany
The Nazi Doctors (Lifton), 197 n.6
Nazi Germany: anti-Semitism in, 58, 69, 96; Aryan wives protest in, 55; contem-

Index

porary fascination with, xii–xiii; Jugend groups in, 24, 177; Protestant Church in, 27, 162; public behavior in, toward Jews, 32–34, 56–59, 63; public responsibility for Holocaust in, 9–13, 15, 69, 96, 100–110; social class in, 5, 6–9, 62, 83–85. *See also* fascism; Final Solution; Gestapo; Hitler, Adolf; Holocaust; National Socialism; SS; Wehrmacht
The Nazi Movement in Baden, 1920–1945 (Grill), 10–11
The Nazi Party (Kater), 3, 5, 7
The Nazi Seizure of Power (Allen), 7, 13
Nazism. *See* National Socialism; Nazi Germany
Nazi Storm troopers (SA), 8, 32, 108–9, 124
The Nazi Voter (Childers), 3–5, 7
Negri, Gen. Paride, 142
the Netherlands, xvi, 32, 98, 144; low Jewish survival rate in, 69, 77–78, 155, 180
Neumann, Heinz, 95
New Republic, ix, xi
Newton, Verne W.: (ed.) *FDR and the Holocaust*, 188
New York Review of Books, ix, x, xi, 16, 67, 94, 163, 169
New York Times, 101, 199 n.2
1984 (Orwell), 13
Nolte, Ernst, 81–82
Norden, Albert, 40
Norway, xvi, 42; Holocaust in, 69, 142–43; Nazi Party in, 19; postwar punishments in, 42
Norway's Response to the Holocaust (Abrahamsen), 142
La Nostra Bandiera, 139
Nuremberg trials, xvii–xviii, 36, 39, 41, 186, 193

Oliner, Samuel P., and Pearl M. Oliner: *The Altruistic Personality*, 203 n.4
"On Polish-Jewish Relations" (Slovenko), 204 n.2
Opsesije i Megalomanije oko Jasenovca i Bleiburga (Zerjavic), 204 n.8
The Order of Terror (Sofsky), 97–98
Ordinary Men (Browning), 104
Ordnungspolizei (Order Police), 187, 189
Orwell, George: *1984*, 13
Osborne, Sir Francis D'Arcy, 170
L'Osservatore Romano, 171
Otwock Ghetto (Poland), 164
Out of the Inferno (Lukas), 92, 143
Ovazza, Ettore, 139–40
Ovazza family (Turin), 139–40

Pacelli, Eugenio. *See* Pius XII
Palestine, 188
Pan Tadeusz (Mickiewicz), 119
Paris peace conference: of 1919–20, 11, 69, 130; of 1946, 132
partisans, xiv, 24, 50, 71, 118, 122, 123, 125, 126, 146, 202 n.1, 203 n.8; Communist, 147, 180, 182, 202 n.2. *See also* resistance movements
Paskuly, Steven: (ed.) *Death Dealer*, 28, 30
Passelecq, George: *The Hidden Encyclicals of Pius XI*, 175–76
Paukstys, Bronius, 125
Pauley, Bruce F.: *From Prejudice to Persecution*, 195 n.1, 196 n.3
Pavelić, Ante, 145, 182
Payne, Stanley G.: "The Concept of Fascism," 19–21
Penkower, Monty: *The Jews Were Expendable*, 185
Perechodnik, Calel: *Am I a Murderer?*, 164, 165
Perlasca, Jorge (Giorgio), 161
Perón, Eva, 182
Perón, Juan, 20, 182
Perpetrators, Victims, Bystanders (Hilberg), 90, 91
Pétain, Philippe, 148, 158
Phayer, Michael: *The Catholic Church and the Holocaust*, 175, 177, 178, 179, 181, 182, 183

Picturing New York (Deák), x
Pièche, Gen. Giuseppe, 141
Pieck, Wilhelm, 36, 39
Pilsudski, Jósef Klemens, 117
Pius VI, 172
Pius VII, 172
Pius IX, 172
Pius X, 174
Pius XI, 67, 75, 177; *Humani Generis Unitas*, 175–76, 178; *Mit brennender Sorge*, 178
Pius XII, 67, 169–84, 204 n.2; anti-Communist views of, 171–72, 176, 182, 183; anti-Jewish views of, 174–75; assistance of, to Nazi war criminals, 175, 182–83; enigmatic personality of, 169–71; institutional weakness of, 171–73, 183–84; intervention of, on behalf of Eastern European Jews, 156, 181–82; timidity of, in face of Nazi aggression, 75, 173, 175–76, 205 n.6 n.8
Plaszów concentration camp (Poland), 70
Pohl, Dieter, 101, 107–8, 109
Poland: assistance of, in Final Solution, xvi–xvii; citizens of, in concentration camps, 75–76, 90, 99; fascism in, 21; Gentile assistance to Jews in, xiv, 71, 127, 191, 202 n.3; Holocaust in, 69, 124, 196 n.4; interwar conflicts in, 86, 88; Jews in disguise in, 24; non-Jewish genocide in, 91, 92, 93, 105, 178–79; postwar conflicts in, 25, 74, 176, 183; union of, with Lithuania, 115–19. *See also* anti-Semitism: Polish; Auschwitz-Birkenau concentration camp; Lódz Ghetto; resistance movements: Polish; Treblinka death camp
Pollak, Abigail, 94
Pollinger, Andrew, 28
Polonsky, Anthony: (ed.) *"My Brother's Keeper?,"* 143–44
Póltawska, Wanda: *And I Am Afraid of My Dreams*, 75–76

Ponar massacre (Lithuania), 126
"A Poor Christian Looks at the Ghetto" (Milosz), 144
"The Poor Poles Look at the Ghetto" (Blonski), 144
Popular Opinion and Political Dissent in the Third Reich (Kershaw), 9–10, 11, 12, 13
Porat, Dina, 114
Pot, Pol, 20
Potočnik, Franc: *Koncentraciisko taborisce Rab*, 202 n.2
The Power of Rome in the Twentieth Century (Rhodes), 174
Prekerowa, Teresa, 202 n.3

Rada Pomocy Zydom (Council for Aid to Jews), 202 n.3
Rajk, László, 181
Rassinier, Paul, 68
Rauca, M. Sgt. Helmut, 122–23, 125
Ravensbrück concentration camp (Germany), 76, 95, 98, 143
Red Cross, 182, 205 n.7
Reich, Wilhelm, 19
Reichenau, Field Marshal von, 27
Reichskommissariat Ostland, 121
Reitlinger, Gerald, 80; *The Final Solution*, 195 n.1
Rendall, Steven, 175
resistance movements: Communist, 72, 78; German, 10; Hungarian, 161; Jewish, 24, 43, 79, 99, 143, 161, 196 n.4, 197 n.5; Norwegian, 143; Polish, 43, 73–74, 143–44, 145, 163–64, 189–90, 202 n.3, 204 n.2
Reuter, Ernst, 36
Rhodes, Anthony: *The Power of Rome in the Twentieth Century*, 174
Ribbentrop, Joachim von, 146
Richter, Helmut, 53, 61, 62–63
Riess, Volker, 26
The Rise of Hitler (Taylor), 6–7
Risorgimento, 142

Index

Roatta, Gen. Mario, 141
Robotti, Gen. Mario, 141
Roll, Evelyn, 103
Romania, 129–36; defection of, to Allies, in 1944, xvii, 132, 135, 160; fascism in, 18, 20, 21, 22, 87, 131, 133–34; Holocaust in, xvi, 15, 29, 105, 131–32, 133–36; interwar nationalism in, 86, 88, 130–31; Jewish survival rate in, 69, 158, 201 n.1; national mythology of, 136; oil refineries in, 191; pre-World War I nationalism in, 129–30; territorial rivalry of, with Hungary, 132–33, 150, 151, 154, 202 n.2; threat of, to release Jews to Palestine, 188
Roosevelt, Franklin D., 69, 156, 181, 188, 190
Rosenberg, Alfred: *The Myth of The Twentieth Century*, 56
Rosenhaft, Eve: *Beating the Fascists?*, 8
Rosenthal, A. M., 198 n.2
Roskies, David G.: (ed.) *The Literature of Destruction*, 197 n.7
Rosselli, Carlo and Nello, 202 n.1
Das Rote Sprachrohr, 78
Roth, Philip, 72
Rotta, Monsignor Angelo, 161, 181
Rozett, Robert, 161
Rubenstein, Richard L., 89–90
Rufeisen, Oswald, xiv, 24, 47–50, 196 n.2
Rumkowski, Mordechai Chaim, 79, 164
Russell of Liverpool, Lord, 198 n.10
Rymanowski, Witold, 144

SA. *See* Nazi Storm troopers
Sakmyster, Thomas: *Hungary's Admiral on Horseback*, 148–58, 204 n.1
Salazar, Antonio de Oliveira, 148
Sarfatti, Margherita, 138
Schleunes, Karl A., 80
Schloss, Eva: *Eva's Story*, 77–78
Schloss, Roslyn, 72
Schmitz, SS Capt. Heinrich, 122
Schoenbaum, David, 101

Schulte, Eduard, 190
Schumacher, Kurt, 36, 38, 41, 42
Schwertfeger, Ruth: *Women of Theresienstadt*, 197 n.7
Scott, Robert, x
Segev, Tom: *The Soldiers of Evil*, 79–80
Serbia, xvi, 86, 91, 174, 176. *See also* Croatia
Sereny, Gitta, 79, 110; *Into that Darkness*, 198 n.10
Seven Thousand Days in Siberia (Stajner), 197 n.8
Shelah, Menachem, 145
Shoah (Lanzmann), 73, 144, 190, 204 n.2
Sierakowiak, David: *The Diary of David Sierakowiak*, 164
Sila-Nowicki, Wladyslaw, 144
Silvers, Robert, xi
Sima, Horia, 134
Skarzysko-Kamienna labor camp (Poland), 99
Slachta, Margit, 181
Slovakia, xvi, 154; Holocaust in, 21, 181
Slovenia, 200 n.1, 202 n.2, 203 n.8
Slovenko, Ralph: "On Polish-Jewish Relations," 204 n.2
Smetona, Antanas, 116, 117–18, 120
Social Democratic Party: in contemporary Germany, 18; in postwar East Germany, 40; in postwar West Germany, 36, 42–43; in Weimar Republic, 6, 7, 8, 37, 38, 195 n.1
Sofsky, Wolfgang: *The Order of Terror*, 97–98
The Soldiers of Evil (Segev), 79–80
Solidarity, 74
Solnit, Albert J., 76
Some Dare to Dream (Frome), 70, 71, 201 n.7
Soviet Union: attitude of, to Hitler and Nazism, 8, 37, 38–39; Bolshevik regime in, compared with Nazi Germany, xv–xvi, 178, 197 n.8; Bolshevik Revolution in, 84–85, 172; concentration

Soviet Union (*continued*)
  camps in, xv, 93, 94, 96–97; German invasion of, 83, 85; occupation of Hungary by, 155, 157, 161; occupation of Lithuania by, 71, 118, 121, 126, 127; occupation of Poland by, 73, 74; occupation of Romania by, 131, 132, 134–35; policy of, toward Israel, 38, 40; Stalinist terror in, 82, 93, 97; suffering of, in World War II, 31, 37, 56–57, 75, 90, 98, 105, 107, 109. *See also* Communism
Spector, Shmuel, 201 n.8
Der Spiegel, 102
SS: Austrians in, 105; concentration camp personnel from, 29, 30, 31, 90–91, 96, 98, 108–9; *Einsatzgruppen* battalions of, 26–28, 85, 122, 187, 201 n.8; *Grosse Aktion* of, in Kovno Ghetto, 122–23; police units associated with, 104–8; postwar advancement of members of, 42; responsibility of, for Final Solution, xvii, 10, 13–15, 69, 94, 186–87
Stajner, Karlo: *Seven Thousand Days in Siberia*, 197 n.8
Stalin, Joseph: criticisms of Israel by, 40; criticisms of Weimar Social Democrats by, 8, 37; destructiveness of, compared with Hitler, 9, 68, 81, 97, 197 n.8, 205 n.8; destructiveness of, in Poland, 92, 163; personality of, compared with Hitler, xv, 20–21; secret agreement of, with Hitler, 81, 118, 205 n.8; victims of, in terror, 82, 93, 198 n.13
Stangl, Franz, 79, 182, 198 n.10
Stein, Edith, 205 n.4
Steinberg, Jean, 34
Steinberg, Jonathan: *All or Nothing*, 139, 141–42, 202 n.2
Stelescu, Mihail, 133
Stella (Wyden), 24, 32–34
Stern, Fritz, 101
Stille, Alexander: *Benevolence and Betrayal*, 137, 138, 139
Streit, Christian, 93

Stroop, SS Maj. Gen. Jürgen, 197 n.5
Suchecky, Bernard: *The Hidden Encyclicals of Pius XI*, 175–76
Süddeutsche Zeitung, 103
Survival in Auschwitz (Levi), 70, 95, 98, 202 n.1
The Survival of Love (Garlinski), 145
Surviving Warsaw (Garlinski), 145
Szálasi, Ferenc, 157
Szeged (Hungary), 150

Taverna, Kathryn: *Lodz Ghetto*, 198 n.9
Taylor, Simon: *The Rise of Hitler*, 6–7
Taylor, Telford, 193
Tec, Nechama: *In the Lion's Den*, 24, 47–50, 203 n.4
Teleki, Pál, 154
Templer, William, 97
"Thanks to Scandinavia" Foundation, 142
Theobald, Roslyn, 95
Theresienstadt concentration camp (Bohemia), 57, 197 n.7, 205 n.6
Thümmel, Paul, 189
Tiso, Monsignor Josef, 20, 181
Tito, 146, 202 n.2, 203 n.7 n.8
Todorov, Tzvetan: *Facing the Extreme*, 94–97, 163, 165
Todt Organization, 99, 122
Tory, Avraham, 113–14, 118, 122–23, 124–26, 127
Transnistria, 135, 201 n.1
Transylvania, 130, 131, 132, 154, 202 n.2; Holocaust in, 134, 135–36, 202 n.1
Trap with a Green Fence (Glazar), 95, 98–99
Treblinka death camp (Poland), 77, 95, 98–99, 189, 198 n.10
Trevor-Roper, Hugh, 26
Trianon Peace Treaty (1920), 151, 155, 158
Trotsky, Leon, 172
Tygodnik Powszechny, 144

Ukraine: collaboration of, in Final Solu-

tion, 10, 74, 89, 98, 109, 165; ethnic divisions in, 15, 24, 25, 92–93; Holocaust in, 27–28; kulaks ("class enemies") in, 82; status of prisoners from, in concentration camps, 99
Ulbricht, Walter, 36, 37, 38, 39
Ulrich, Volker, 199 n.6
Unanswered Questions (ed. Furet), 80, 198 n.13
Unbroken (Crome), 78
Under His Very Windows (Zuccotti), 179, 180
Unholy Trinity (Aarons and Loftus), 205 n.8
United States, 185–93; anti-Semitism in, xvii, 25, 106, 185, 187, 204 n.1; denazification effort of, 41; Holocaust documents captured by, 67; involvement of, in "Rat Line," 182; Jewish citizens of, in occupied Europe, 73; Jewish immigration into, 188, 195 n.1; wartime knowledge of Holocaust in, xvii, 188–92, 193
United States Holocaust Memorial Council, 74, 89, 101
United States War Refugee Board, 186, 193
The Unmasterable Past (Maier), 198 n.12 n.13 n.14
Ustasha (Croatian fascist militia), 21–22, 141, 145–47, 179, 202 n.2, 203 n.7, 204 n.8

Vaickus, V., 125
Vatican. *See* Catholic Church
The Vatican and the Red Flag (Luxmoore and Babiuch), 172, 176, 183
Vergangenheitsbewältigung, 43, 102
Vienna, 105, 196 n.3
Vierteljahrshefte für Zeitgeschichte, 107
Vilnius (Vilna, Lithuania), 72, 115, 117, 118, 119, 121, 128
Vitvitsky, Bohdan, 92
Voldemaras, Augustinas, 116, 117, 120

Volkov, Shulamit, 80
Vytautas, grand Duke (of Lithuania), 115, 118

Wagner, Richard, 6
Waitzman, Haim, 79
Wallachia, 129, 134
Wallenberg, Raoul, 161, 186, 192
Wannsee Conference, 28, 187, 189
The War Against the Jews (Dawidowicz), 195 n.1
Warsaw: Ghetto Uprising (1943), 43, 73, 144, 161, 163, 197 n.5, 204 n.2; Jews in disguise in, 71; Uprising of the Polish resistance (1944), 43, 164, 204 n.2
Wartime Lies (Begley), 23–24, 49
Web, Marek, 79
Wehler, Hans-Ulrich, 101, 104, 199 n.8
Wehrmacht, xvii, 26, 27, 42, 94, 104, 122, 178
Weil, Jiří: *Life with a Star*, 71–72
Weimar Republic: Communist Party in, 8–9, 37; National Socialist Party in, 3–9, 17–18, 195 n.1; Social Democratic Party in, 6, 7, 8, 37, 38
Weiss, Aharon, 92
West Germany: attitude of, toward Israel, 35–36; attitude of, toward Nazi past, xvii–xviii, 36, 38, 40–43; stability of, 5
What Is to Be Done (Lenin), 164
What the Nazis Planned, What the British and Americans Knew (Breitman), 185–93
While Six Million Died (Morse), 185
Who Voted for Hitler? (Hamilton), 4, 5, 17–18, 195 n.1
Who Were the Fascists (ed. Larsen), 16–17, 18–22
Why Did the Heavens Not Darken? (Mayer), 67–68, 69–70, 83–88, 123
Wiesel, Elie, 101
Wieseltier, Leon, xi
Wills, Gary, 175, 176
Wirth, Andrzej, 197 n.5

Wistrich, Robert, 101
Wladyslaw II Jagiello, King (of Poland), 115
Wolff, SS Gen. Karl, 186–87
Women of Theresienstadt (Schwertfeger), 197 n.7
World War I: collapse of Habsburg monarchy following, 130, 148–50, 151, 152, 172; ethnic conflicts following, 20, 25, 85–87, 116; German barbarism during, 187–88; German discontent following, 11, 69; Jewish support for Germany during, 81, 106; sinking of *Lusitania* in, 185–86
Wyden, Peter: *Stella*, 24, 32–34
Wyman, David S.: *The Abandonment of the Jews*, 185
Wyszynski, Cardinal Stefan, 183

Yad Vashem, 63, 73, 143, 203 n.3
Yerushalmi, Yosef, 16

YIVO Institute for Jewish Research, 72
YMCA, 204 n.1
The Yugoslav Auschwitz and the Vatican (Dedijer), 145–47
Yugoslavia, 152, 203 n.6; breakup of, 152; concentration camps in, 142, 204 n.8; Holocaust in, 132, 141; Hungarian-led massacres in, 158; wartime casualties in, 203 n.8. *See also* Croatia; Serbia

Zegota (Council for Aid to Jews), 143, 202 n.3
Die Zeit, 102
Zerjavić, Vladimir: *Opsesije i Megalomanije oko Jasenovca i Bleiburga*, 204 n.8
Zionism, 32; in Hungary, 161–62; in Italy, 138, 140; in Lithuania, 48, 50, 120; Victor Klemperer's views on, 54, 56
Zuccotti, Susan: *The Italians and the Holocaust*, 139, 204 n.3; *Under His Very Windows*, 179, 180